WALKING *in the* FULLNESS *of* I AM

Awakening the Story of Us and the Gospel of the Kingdom

GARY R. MANESS

WESTBOW PRESS®
A DIVISION OF THOMAS NELSON & ZONDERVAN

WestBow Press books may be ordered through booksellers or by contacting:

WestBow Press
A Division of Thomas Nelson & Zondervan
1663 Liberty Drive
Bloomington, IN 47403
www.westbowpress.com
844-714-3454

ISBN: 978-1-6642-6919-4 (sc)
ISBN: 978-1-6642-6920-0 (hc)
ISBN: 978-1-6642-6918-7 (e)

Library of Congress Control Number: 2022911152

Print information available on the last page.

WestBow Press rev. date: 07/06/2022

DEDICATION

To my wife Cindy. Along with God, you continue to make all things good in my life. Thank you for being the wonderful person you are and an inspiration to me and all who meet you.

To my parents, Leamon and Shirley. I was so blessed to have wonderful parents to mold and shape my life. Mom taught me about God and never giving up. Dad taught me about character, how to love, and how to care for others. Your legacies live on each and every day.

To our eight wonderful children and thirteen grandchildren. You are each amazing and keep life filled with laughter, love, and excitement.

KEY SCRIPTURES

"And God said unto Moses, I AM That I AM: and he said, Thus shalt thou say unto the children of Israel, I AM hath sent me unto you" (Exodus 3:14 KJV).

"For the earnest expectation of the creation eagerly waits for the revealing of the sons of God" (Romans 8:19 AMPC).

"To know the love of Christ which passes knowledge; that you may be filled with all the fullness of God" (Ephesians 3:19 NKJV).

The Seven I AM Statements of Jesus (NKJV):

1. "I AM the bread of life" (John 6:35).
2. "I AM the light of the world" (John 8:12).
3. "I AM the way, the truth, and the life" (John 14:6).
4. "I AM the good shepherd" (John 10:11).
5. "I AM the true vine" (John 15:1).
6. "I AM the door" (John 10:7).
7. "I AM the resurrection and the life" (John 11:25).

CONTENTS

PREFACE

The Fullness (Pleroma) of God

More! Have you ever wanted more? Are you satisfied with the circumstances of your life and relationship with God and others, or do you want more? God wants you to live an abundant life, reach into the heart of heaven, and pull it into the here and now. He wants you to live life full rather than half empty. The good news of the gospel is that God has more for you.

By all accounts I have lived a wonderful life, and I am thankful to God for his many blessings. I gave my life to Christ at the age of thirteen, and I began following him from that day. I have experienced supernatural encounters with God and seen his goodness over and over again. My wife and I have eight wonderful children and thirteen grandchildren. God has blessed me with a successful career in finance over the past 30 plus years. I have had opportunity to provide internal audit, risk management and consulting services to government leaders, Fortune 500, and other corporate companies. Besides my professional career, I had the privilege of being a Pastor and church planter. In 1991, I planted a church in Midlothian, Virginia and served as its founder and Senior Pastor. Clover Hill Church continues to thrive and is growing and touching many lives. My wife and I still live in Virginia. We are active in our local church, and hopefully we're making a difference in the lives of those we meet. Yet, I feel in my spirit there is more. God wants something greater for me, for you, and his church.

As a child, I was blessed to grow up with incredible parents that served as role models. They were not perfect, but they displayed tremendous love for my brother and me and played an important role in who we turned out to be in life. I remember on one occasion saying, "If I could only be half the man my father is." You see, he was my dad, and his DNA was not only in me but his actions along with my mother's helped mold my life. I knew if I could be like them, my children would have the privilege of experiencing the rich heritage I experienced.

Many of you have been blessed with parents like mine or others who became your heroes to model your life after. Role models are a blessing to society and their lives impact countless generations. While many people have become heroes and role models, if you want more, you need to consider the importance of God in your life. After all, he is your creator, and you are his child. What if your hero and the one you patterned your life after was God, and what if he has more for you? Consider for a moment the possibility of not only patterning your life after him but being filled with all his fullness. Instead of being "half the man" your heavenly father is, what if you could have the full measure of God inside you? What impact would that have on who you are, the choices you make, and your interactions with the world?

This was the challenge God gave me while attending a Supernatural Life Conference in September 2015. After one of the guest speakers finished, we concluded with prayer and reflection. During those moments, the Holy Spirit said to me, "*Walk in the fullness of I AM.*" I've heard God speak to me before, but I was taken aback by those words and wasn't quite sure what they meant. As I continued in prayer, I began to receive more, and the Holy Spirit began giving me downloads of insight for this book.

During that encounter, God shared with me that his plans for his children has not changed since he planned his kingdom. The depths of the revelation of God as our Father, his love for us, and our identity in him is only beginning to unfold. He began to show me that the Great Commission Jesus gave his disciples was not new but had originally been given to Adam and Eve in the Garden of Eden, and God wants our lives to radiate his fullness. Some have had glimpses of the fullness of God, but the truth is he has much more.

Many years ago, a man named Moses had an encounter with God that changed his life and the world. During that divine appointment, God revealed himself to Moses in a burning bush as I AM. From that day, Moses was never the same, and he began to walk in a measure of the fullness of God. What Moses experienced in measure you and I can experience in its fullness. The coming of Christ and the giving of the Holy Spirit on the day of Pentecost activated the fullness of God in all who receive Jesus Christ as Lord. In the coming days, we will see Christians walk in the fullness of God that includes not only the supernatural encounters Moses had, but also the works of Jesus, and the miracles seen during the days of the early church, and even more. Believers are being awakened and filled with the same fire of love God has for his children, and their lives are being radically changed.

Each of us are uniquely designed by God. From the foundations of the world, God planned your life. Psalm 139:16 (NIV) says, "Your eyes saw my unformed body; all the days ordained for me were written in your book before one of them came to be." God's individualized plan for your life is who you really are, and you can walk in the fullness of that plan. To discover who you are, you must fully discover God.

Many define themselves by their old nature and behaviors before they became a believer in Christ. Our subconscious way of thinking always leads us to the same old patterns of behavior, but God's word should change our views on who we are. Unfortunately, many still define themselves by how they feel, what they have, what they do, or their accomplishments.

Walking in the fullness of I AM does not involve working or trying hard. If that were the case, 20 years from now you would still be trying to reach a higher spiritual plane of existence. Trying hard is a works-based form of relationship with God that always sets you up for failure and disappointment. If you are going to learn to walk in the fullness of God, you must have an expectation and an anticipation of your future with God. Walking in the fullness of I AM involves changing the way you think, believe, and interact with God and the realms of the spirit. In short, it involves faith, repentance, love, and encounters with God. Before those religious words side-track you to thinking this will never work, let me explain. Faith is simply believing or recognizing something is true. Repentance is changing the way you think about something. Love involves the deeply rooted love of God as the foundation of your life. And finally, encounters with God naturally occurs when you spend time in the presence of God, and the Holy Spirit begins to move upon your heart and life.

Romans 12:2 (NKJV) says, "do not be conformed to this world, but be transformed by the renewing of your mind, that you may prove what is that good and acceptable and perfect will of God." The word "transformed" in the Greek is *metamorphoo*[1] and it means "to change into another form," "to transfigure." It is where we get the word metamorphose. This word is used four times in scripture. It was used twice in describing Jesus' transfiguration on the mountain top in front of some of the disciples, once in the scripture we just cited, and the 4th time in 2 Corinthians 3:18 (NKJV) where it says, "we all, with unveiled face, beholding as in a mirror the glory of the Lord, are being transformed into the same image from glory to glory, just as by the Spirit of the Lord."

The transformation of your heart begins with a revelation of God and his kingdom. Once you receive a revelation of truth, your spirit and soul gain the capacity to align with God's word and walk in the fullness of that revelation. When the Holy Spirit said to me "*Walk in the fullness of I AM*," I spent the next several years trying to conform to that identity. Finally, the Holy Spirit helped me realize I did not have to perform, act, feel, or think a certain way to walk in that promise. I realized that I AM who God says I AM, independent of any other circumstance.

Before we discuss the application of these truths, let's begin with an understanding of what the Bible means by God's fullness. The Greek word for "fullness" is *pleroma*[2] and it means "that which is (or has been) filled" (i.e., the container) or "that which fills or with which a thing is filled" (i.e., the contents). In other words, the Fullness of God means the complete fullness of who God is has been poured completely into the life of the believer. It means you can be filled up to the brim, with no room to spare, with the completeness of God. Would you like to live this way?

This seems too good to be true and beyond anything most of us have heard. God created you to be totally saturated with all of himself. If you want to know what that looks like, look at Jesus. In John 14:9 (NIV), Jesus said, "Anyone who has seen me has seen the Father." Jesus was saying there was no distinction between himself and the Father. In fact, the Bible says just as Jesus is the fullness of the Godhead, we are the fullness of Christ (Ephesians 1:23).

While most of us have no trouble believing the Father, Son, and Holy Spirit are one, we are taken aback by the proposition that we are included in that circle. However, Jesus declared this in John 17:20-23 (NKJV):

> "I do not pray for these alone, but also for those who will believe in Me through their word; that they all may be one, as You, Father, are in Me, and I in You; that they also may be one in Us, that the world may believe that You sent Me. And the glory which You gave Me I have given them, that they may be one just as We are one: I in them, and You in Me; that they may be made perfect in one, and that the world may know that You have sent Me, and have loved them as You have loved Me."

All we can say is a reverenced and in awe WOW! Jesus made it clear, the glory which the Father gave the Son, he has given us. Jesus proclaimed he is in us just like the Father is in him, and we have all been made one. Jesus said he loves us with the same love the Father has for him. As amazing as this is, how many of us live this way or are even aware of these truths?

The concept of the fullness of God in our lives has been a mystery hidden since before creation. On seventeen occasions, the New Testament uses the word fullness and in those instances reveal to us the applications of these truths. Let's consider a few of them:

1. All the fullness of the godhead (the sum of God's perfection, powers, and attributes) permanently dwells in Christ, the Son of God (Colossians 1:19).
2. All this fullness dwells in bodily form in Christ (Colossians 2:9).
3. Out of his fullness, we have received the superabundance of his grace, truth, spiritual blessings, favor upon favor, and gifts heaped upon gifts (John 1:16).

4. As believers, we are the body of Christ and in us lives the full measure of Christ, who makes everything complete and fills us with himself (Ephesians 1:23).
5. As believers, we can personally experience the love of Christ and have our entire being filled up with the full measure of God (Ephesians 3:19).
6. As believers, we are perfected, fully equipped, and made complete as we learn, grow, mature, and experience for ourselves the full measure of Christ (Ephesians 4:11-13).

The application of these truths is life changing and will revolutionize the church and our world. The question is, why haven't we been taught these truths? Why hasn't the church focused on these teachings? The answer is that the knowledge of these truths has been unfolding through the ages, just as God planned. They have been hidden until the appointed times.

As proof of this assertion, consider Galatians 4:4 (KJV), "But when the fulness of the time was come, God sent forth his Son, made of a woman, made under the law." The revelation of Jesus, the Son of God, coming in the flesh as the Son of Man was not manifested until the appointed time. There were multiple Old Testament prophesies that spoke of the coming of the Messiah, but it wasn't manifested until the appointed time. And when Jesus came, many still did not receive him because they did not understand the times in which they were living. Ephesians 1:9-10 (KJV) says, "Having made known unto us the mystery of his will, according to his good pleasure which he hath purposed in himself: That in the dispensation of the fulness of times he might gather together in one all things in Christ, both which are in heaven, and which are on earth; even in him." This scripture makes it clear; the mystery of God's plans has been and will continue to be revealed to us at his appointed times. I believe this is the explanation for why the truth of our identity and the kingdom hasn't been fully unfolded.

God's amazing love for us is so deep it is difficult to understand his desire to fill us with all of himself; however, this is a key aspect of the story of humanity and the gospel of the kingdom. For many, this seems out of reach, a lofty goal, or just impossible. Some may even see this as prideful or blasphemous; yet it is what the Apostle Paul said in Ephesians 4:11-13 (NKJV):

> "And He Himself gave some to be apostles, some prophets, some evangelists, and some pastors and teachers, for the equipping of the saints for the work of ministry, for the edifying of the body of Christ, till we all come to the unity of the faith and of the knowledge of the Son of God, to a perfect man, to the measure of the stature of the fullness of Christ."

As Paul explains it, the fulfillment of these promises does not happen automatically. It is a process that comes with maturity through what I call experiential knowledge. When Paul speaks of the knowledge of the Son of God, it means you and I can personally experience these truths. Maturity begins with an understanding that God designed you to be filled with all of himself; and through the process of first-hand encounters with him, you are transformed, perfected, and filled with the abundance of Christ. Some lessons can be taught while others are only learned when they are experienced.

To clarify any potential misunderstandings, there is only one God, and he is expressed in the trinity as Father, Son, and Holy Spirit. However, as his children, we have been created in his image and likeness and can be filled with the complete fullness of our father. This is how we should naturally think of ourselves. Consider what Paul wrote in Philippians 2:5-7 (NKJV), "Let this mind be in you which was also in Christ Jesus, who, being in the form of God, did not consider it robbery to be equal with God, but made Himself of no reputation, taking the form of a bondservant, and coming in the likeness of men." Paul taught the Philippians they should have the same mindset as Christ and see themselves the same way Jesus saw himself. As the Son of Man, Jesus was in the same form and likeness of God the Father, and his sonship was secure and forever settled; however, that did not take away from the deity of God. Rather, he took upon himself the form of a servant.

As we continue our discussions, we are going to dig deep into the story of humanity and into the mysteries of God that have been hidden since creation. We will explore the ancient of days before time, a period God calls "in the beginning" (Genesis 1:1 KJV). We will discuss God's unfolding of his plans through the ages, his plans for our lives in this present age, and the ages to come.

It is my hope that as we journey back to the beginning and discuss the creation of heaven and earth, it will begin a revealing and an awakening of who we are, who God is, and our relationship together. As we move forward through the dispensations of time, the unveiling of these truths will help unfold the context of our lives in God's plan and how he wants us to experience an abundant life and walk in his glory and kingdom.

I realize some of the things we will discuss will be new to some, controversial to others, seem too good to be true, or even scary. I don't claim to have all the answers or present everything God has planned for us. Instead, I approach these topics with the lens of an auditor and the heart of a Pastor and Teacher. I hope to share intriguing information, questions, and hopefully insight to some of the answers or possible answers to life's biggest mysteries.

As we catch glimpses of who God is and who we are, hopefully, this will become a small part of a great awakening God wants for his Church and planet earth. I believe we have entered a time of shaking and the beginning stages of a greater revelation of God. It is the beginning stages of the revealing of the sons and daughters of God. As we continue in the End of Days, God wants his children to mature, grow, and present ourselves as a glorious church without spot or blemish. It will cause many to question their beliefs and man-made traditions. Many will have to step outside the norms of institutions and yield to the heart of God. As children of the Most High, we will begin to learn the concepts of how to ***Walk in the Fullness of I AM*** and gain new passions for our identity as his sons and daughters.

INTRODUCTION

The I AM Statements of Jesus

As we begin our journey together, I want to introduce our discussions with some thought-provoking questions. What is normal and natural, and what does that look like? When we think about normal, we think about things that are routine or ordinary. Similarly, when we think about natural, we think about things that occur naturally and not a result of people. In other words, the things that are normal and natural should be routine and expected as they were created to be.

But what would most people say is normal and natural? Many would say it looks different for each person. Some would say it depends on where or when you were born, who your parents are, your economic status, your culture, your beliefs, and so on. Many would argue there is no such thing. But is that true? I would argue that while God loves diversity, there are a core set of principles and way of life that should be normal and natural to us all. Life may look different for each person due to circumstances; however, it should fit within the boundaries of what should be routine.

To explore this concept a little further, consider a few more questions. Is it natural to experience poverty, sickness, and death? Is it normal to be loved, happy, and experience joy and peace; or is it natural to experience discord and strife, fight battles and wars, and face problems without solutions? Should it be normal to face the future with excitement and anticipation, or should we face it with fear and uncertainty? Why was I born? Why am I here?

We have all pondered such questions at some point in our life; however, I want to share with you a mindboggling truth. The revelation of these mysteries is contained in the Bible and God wants to reveal them to you. In fact, the Apostle Paul tells us in Ephesians 3:2-5 that God revealed to him and the Apostles the mysteries hidden from us since the world began. That's an amazing statement. He also said God can reveal those same secrets to you. "Now to Him who is able to establish you according to my gospel and the preaching of Jesus Christ, according to the revelation of the mystery kept secret since the world began" (Romans 16:25 NKJV).

We are living in the most exciting time in all of history. Our generation is witnessing God's plans unfold. As these secrets and mysteries are unveiled and you begin to walk in them, there will be little room for darkness or the enemy in your soul. I don't know about you, but this is something I am interested in.

As we begin to uncover these mysteries and ponder what is normal and natural according to God, we will quickly discover the story of humanity and what Jesus called the gospel of the kingdom. In the chapters ahead, we will discuss more fully the gospel of the kingdom; however, let's begin with a few introductory thoughts. The word gospel means good news. It is the good news of God's word, plans, and designs for your life and all of humanity. The concepts of the kingdom originated before the foundations of the earth. Therefore, what is normal and natural must be viewed in light of God's plan for the kingdom. As we begin to fully understand these truths, it will give us context for the real story of humanity, the work of Christ, and God's plans for us all. As we gain insight to these plans, we come to understand God is in the process of restoring all things to his original design recorded in Genesis 1:1. Acts 3:21 (NKJV) expresses that plan perfectly, "whom heaven must receive until the times of restoration of all things, which God has spoken by the mouth of all His holy prophets since the world began."

What I am suggesting is that the way God originally created everything is in fact Normal and Natural, and everything in life should be measured against that standard. However, something happened to change life from Normal to Ab-Normal, and the way many of us experience life is now filled with Ab-Normal-Ities. But these actions did not catch God off guard. He is all knowing and has kept hidden some of the most amazing truths and knowledge until the final unfolding of his plans.

As we discuss the amazing acts and plans of God, at times we will take a hard-academic look at the text of the Bible. At other times, we will allow the Holy Spirit to shine light on what has been set before us all along, hidden in plain view. Together, we will uncover startling truths about the way God intended life to be lived and his plans for the kingdom.

As we uncover these truths, I want to challenge you to question your life and beliefs. Ask yourself the following questions:

1. Have I become so entrenched with my way of life that I can't see the bigger picture?
2. Am I stuck in Ab-Normal-Ities when in fact there is a much bigger world around me?
3. Is my Normal really Ab-Normal and Un-natural when compared to how God intended life to be lived?

As we begin to crack the door to what is beyond our routine, we are going to see the way God intended life to be lived is very different than it is now. We are going to see the mysteries of his plans have been concealed in a fellowship between God the Father, Son, Holy Spirit, and the sons and daughters of God. For us, it hasn't been routine because what God created to be normal and natural is only intermittently seen. It is feared by Satan, and many do not understand or fathom its possibilities. What was once accepted as truth has been discarded by many as fable, and the hidden depths of God's original blueprint has remained hidden until the advent of Christ and our approaching the end of days.

To guide us through these discussions, this book is divided into seven sections, each corresponding to one of the seven I AM statements of Jesus in the Gospel of John. Concealed within the I AM statements of Jesus is the plan of God for the ages, the story of humanity, and the context for us to walk in the fullness of God. We will begin each section with a discourse on one of the I AM statements and then look to portions of scripture to fully explore the depths of these mysteries.

John records in his Gospel seven astonishing proclamations Jesus made about himself (taken from the NKJV):

1. "I AM the bread of life" (John 6:35).
2. "I AM the light of the world" (John 8:12).
3. "I AM the way, the truth, and the life" (John 14:6).
4. "I AM the good shepherd" (John 10:11).
5. "I AM the true vine" (John 15:1).
6. "I AM the door" (John 10:7).
7. "I AM the resurrection and the life" (John 11:25).

As we explore the good news of the kingdom within these statements, we are going to pull back the curtain and reveal the truth about God. He is good all the time, he is a kind loving Father, and he is in control. He is not panicking about the state of our world, and has never been caught off guard. We are going to see how an enemy arose and committed high treason to sabotage creation and twist what God designed. But God is so in love with us his children, he took extraordinary measures before the creation of the world to secure our future.

As we begin to unlock the truths of the fullness of I AM and the real story of humanity, we are going to Awaken and see how we should live, think, and act as children of the kingdom. However, I want to share with you a word of caution. As we discuss the amazing acts and truths of God, if all you get from this book is the wow factor of mysteries and secrets, then you will have missed the real intentions of this book. I want to challenge you to look beyond the powerful acts of God and see his heart. I want you to see his ways, come to know who he really is, and understand how much he loves you. Allow the King of creation to have encounters with you and deepen the relationship he has with you. Along the way you will discover the ways of God, who you really are, and who you were created to be. This is our story, the real story of humanity. It is exciting and much bigger than you imagined. God is in the process of bringing to pass his intentions and designs and he wants you to have a part in the unfolding of his plans. Are you ready for what is ahead?

SECTION I
I AM the Bread of Life

"And Jesus said to them, I AM the bread of life" (John 6:35 NKJV).

The Greek word for "bread" is *artos*[3] and while it means "food composed of flour mixed with water and baked," it also means "to fit, put together." The root of the word means "to raise from the ground." The Greek word for "life" is *zoe*[4] and it means "the absolute fullness of life, both essential and ethical, which belongs to God."

In this section, we will discover God is the creator and architect of heaven and earth. Every design of creation came from his mind and was planned by him before anything took place. He began with heaven, the epicenter and template for his kingdom and all of creation. As his plans progressed, he spoke the earth into existence and placed it within heaven's atmosphere. Eden was the starting point of what is good, normal, and natural. But as God's plans began to unfold, an existential threat arose to undo his plans. But nothing took God by surprise. He saw the end from the beginning, and as the bread of life, God is the sustainer and restorer of creation. As we learn to *Walk in the fullness of I AM*, we come to understand that the bread of life lives within us, and our life and the world around us can be brought into agreement with the absolute goodness of God. He is the only one able to fill the innate hunger and thirst within every man and woman to embrace the fullness of life. As the Son of God, Jesus is the bread of life, the source of all we need, and the restorer of all things.

THE EDEN CONNECTION

CHAPTER 1

In the Beginning

"In the beginning God created the heaven and the earth" (Genesis 1:1 KJV).

As we begin our discussions of *Walking in the Fullness of I AM*, we must begin with a deep look at the very beginning of creation. Every story has a beginning. Have you wondered how our story began? Will it come to an end? Understanding our beginning gives us context for our lives today. The scientific community has concluded that we are here by chance, through evolution. If this is true, our lives are insignificant when compared to every person that has been or will be born. When compared to history and the vast expanse of the universe, our individual lives could appear as nothing more than a grain of sand in time. But is that true?

As we begin the examination of our story, let's consider the proposition that each of us is far more important than we think. The amazing truth is God has personally known you from the beginning. Before time began, he engineered your life with a mission and purpose. He designed you with gifts and talents and a uniqueness that is not shared by any other person who has ever lived or ever will live. Ages ago, God planned you to be part of his family. He gave you a name and recorded it in the registry of heaven and fell in love with the real you. He planned your life, including when and where you would be born.

You are not an accident. People can make mistakes, but your life is part of the plans of God. The magnificent truth of this mystery is hidden in the very first verse of the Bible.

From the Mind of God

"In the beginning, God created" (Genesis 1:1 KJV). This one phrase has been debated and studied for ages. It is hard for us, with our limited understanding, to grasp the significance of these words. Does this mean God had a beginning? Of course not, in the beginning God was already present. He is the Ancient of Days and existed before time. We learn this truth from the meaning of the name of God. The word "God" in Hebrew is *elohim.*[5] It is a plural noun and means "rulers, judges," "divine ones," "angels," "gods," "the (TRUE) god." The word refers to those in the spirit realm and can refer to God, angels, or even the spirits of humans. Since Genesis 1:1 describes the very beginning before any of God's creation, it refers to God himself.

Genesis 2:4 (KJV) gives us more insight about God. It says, "These are the generations of the heavens and of the earth when they were created, in the day that the Lord God made the earth and the heavens." In this verse, God introduces himself to us as "Lord." It is the first time this word is used in the Bible. The Hebrew word used is *Yehova*[6] and it means "the existing One," "(the) self-Existent or Eternal." In the beginning, God was already here and existed since eternity past. He had no beginning of days and will have no end of days.

To describe God's unfolding plan, the Bible simply says, "In the beginning, God created the heaven and the earth" (Genesis 1:1 KJV). Settling this one point in your mind will make everything else clear. If not, questions will linger with no satisfactory answer. Many believe life evolved and there is no God. Some view God as stepping into evolution as a benevolent Father taking pity on fledgling life. Others believe God set things in motion and took a back seat to watch how it all turns out. The truth is all of creation was in the heart of God before the beginning. All of creation, including you, were created by design and with purpose. Coming to a place of understanding and acceptance of this truth changes the whole conversation of who we are, life, eternity, and the story of humanity. It all starts with an understanding that in the beginning God created.

The word "created" in Genesis 1:1 (KJV) is the Hebrew word *bara*[7] and it means "to create, shape, form." Hebrews 11:3 (KJV) says, "Through faith we understand that the worlds were framed by the word of God, so that things which are seen were not made of things which do appear." This may be a shock to evolutionist, but from these scriptures we learn God spoke heaven and earth into existence out of nothing. It is the theological concept known as ex nihilo, a Latin phrase meaning "out of nothing."[8]

God spoke life into existence, and all of creation stays held together by him. Colossians 1:17 (NIV) says, "He is before all things, and in Him all things hold together." The elusive God particle that scientists are desperately trying to discover can be found in God's spoken word. As Isaiah 55:11 (NIV) declares, "So is my word that goes out from my mouth: It will not return to me empty but will accomplish what I desire and achieve the purpose for which I sent it." This is an eternal truth and principle of the kingdom of God.

Some find it hard to conceptualize that there was a beginning and how that relates to time and eternity. How can God be eternal or exist before time? From our vantage point, we tend to view eternity as an infinite amount of time; however, this is not the case. Time had a beginning and was created by God. God is eternal, not because he has an infinite amount of time but because he stands outside of time. He is not constrained by the boundaries of time and space. As we shall see when we discuss the six days of creation, God created time and space. As time proceeded, he stepped into creation through his Son to dwell in the time he created on the earth he spoke into existence. How incredible is that? It explains how he can see the ending from the beginning and his omnipresence. He stands outside of time and space beholding it all.

To help explain this, imagine a single plane represented by a piece of paper. On that plane are two people with space between them. It does not matter how far apart the space is, it can be close together or far apart.

Standing on the outside of the piece of paper you can see both people at once, no matter how far apart they are in time because you are outside the boundaries of space and time. I know this is just a simple illustration and it by no means explains the eternity of God. The truth is, God is beyond our comprehension or explanation. He simply is eternal past, present, and future. And let me share with you another secret. Although you had a beginning, since God's Spirit is in you, you are an eternal being as well. You were in the mind of God before time began, and you will have no end of days. You are eternally his. The question is, where will you live in eternity?

Genesis 1:1 should be viewed as a reference to the very beginning, a period before time. Let's look deep into this phrase: "In the beginning" (Genesis 1:1 KJV). When we look at the original Hebrew text, we find something extremely interesting. We find that this is not a phrase at all; rather, it is a single Hebrew word, *re'sit.*[9] Some text list the word as *bereshit.* It means "first, beginning, best, chief." It comes from the Hebrew root word *ros,*[10] which means "head," "top," "chief, choicest, best," and "sum." In other words, the very first phrase in the Bible could be read, "In/from the head, God created." While the word means first or beginning, it implies the concept of forethought as though you are looking at the sum total of everything at one time in the beginning. The entirety of creation came from the mind and thoughts of God before it began. Isaiah 46:10 (NIV) says, "I make known the end from the beginning, from ancient times, what is still to come. I say, my purpose will stand, and I will do all that I please." Do you realize the significance of this statement? God saw the entirety of creation including your life before it began. He foresaw every thought you would have, every decision, and every action you will take. He has seen all your mistakes and failures as well as your triumphs and successes. He foresaw every war that would be fought and the tragedy of sin and evil before it began. He has given us free will to choose and make decisions, and by foreseeing all that will happen, he has planned a way for you to walk in the fullness of who you really are and will be with you through all things. In the end, his plans and purposes will come to pass. This is mindboggling when you consider the implications of this truth.

In addition to meaning head, *bereshit* also means "first of its kind," or "firstfruits." In other words, the creation of heaven and earth were the firstfruits, the first of its kind. God had never done anything like this before. For all those who have wondered if God created worlds and universes prior to Genesis 1:1, the answer is no. This is the very first of his creation.

The Bible tells us in John 4:24 (KJV) that "God is a spirit." This does not mean he is not real or that he does not have physical features. In fact, the spiritual world has more substance than the physical world. God is real and his first act of creation was to create a tangible place for everything that is spiritual and physical to dwell. It was the beginning stages of God's kingdom.

Since heaven and earth are the first fruits of creation, this is significant. Firstfruits imply a tithe, a covenant, and a promise between God and creation. Psalm 24:1 (KJV) says, "The earth is the Lord's, and the fullness thereof; the world, and they that dwell therein."

Before the creation of heaven and earth, God planned and designed a kingdom that will one day be inherited by his children. Genesis 1:1 is the beginning stages of that plan. Think about that for a moment. From the beginning of creation, God had an end game in mind. What does a builder do when they build a foundation? The first stone set in place is the cornerstone. All the other stones will be placed in relationship to this foundation stone. This theme is emphasized in Psalm 118:22 (NKJV), "The stone which the builders rejected has become the chief cornerstone." From the beginning, Christ is referenced as the chief architect of the kingdom. The Gospel of John confirms this amazing truth in John 1:1-3 (NKJV), "In the beginning was the Word, and the Word was with God, and the Word was God. He was in the beginning with God. All things were made through Him, and without Him nothing was made that was made."

Before the world began, God made a covenant with creation, and Jesus as the cornerstone of the kingdom revealed this covenant and its promises to his disciples. In Matthew 6:9-13 (KJV) Jesus said, "After this manner therefore pray ye: Our Father which art in heaven, Hallowed be thy name. Thy kingdom come, thy will be done in earth, as it is in heaven. Give us this day our daily bread. And forgive us our debts, as we forgive our debtors. And lead us not into temptation, but deliver us from evil: For thine is the kingdom, and the power, and the glory, for ever. Amen."

It is interesting to note that the Greek word for "ever" is *aion*[11] and it means "an unbroken age, perpetuity of time, eternity." It includes eternity past, present, and future. It confirms that from eternity past, God had a plan for creation including heaven and earth, a kingdom, a family, and a king. It was all in the heart of God before there was anything.

Many have wondered what creation looked like. We learn from Genesis 1:1 and other scripture that God created heaven first, then the inhabitants of heaven before he created earth. In other words, they were not created simultaneously but in sequence. Like a master architect and builder, God created his design in a series of steps, and the first in his sequence of creation was heaven itself. With this in mind, let's look closer at the creation of heaven. As we do, we are going to uncover things that perhaps you have never known before, and it will answer questions humanity has wrestled with and debated for ages.

Reflections of Who I AM

1. How long ago was "in the beginning" (Genesis 1:1 KJV)?
2. What does "in the beginning" (Genesis 1:1 KJV) mean in Hebrew?
3. Did God know us before he created heaven and earth, and what are the implications of this truth?
4. What does the word "created" mean in Hebrew?
5. Since God created heaven and earth in a sequence rather than simultaneously, what does that imply about the past, present, and future and the trustworthiness of God?
6. Jesus said, "I AM the bread of life" (John 6:35 NKJV). How can the information discussed in this Chapter help you apply the fullness of that truth in your daily life?

Prayer of Activation

Our Father in heaven, I stand in awe of your magnificence. Your handiwork can be seen in creation and in me. I pray your purposes and promises for my life will be fulfilled. When life becomes difficult and hard to understand, I will choose to trust you. When things seem to not go well, I will choose to trust you have a plan and purpose for me. Help me make good choices that align with your purposes. Let my life glorify you in all I say and do. The life you gave me, I give back to you so you can direct and lead me in the eternal purposes you have for me. Fill my life with all of who you are. I choose you to be Lord of my life. I pray this in Jesus's name, Amen.

CHAPTER 2

God Created Heaven

"In the beginning God created the heaven…" (Genesis 1:1 KJV).

Since the beginning of time, humanity has looked for and wondered about heaven. When God told Abraham to go to the land of promise, Hebrews 11:10 (AMP) says this about his mindset, "For he was [waiting expectantly and confidently] looking forward to the city which has foundations, [an eternal, heavenly city] whose architect and builder is God." Abraham did not know where he was going but in his mind he was looking for an eternal city of promise.

In our modern society, many have wondered if heaven is real. We tell our children it is the place they go when life is over, but do we believe this is true? A study conducted by the Pew Research Center in 2014[12] showed that 72% of Americans believe in heaven and 58% believe in Hell. But what does the Bible say? Our beliefs do not alter what's true. The greatest story ever told is not a fairy tale, and it all began in a real place the Bible calls heaven.

Why did God create Heaven first?

One day I asked God to show me something new that I had never seen before. He spoke this question to my heart, "*why did I create heaven first*?" I had never thought about that question before and didn't have an answer. Then the Holy Spirit said, God created heaven first to provide a blueprint and design for the rest of creation and to establish the eternal principle that every good and perfect gift is from above. This was a reference to James 1:17 (NKJV), which says, "Every good gift and every perfect gift is from above, and comes down from the Father of lights." From this insight, we can conclude everything that is good proceeds from his presence, and God's presence is an open door to the treasures of heaven.

The Creation of Heaven

God's first creative act was heaven and in this first stage of creation, there was no earth, planets, or stars. The Hebrew word used for "heaven" is *shamayim*.[13] It has two meanings. The first is "sky" and the second is the "abode of God." It comes from a singular variant of the word that is not used. In Hebrew, this is a dual word which denotes a pair. However, the usage of this word does not have to present itself as a pair and should be translated as singular, plural, or dual depending on the context. Therefore, in the context of Genesis 1:1, God's first act of creation was the physical abode of God called heaven, surrounded by the empty sky or atmosphere. Nothing else had been created at this point.

God's beginning acts of creation is further described in Job 26:7 (KJV), "He stretcheth out the north over the empty place, and hangeth the earth upon nothing." Job uses the word "north" to reference heaven. In the ages past when there was nothing, from his mind, God spoke heaven into existence. He began by speaking the sky and atmosphere into reality, and in the northern parts of this space he stretched out his abode, the literal physical place called heaven.

Can you picture the excitement God must have felt in that moment? Seeing the end from the beginning, he created the awe and wonder of heaven, a place of eternity where his presence would reside. It would be the place from which all his goodness would proceed, the place of his glory and treasures that the rest of creation would be patterned after.

Location and Division of Heaven

Many have asked about heaven's location. Genesis 1:1 tells us God created heaven and subsequently the earth. Job tells us that after creating heaven, God hung the earth upon nothing. At that point, one could stand on the earth and look directly into heaven and see the throne of God. The only thing between earth and heaven was open sky and atmosphere. There was no darkness, planets, or stars, only heaven and earth.

As we survey scripture, the Apostle Paul tells us in II Corinthians 12:2 (KJV) he was "caught up to the third heaven." By implication, there must be a first heaven, second heaven, and third heaven. Does this mean there are three heavens? To answer this question, we must go back to our original discussion of the Hebrew word used for heaven, *shamayim*. Most Bible translations says in the beginning God created the "heavens" (plural). However, the King James Version rightly translates the word in its singular form as "heaven." This is important because it gives us insight to heaven in its original form before the fall of Lucifer and the birth of darkness.

As we further examine this word, we discover another hidden treasure. This word is a compound of the Hebrew word *mayim*,[14] which means "waters." You may recall in Genesis 1:7-8 (KJV), God "divided the waters which were under the firmament from the waters which were above the firmament....and God called the firmament heaven." In other words, there was one singular heaven that God divided into thirds by the firmament. There are now waters (heaven) above the firmament and waters (heaven) beneath the firmament. From the second day of creation onward, we have a first, second, and third heaven. From this point forward, the Hebrew word *shamayim* should rightly be translated in the plural form as "heavens."

From a scientific viewpoint, the first heaven consists of the earth's troposphere, stratosphere, and mesosphere. It begins with the earth's surface and extends upward until we reach outer space. Although there is no firm boundary where the earth's atmosphere ends and the second heaven begins; conventionally, outer space begins at the Karman line, an altitude of about sixty-two miles above sea level. This is the point at which the atmosphere becomes too thin to support aeronautical flight. Therefore, the first heaven is the atmosphere and sky surrounding the earth.

The second heaven, or firmament, is outer space, the universes. On the fourth day of creation, it became the place where God would put the planets, sun, moon, and stars. We don't know how many miles this area includes. Science measures space in terms of light years and some believe outer space continues to expand faster than the speed of light. However, some physicists correctly believe space is finite and has an edge. Although it may be expanding, outer space has an end point that corresponds with the biblical account of the third heaven.

The third heaven is where God resides, and it begins above the firmament of the second heaven. But where is heaven, the abode of God? Is there a location we could point to that we would call heaven? We could all point up but depending on where we are on earth we would all be pointing in a different direction. From both a scientific and biblical perspective, heaven appears to be located in true north.

From a scientific viewpoint, the earth and our universe rotate around true north. In the northern skies is Polaris or the North Star. It is the one fixed point in the heavens that always points to true north and has guided sailors, astronomers, and travelers for centuries. Polaris also has its own circle around the precise spot of true north. It is slightly off center of celestial true north. In fact, scientists tell us there is a hole or an empty space in the northern most part of the universe. Could this be the direction of the empty space where God created the physical abode of heaven, the place where there are no stars and planets, a place where outer space ends?

From a biblical viewpoint, scripture supports the assertion that heaven is located in true north. We have already discussed Job's account of heaven being stretched out over the north; however, there are additional references to support this belief. Hebrew priests in the Old Testament made sacrifices to the Lord toward the north. Leviticus 1:11 (KJV) says, "And he shall kill it on the side of the altar northward before the Lord." As ancient priests made their sacrifices, they looked toward the north as the location of God. Additionally, and perhaps the most definitive proof of the location of heaven is provided to us in the description of Lucifer's fall. In Isaiah 14:13 (AMP), Satan identified the location of heaven, "But you said in your heart, 'I will ascend to heaven; I will raise my throne above the stars of God; I will sit on the mount of assembly in the remote parts of the north." From scientific and scriptural evidence, it appears that the abode of God is located above the second heaven in the area of true north.

Descriptions of Heaven

Now that we've identified the location of heaven, let's discuss its description. What does heaven look like? The Bible discusses physical and geographical attributes in heaven just like there are on earth. In Genesis Chapter 1:6 (KJV), the Hebrew word for "firmament" is *raqiya*[15] and means an "extended surface, (solid) expanse," "flat expanse," "the vault of heaven," "supporting waters above it." The meaning of the word lets us know there are physical properties to the ceiling of the second heaven and the floor of the third heaven. In fact, some Hebrew scholars teach there is an ocean of water above the expanse resting on the solid surface of the third heaven. Let's discuss some of the descriptions of heaven mentioned in the Bible:

Mount Zion – Hebrews 12:22 (AMP) says, "But you have come to Mount Zion and to the city of the living God, the heavenly Jerusalem." At the center of heaven is Mount Zion. It is where the city of God, the heavenly Jerusalem is located. It is called the mountain of the Lord. God describes this place in Psalm 50:2 (KJV), "Out of Zion, the perfection of beauty, God hath shined." The word perfection means complete, perfect, and perfectly beautiful. It is the crown of perfection in heaven and beautiful beyond words to describe.

Heavenly Jerusalem or New Jerusalem – Revelation 21:2 (KJV) says, "And I John saw the holy city, new Jerusalem, coming down from God out of heaven, prepared as a bride adorned for her husband." How many of you want to live in this inner city? Most cities today aren't very pleasant; however, this is not the case with the New Jerusalem. The heavenly Jerusalem will one day descend from heaven and be presented to the saints of God on earth.

Its construction began before the creation of earth. This is confusing to some because in addition to being called the heavenly Jerusalem, it is also called the New Jerusalem. But when you look closely at the text, it is quickly explained. The Greek word for "new" is *kainos*[16] and while it can mean "recently made" as in new, it also means "unused." There is coming a day when the saints of God will possess an eternal city that is unused and has never been inhabited.

Revelation Chapter 21 describes the splendor of this city. It is 1,400 miles long, wide, and high. The base of the city covers nearly two million square miles. Some have described the city as a cube, and others say it is a pyramid, but either way it is of tremendous size. The city has twelve foundations, each garnished with a precious stone engraved with one of the names of the twelve Apostles. Surrounding the city is a massive two hundred feet high wall made of jasper. The walls have twelve gates, three on each side made from a single pearl engraved with the name of one of the twelve tribes of Israel. As if this was not luxurious enough, the streets of the city are of pure gold and looks like transparent crystal.

It is unclear if the names engraved in the foundations and gates were placed there before the creation of humans. Either God foresaw the history of humanity and had these twenty-four names carved on the foundations and doors before he created the earth, or they were added as the story of humanity unfolded. Either way, it shows the extent of God's love for us as he planned out every detail of creation. One day, this city will be our inheritance.

The Throne of God - II Chronicles 18:18 (KJV), "I saw the Lord sitting upon his throne, and all the host of heaven standing on his right hand and on his left." Ezekiel 10 describes the throne as being mobile and made of sapphire with four wheels made of beryl. Attached to the throne are six cherubim. Four gives mobility to the throne at God's command and two on each side face inward and cover God's glory.

River of Life and Tree of Life – Revelation 22:1-2 (KJV), "And he shewed me a pure river of water of life, clear as crystal, proceeding out of the throne of God and of the Lamb. In the midst of the street of it, and on either side of the river, was there the tree of life." Imagine if you will the most beautiful throne room, and from the throne proceeds a pure river of life that flows through the city. The river is pure, clean, and free from anything unclean, and it gives its recipients the absolute fullness of eternal life that belongs to God. Amazingly, this eternal life of God is in both the River of Life and the Tree of Life. The Tree of Life produces twelve varieties of fruit, one for each month. The fruit from the tree yield eternal life, and the leaves of the tree are for the healing of the nations.

Mansions in Heaven – "In my Father's house are many mansions: if it were not so, I would have told you" (John 14:2 KJV). Jesus told his disciples that heaven includes dwelling places that God's children will be able to go to and live in.

Light and Darkness

As we conclude our discussion of heaven, we need to pause for a moment and think about light and darkness. At first this may seem odd but as we continue with the story of humanity, it will provide clarity. I John 1:5 (KJV) says, "This then is the message which we have heard of him, and declare unto you, that God is light, and in him is no darkness at all." James 1:17 (ASV) says, "Every good and perfect gift is from above, coming down from the Father of lights, with whom can be no variation, neither shadow that is cast by turning."

There is no darkness in God. In the beginning of creation, darkness did not exist. Think about that for a moment. I Timothy 6:16 (NKJV) says, "who alone has immortality, dwelling in unapproachable light." God is light and dwells in light. In him is no darkness nor a shadow causing darkness. Since God was present in the beginning, the original state of existence was light. Therefore, darkness had a beginning. This is a profound statement and contrary to what many teach.

When God said, "Let there be light" in Genesis 1:3 (KJV), some have incorrectly interpreted this to mean God created light. However, this is an incorrect interpretation. As we shall discuss later, something happened to conceal the light of God. When God said, "Let there be light" (Genesis 1:3 KJV), he pierced the darkness with his light and would no longer permit darkness to prevail.

In the beginning, God created heaven and earth and all of creation dwelled in light. This is the beginning of our story.

Reflections of Who I AM

1. Why did God create heaven first?
2. What are the three heavens mentioned in the Bible?
3. Where is heaven (the abode of God) located?
4. Since God is light and in him is no darkness, what are the implications regarding darkness?
5. In the descriptions of heaven, what does the Bible teach about the tree of life and the river of life?
6. Jesus said, "I AM the bread of life" (John 6:35 NKJV). How can the information discussed in this Chapter help you apply the fullness of that truth in your daily life?

Prayer of Activation

Our Father in heaven, I thank you for the creation of heaven and the assurance that you created for us a place of eternity. Help me to realize that you are light, and every good and perfect gift comes from you. Help me to live in your presence each day and let it be a doorway to the riches of heaven in my life. I pray this in the name of Jesus, Amen.

CHAPTER 3

The Inhabitants of Heaven

"By the word of the Lord were the heavens made; and all the host of them by the breath of his mouth" (Psalm 33:6 KJV).

After the creation of heaven and prior to forming the earth, God made the inhabitants of heaven. The subject of angels is one of the major themes of theological study, and yet the topic is often ignored. I imagine the subject is overlooked because it is a topic of much speculation and biblical text leads us to uncomfortable places. Who were these original residents of heaven and what are their purposes? Most of the angelic host maintained their loyalty to God but one-third of them rebelled and fell from their original state. In his chapter we will discuss some of these areas of mystery and dare tread where many will not go.

Angels are Created Beings with Diverse Responsibilities

The angelic host were spoken into existence by the word of God. Job 38:7 confirms to us they were created before the earth since they watched God create our planet and shouted for joy at what they were beholding. The host of heaven includes the angels around the throne and all the heavenly host that go forth to wage war and serve God.

This does not mean all the angelic host are waring angels. The Hebrew word normally used for "angel" is *malak*,[17] which means "messenger." The Bible describes a hierarchy among the angels and their description often refers to their function or assignment. For example, consider the following:

1. Archangels or Watchers – These are the chief, prince, or leader angels referenced in I Thessalonians 4, and Jude. We get a further description of these angels in Enoch XX: 1-8:

    > "And these are the names of the holy angels who watch. Uriel, one of the holy angels, who is over the world and over Tartarus. Raphael, one of the holy angels, who is over the spirits of men. Raguel, one of the holy angels who takes vengeance on the world of the luminaries. Michael, one of the holy angels, to wit, he that is set over the best part of humankind and over chaos. Saraqael, one of the holy angels, who is set over the spirits, who sin in the spirit. Gabriel, one of the holy angels, who is over Paradise and the serpents and the Cherubim. Remiel, one of the holy angels, whom God set over those who rise."[18]

2. Cherubim or Living Creatures – Cherubim are first referenced in Genesis as guarding Eden after Adam and Eve were expelled. They are described in Ezekiel as having four wings and four faces including the face of a man, the face of a lion, the face of an ox, and the face of an eagle. Their appearance is as burning coals of fire and they move as flashes of lightening. They cover God's throne and give it mobility. The most famous of the Cherubim is Lucifer.
3. Seraphim – They are burning angels of fire described in Isaiah 6 and they hover above God's throne. They have six wings and cry out holy, holy, holy, is the Lord of host. Perhaps they cry out

as they continuously see something new about the splendor and glory of God.

4. Thrones, Dominions, Principalities, Powers – These are ruling angels and are referenced in Colossians 1, Ephesians 1, and Ephesians 3.

It is clear from scripture that the host of heaven were created by God and assigned specific purposes. So why did God create angels? Hebrews 1:13-14 (KJV) says, "But to which of the angels said he at any time, Sit on my right hand, until I make thine enemies thy footstool? Are they not all ministering spirits, sent forth to minister for them who shall be heirs of salvation?"

From their inception, the angelic host were created to minister, serve, and give aid to a race of beings that had not yet been created. Humans would become the heirs of salvation, and the angels were designed specifically to assist God to minister to them. What's most remarkable about this statement is when the angels were first created, there was no such thing as sin, rebellion, humans, or the need for salvation. These were foreign concepts. This tells us God had a grand design and the end game was in his mind from the beginning. Before the creation of earth or humanity, God create the angelic host so they could one day minister to his children who would become the heirs of salvation. Seeing the end from the beginning, God knew one-third of the angelic host would rebel against him and so the mystery of God's relationship to humanity was kept hidden. Therefore, in his genius, God withheld from the angels his full plan. This is documented to us in the following scriptures:

> "And to make all see what is the fellowship of the mystery, which from the beginning of the ages has been hidden in God who created all things through Jesus Christ; to the intent that now the manifold wisdom of God might be made known by the church to the principalities and powers in the heavenly places, according to the eternal purpose which He accomplished in Christ Jesus our Lord" (Ephesians 3:9-11 NKJV).

> "Unto whom it was revealed, that not unto themselves, but unto us they did minister the things, which are now reported unto you by them that have preached the gospel unto you with the Holy Ghost sent down from heaven; which things the angels desire to look into" (I Peter 1:12 KJV).

The Divine Council

As we think about the responsibilities of the host of heaven, we need to mention the Divine Council. For most Christians and churches, this is a topic not discussed. Most have never heard of it or choose to ignore it. As you might expect, the subject is controversial and often misunderstood. While there is academic study on this topic, for our purposes, I will provide a very brief overview.

At some point during creation, biblical text discusses God's establishment of a Divine Council from among the heavenly host. While God is sovereign and can do all things, it has always been his pattern to use creation to carry out his will and purposes. To that end, it appears the Divine Council was established to assist God in the administrative activities over creation.

To confirm the existence of such a council, here are a few passages of scripture:

- "God has taken his place in the divine council; in the midst of the gods he holds judgment" (Psalm 82:1 ESV).
- "For who hath stood in the counsel of the Lord, and hath perceived and heard his word" (Jeremiah 23:18 KJV)?
- "Were you present to hear the secret counsel of God? And do you limit [the possession of] wisdom to yourself" (Job 15:8 AMPC)?
- "For who in the heavens can be compared to the Lord? Who among the mighty [heavenly beings] can be likened to the Lord, A God greatly feared and revered in the council of the holy (angelic) ones, and to be feared and worshipfully revered above all those who are round about Him" (Psalm 89:6-7 AMPC)?

Of the above scriptures, Psalm 82 speaks most clearly to the topic of the Divine Council. Let's look closely at this scripture and the Hebrew text used in Psalm 82:1 (ESV), "God (Elohim) has taken his place in the divine council (Edah); in the midst of the gods (Elohim) he holds judgment." Before this becomes confusing or causes panic, rest assured the Bible is not suggesting there are other Gods beside the Father, Son, and Holy Spirit. Isaiah 45:5 (KJV) says, "I am the Lord, and there is none else, there is no God beside me."

As we have previously discussed, the Hebrew word *elohim* refers to those in the spirit realm. Regarding the Divine Council, the Hebrew word used is *Edah*[19] and it means a "congregation," "assembled together by appointment," a "company of angels." In other words, the members of the Divine Council consisted of *elohim* appointed by God. They meet, discuss the plans and purposes of God, and assist him in the affairs of creation. We know little about the divine council, some scholars believe Lucifer was a ranking member. Even if this were not true, he is a central figure in our story and God's plans for the kingdom.

Who is Lucifer/Satan?

Before his rebellion, Satan's name was Lucifer. From all accounts, he was an angel of importance and believed to be the first angel God created. The name Lucifer is mentioned only one time in scripture. Isaiah 14:12 (NKJV) says, "How you are fallen from heaven, O Lucifer, son of the morning! How you are cut down to the ground, You who weakened the nations!"

The Hebrew word for "Lucifer" is *heylel*[20] and it means "shinning one," "bright star" or "morning star." It implies a light-bearer and his name is a reference to one of the functions he served in heaven. Ezekiel 28:14 (KJV) says, "Thou art the anointed cherub that covereth." The word "anointed" is *mimshach*[21] and it is the only time this form of the word is used in scripture. It means an "expansion with extended wings." It is a reference to the Cherubim that covered the Mercy Seat atop the Ark of the Covenant. When God gave Moses the design of the tabernacle, he instructed him to pattern it after what was in heaven (Hebrews 8:5). Covering the Mercy Seat were two cherubim with outstretched wings that covered the glory and presence of God. Accordingly, it appears as though one of Lucifer's original functions was to cover the glory and presence of God upon his throne.

What else do we know about this angel before his fall? Ezekiel 28:12, 14-15 (KJV) says, "You were the seal of perfection, Full of wisdom and perfect in beauty.... You were the anointed cherub who covers; I established you; You were on the holy mountain of God; You walked back and forth in the midst of fiery stones. You were perfect in your ways from the day you were created, Till iniquity was found in you." The Bible says Lucifer was the seal of perfection. Ezekiel 28:12 (AMPC) says, "You are the full measure and pattern of exactness [giving the finishing touch to all that constitutes completeness]." He was entirely and perfectly beautiful. He was a step above in both appearance and intellect. He was full of wisdom and perfect in all his ways from the day he was created. In other words, no other angel was his equal.

The Mystery of the Precious Stones

If this were not enough, Ezekiel gives us another intriguing description of Lucifer and brings up one of the mysteries in the Bible, namely, the mystery of the precious stones. Ezekiel 28:13 (KJV) says:

> "Thou hast been in Eden the garden of God; every precious stone was thy covering, the sardius, topaz, and the diamond, the beryl, the onyx, and the jasper, the sapphire, the emerald, and the carbuncle, and gold: the workmanship of thy tabrets and of thy pipes was prepared in thee in the day that thou wast created."

When God created Lucifer, the Bible says he was prepared, fitted, or fashioned with tabrets and pipes. Tabrets imply a musical instrument like a drum or tambourine. It is believed Lucifer was responsible for leading the choirs of heaven and led the angelic praises as God created the earth. Job 38:4, 7 (NIV) says, "Where were you when I laid the earth's foundation? .... while the morning stars sang together and all the angels shouted for joy?"

But what were the "pipes" Ezekiel spoke about? The Hebrew word used is *neqeb*[22] and it means a "socket or setting a gem." These are the hollow sockets a jeweler fashions to hold precious stones. In fact, Ezekiel says every precious stone was his covering. Why then was Lucifer covered with gemstones? The Hebrew word for "covering" is *mecukkah*[23] and it means a "garniture." It is an ornament or decoration used to adorn. At times, they were for memorials or a reward for achievement or position. In other words, Lucifer's covering had nine precious stones as decorations or rewards for achievement.

To deepen this mystery further, these were not just any stones. They were included in the breastplate of the High Priest when he entered the Holy of Holies. According to Exodus 28:17-21, the breastplate of the High Priest included twelve precious stones that were engraved with the names of the twelve tribes of Israel. Interestingly, nine of these twelve stones were the same stones used for Lucifer's covering. Is this just a coincidence? I think not. Furthermore, when we compare the precious stones on the breastplate of the High Priest against the precious stones covering Lucifer, we find Lucifer is missing one full row of stones.

High Priest's Stones (Exodus 28:17-21)			
Column 3	**Column 2**	**Column 1**	**Rows**
Carbuncle	Topaz	Sardius	Row 1
Diamond	Sapphire	Emerald	Row 2
Amethyst	Agate	Ligure	Row 3
Jasper	Onyx	Beryl	Row 4

Lucifer's Stones (Ezekiel 28:11)			
Column 3	**Column 2**	**Column 1**	**Rows**
Diamond	Topaz	Sardius	Row 1
Jasper	Onyx	Beryl	Row 2
?	?	?	Row 3
Carbuncle	Sapphire	Emerald	Row 4

The mystery of the missing stones does not stop here; rather, it intensifies when we realize these same twelve stones on the breastplate of the High Priest correspond to the stones used in the foundations of the New Jerusalem. Those twelve foundation stones are described to us in Revelation 21:19-20. Let's compare the precious stones in the New Jerusalem with Lucifer's covering stones.

New Jerusalem Foundation	Precious Stone	Lucifer's Covering
1st Foundation	Jasper	Jasper
2nd Foundation	Sapphire	Sapphire
3rd Foundation	Chalcedony (Carbuncle)	Carbuncle
4th Foundation	Emerald	Emerald
5th Foundation	Sardonyx (Onyx)	Onyx
6th Foundation	Sardius	Sardius
7th Foundation	Chrysolyte (Diamond)	Diamond
8th Foundation	Beryl	Beryl
9th Foundation	Topaz	Topaz
10th Foundation	Chrysoprasus (Agate)	?
11th Foundation	Jacinth (Ligure)	?
12th Foundation	Amethyst	?

Once again, there are three stones missing. The one full row missing from the breastplate of the High Priest also corresponds to the top three floors or foundations of the New Jerusalem? This is more than a coincidence. Remember our definition of the Hebrew words used to describe the stones used for Lucifer's covering. They were stones given to him as rewards for achievement.

What could explain the mystery of the missing stones? We have already established that Lucifer was one of the covering angels that covered the throne of God. Just like the High Priest would go into the holy of holies to stand before the Ark of the Covenant and the Mercy Seat that represented the throne of God, Lucifer was one of the covering angels that surrounded God's throne. The High Priest would wear a breast plate of twelve precious stones, nine of which adorned Lucifer as he covered God's throne.

We have already shown that according to Hebrews 8:5 the temple on earth was patterned after what was in heaven. Therefore, as a member of the Divine Council and a covering angel, Lucifer had access to the holy of holies in heaven, a place that was limited to only the High Priest on earth. Could their roles have also been similar? Let's examine this possibility by looking at the responsibilities of the High Priest.

When God gave Moses the design for the breastplate, he called it a breastplate of judgment (Exodus 28:15). Aaron eventually became the High Priest and would wear the breastplate when he entered the Holy of Holies. But there are two more stones associated with the breastplate. They are mentioned in Exodus 28:29-30 (NKJV):

> "So Aaron shall bear the names of the sons of Israel on the breastplate of judgment over his heart, when he goes into the holy place, as a memorial before the Lord continually. And you shall put in the breastplate of judgment the Urim and the Thummim, and they shall be over Aaron's heart when he goes in before the Lord. So Aaron shall bear the judgment of the children of Israel over his heart before the Lord continually."

What are the Urim and Thummim stones? They are said to be among the mysteries handed down from God to Moses and the Jewish sages. While there are multiple thoughts on how they were used, recent scholars studying I Samuel 14:41 believe they were used for casting lots. It is believed the Urim was a black stone and if selected would mean a "No" answer; however, if the Thummim or white stone was selected, it would mean a "Yes" answer. Others believe that as God's glory filled the temple, his light would shine through the stones upon the engraved letters to spell out God's will.

As a side note, it is interesting to compare these Old Testament practices with the New Testament. Paul instructs the church in Ephesians 6:14 (NKJV), to "Stand therefore, having girded your waist with truth, having put on the breastplate of righteousness." Notice that under the Old Covenant it was a breastplate of Judgment, but under the New Covenant it is a Breastplate of Righteousness. The Apostle John in Revelation 2:17 (NKJV) says, "To him who overcomes I will give some of the hidden manna to eat. And I will give him a white stone, and on the stone a new name written which no one knows except him who receives it." Notice the reference to a white stone and the symbolism to acceptance or a "Yes" answer.

While this is intriguing, we still haven't answered the question why Lucifer was missing three stones. The answer I believe lies in the purpose of the stones. Remember, the stones were given as rewards for accomplishments. Consider I Corinthians 3:10-14 (NKJV):

> "According to the grace of God which was given to me, as a wise master builder I have laid the foundation, and another builds on it. But let each one take heed how he builds on it. For no other foundation can anyone lay than that which is laid, which is Jesus Christ. Now if anyone builds on this foundation with gold, silver, **precious stones**, wood, hay, straw, each one's work will become clear; for the Day will declare it, because it will be revealed by fire; and the fire will test each one's work, of what sort it is. If anyone's work which he has built on it endures, he will receive a reward."

As a member of the Divine Council and ranking angel in heaven, Lucifer may have taken part in the construction of the New Jerusalem; and as a reward, given a precious stone for each foundation he helped construct. Remember what Ezekiel 28:14 (KJV) says of Lucifer, "Thou art the anointed cherub that covereth; and I have set thee so: thou wast upon the holy mountain of God; thou hast walked up and down in the midst of the stones of fire." Could the stones of fire be connected to the precious stones and the Urim and Thummim? Gemologists tells us precious stones are born out of fire and heat. Perhaps the holy mountain of God was the place where the precious stones were created and were coverings of achievement or ornaments that adorned. If this is true, why is Lucifer missing three stones, which happens to correspond to the top three floors of the New Jerusalem?

As we are going to discuss in a later chapter, there came a moment when Lucifer learned of God's plans concerning the creation of humanity and decided to rebel against him. That was the moment the kingdom of darkness was born, and Lucifer became Satan, the adversary. Is it possible Lucifer's rebellion occurred after construction of the ninth foundation of the New Jerusalem but before completion of the top three floors? This is a possibility. But perhaps, there are other reasons Lucifer did not help construct the top three floors.

I believe completion of the top three floors of the New Jerusalem were reserved for Jesus, our eternal High Priest and only one worthy to complete the project. Hebrews 4:14 (NKJV) says, "Seeing then that we have a great High Priest who has passed through the heavens, Jesus the Son of God, let us hold fast our confession." In addition, Jesus told his disciples he was going to take part in the construction of the New Jerusalem. John 14:2-3 (KJV) says, "In my Father's house are many mansions: if it were not so, I would have told you. I go to prepare a place for you. And if I go and prepare a place for you, I will come again, and receive you unto myself; that where I am, there ye may be also." This is remarkable. Jesus told his disciples he would go to heaven and prepare a place for them. No doubt, he is referring to the New Jerusalem.

Why did Jesus have to complete the top three floors? Why was no one else qualified? The answer lies in the meaning of the stones used for each foundation.

The 10th Foundation Stone - Chrysoprasus (Agate) – While the Greek word for this stone tells us it is greenish yellow in color, the Hebrew word for "Agate" comes from two root words, *shabah*[24] and *shabiyb*[25]. These two root words gives us the hidden meaning of the 10th foundation of the New Jerusalem.

The first root word is *Shabah*, and it means "to take, or lead away captive." When we think about Jesus the High Priest, the Bible says in Hebrews 4:8 (KJV), "When he ascended up on high, he led captivity captive, and gave gifts unto men." This image is further described to us in Colossians 2:15 (KJV), "And having spoiled principalities and powers, he made a shew of them openly, triumphing over them in it." These scriptures describe Jesus as the conqueror over death, hell and the grave as he first descended into hell to defeat the powers of darkness. As he did, he made an open shame of the kingdom of darkness. Leading captivity captive is a phrase used to describe an ancient custom of the defeat of another kingdom. The defeated leader would be stripped and lead around in a public display of shame. For this reason alone, Lucifer could never qualify to complete the 10th floor of the New Jerusalem.

The second root word is *Shabiyb*, and it means "flame as split into tongues." It is a foreshadow of Acts 2:3 (KJV), "And there appeared unto them cloven tongues like as of fire, and it sat upon each of them." This occurred on the Day of Pentecost when the Holy Spirit descended and filled the upper room. When John the Baptist was baptizing, he said in Matthew 3:11 (NKJV), "I indeed baptize you with water unto repentance, but He who is coming after me is mightier than I, whose sandals I am not worthy to carry. He will baptize you with the Holy Spirit and fire." On the Day of Pentecost, the wind or breath of God filled the upper room. This was the same wind or breath of the God that hovered over the face of the deep at creation. The only way to the Father is through Jesus. He alone is qualified to baptize his children with tongues of fire. Again, this is an accomplishment and position Lucifer could never achieve.

The 11th Foundation Stone - Jacinth (Ligure) - The Greek word indicates this is a dark blue stone like a sapphire. The Hebrew word for "Ligure" is *Ishem*[26] and while it means "a precious stone," the precise meaning is unknown. The stone represents the tribe of Dan. It is believed by some that the flag for the tribe of Dan was of sapphire color and Genesis 49:17 (NIV) says, "Dan will be a snake by the roadside." The sapphire color matches the color used for the High Priest's robe. The snake on Dan's flag is no doubt symbolic of the snake in the garden and an enemy of Israel. For these reasons, Lucifer could not fulfill the qualifications for this stone.

The 12th Foundation Stone - Amethyst - The root of the Hebrew word for "Amethyst" is *halam*[27] and it means to "be healthy, strong" and to "dream." This was not the characteristics of Lucifer. The Greek word for Amethyst comes from two root words, *alpha*[28] and *methyo*.[29] *Alpha* is the first letter of the Greek alphabet and is used to signify the beginning. Jesus said in Revelation 1:8 (KJV), "I am Alpha and Omega, the beginning and the ending." *Methyo* has two meanings. The first meaning is "to drink to intoxication." The word was used in Acts 2:15 describing those who had been filled with the Holy Spirit. The second meaning is "one who has shed blood profusely." It is a picture of how

Christ shed his blood for us. The word is also used in Revelation 17:6 to describe the martyrs of Christ. Lucifer could never become a martyr for Christ, and he did not shed his blood for others. Therefore, he could have never received this reward.

No one except Jesus was qualified to complete the top three floors of the New Jerusalem. While the angelic host may have assisted God, only Jesus was worthy to finish the work.

Other Purposes of Angels

While one-third of the angelic host rebelled against God, two-thirds continued to be ministering spirits for the heirs of salvation and aids to God in his kingdom. We could exhaust the rest of this book describing the work of the angels; however, we'll conclude with a couple of positive notes about their work. Psalm 91:11 (NKJV) says, "For He shall give His angels charge over you, To keep you in all your ways." Luke 16:22 (KJV) says, "And it came to pass, that the beggar died, and was carried by the angels into Abraham's bosom."

Reflections of Who I AM

1. Who were the host of heaven created by God in Psalm 33:6?
2. Why were three stones missing from Lucifer's covering?
3. Who is our eternal High Priest?
4. How do the angels minister to or help believers?
5. Who did Jesus say would be the future inhabitants of the city of God?
6. Jesus said, "I AM the bread of life" (John 6:35 NKJV). How can the information discussed in this Chapter help you apply the fullness of that truth in your daily life?

Prayer of Activation

Our Father in heaven, I thank you for your Son Jesus, our eternal High Priest. I thank you that upon his death, resurrection, and ascension, he has prepared a place for us to be with you throughout eternity. You have gone to such extraordinary measures and painstaking actions to secure my future as your son/daughter. Help me to walk in the light of your truth. I choose to keep my eyes fixed on you and I am confident you will protect me from all the onslaughts of the kingdom of darkness. Christ alone was worthy to complete the preparations in his Father's house and I choose to follow you all the days of my life. I pray this in the name of Jesus, Amen.

CHAPTER 4

Earth, Heaven's Frontier

"In the beginning God created the heaven and the earth" (Genesis 1:1 KJV).

"Space: the final frontier. These are the voyages of the starship Enterprise. Its five-year mission: to explore strange new worlds. To seek out new life and new civilizations. To boldly go where no man has gone before!"[30] These words introduced every episode of the Star Trek series as Captain Kirk and his crew explored the unknown. Think about an age when there were no planets or star systems, only heaven, the atmosphere surrounding it, and the angelic host. Imagine heaven's excitement when God announced his plans to create earth.

Earth was not only a new frontier; it was heaven's only frontier. Patterned after heaven itself, the earth was God's design for his kingdom on display. It would be a physical world patterned after the spiritual and natural realms of heaven. It would be among the first fruits of creation, the dwelling place for a race of humans that had not yet been created, and the future home of the New Jerusalem and inheritance of the Saints. The earth plays a significant role in the kingdom of God and the story of humanity. So, how did it begin?

Ancient of Days

God began creation with the end game in mind. It is recorded in Matthew 25:34 (KJV), "Then shall the King say unto them on his right hand, Come, ye blessed of my Father, inherit the kingdom prepared for you from the foundation of the world." The Greek word for "foundation" is *katabole*[31] and it means "a throwing or laying down." The word is used to describe the laying down of a foundation and also the depositing of seed in the womb. In other words, it speaks to the origins of the earth before its completion.

This concept is reaffirmed to us in Daniel 7:22 (KJV), "Until the Ancient of days came, and judgment was given to the saints of the Most High; and the time came that the saints possessed the kingdom." The Prophet Daniel wrote about a future event when the Ancient of Days would come, and the saints would possess the kingdom of God. But who is this Ancient of Days? The phrase is a title describing the timelessness of God. It is also a description of a period before time began, in the age's past. In other words, the ancient of days was the period before time, before the measurements of days, weeks, months, and years. This was the period before Genesis 1:2 when the earth was in its original state prepared as the kingdom of God.

In God's planning of the kingdom, in the eon's past, he wanted to share his kingdom, authority, and leadership with a people who would rule and reign with him. They would be a people of kings, priests, and overcomers. Looking through history, God saw every person that would ever be born. He gave each of us a name and penned it in a Book of Life (Revelation 17:8). This Book of Life is the registry of the citizens of heaven; and to each one, he gave a special name reserved for the day it would be revealed to them. God foresaw and planned a day of celebration when all he prepared would be revealed. Before there was anything, God had you and me in mind and he knew us all by name. How amazing is that?

Eyewitness Accounts

The angelic host were eyewitness accounts of God's creation of the earth, and they shouted for joy as he created. What did they see? What does the Bible tell us about God's creation of the earth? Every construction project begins with laying a foundation. In God's discourse in Job 38:4-7 (NIV), he says, "where were you when I laid the earth's foundation? Tell me, if you understand. Who marked off its dimensions? Surely you know! Who stretched a measuring line across it? On what were its footings set, or who laid its cornerstone—while the morning stars sang together and all the angels shouted for joy?" No wonder the angels shouted for joy as they watched God lay out the dimensions of earth. Job declares that the footings of the earth hung upon nothing but empty space.

After creating the foundation and setting its footings, God laid the first cornerstone and carved out the earth's surface, mountain ranges and waters of the earth. It is recorded in Isaiah 40:12 (NIV), "Who has measured the waters in the hollow of his hand, or with the breadth of his hand marked off the heavens? Who has held the dust of the earth in a basket, or weighed the mountains on the scales and the hills in a balance?" What an amazing description of God creating the earth. Imagine God scooping up water in the hollow of his hand and using that to measuring the amount of water needed for the earth. Imagine God using the breadth or span of his hand to mark off the heavens. A span was the measurement from the thumb to the little finger when spread out. It was a measurement of nine inches. God used the breadth of his hand (about nine inches) to measure the heavens. Imagine God taking a basket, filling it with dust, and using that to measure the amount of dust needed to create the earth. Finally, imagine God taking a set of scales and with a pinch of dirt and rock measuring the weight of the mountains and hills. God is the ultimate architect and master builder.

Eden - In Earth as it is in Heaven

We can only imagine what it looked like to behold creation. In the Lord's prayer, Jesus gave us a clue of God's original design for earth. Matthew 6:10 (KJV) says, "Thy kingdom come, Thy will be done in earth, as it is in heaven." In this passage, Jesus discussed the concept of heaven on earth and confirmed for us that the earth was patterned after heaven.

When God created the earth, he began in the geographical center, Eden. Did you know Eden existed prior to God planting the garden for Adam and Eve? Genesis 2:8 (NKJV) says, "The Lord God planted a garden eastward in Eden, and there He put the man whom He had formed." Notice that the Garden's name isn't Eden. Instead, the garden was planted in Eden, a geographical area referenced by God himself. While the location of Eden has been debated for ages, biblical texts and the teachings of the sages confirms its boundaries with the center being located on the temple mount in Jerusalem. This is confirmed in the Book of Jubilees 89:19, "And he knew that the Garden of Eden is the holy of holies, and the dwelling of the Lord, and Mount Sinai the centre of the desert, and Mount Zion -the centre of the navel of the earth: these three were created as holy places facing each other."[32] This teaching says that the center of the earth is Israel, the center of Israel is Jerusalem, and the center of Jerusalem is the Temple Mount.

If you were to travel to Israel today and visit Jerusalem, you would see the Temple Mount and the present-day Dome of the Rock. Under this dome lies a huge stone. It is called the Foundation Stone or Foundation Rock. This is how the Dome of the Rock got its name. It is taught that this is the cornerstone referenced in Job 38 when God set the first cornerstone of the earth during creation. No wonder Jerusalem has such significance even in this present day. It is the most contested piece of real estate on Earth and central to the plans of God.

Eden was the center of the kingdom. In the center of Eden was a mountain, and on the sides of the north was a place called Mount Zion. Resting upon Mount Zion is the foundation stone, the corner stone upon which all the earth was created. Setting on the foundation stone was a throne upon which a King would sit to rule and reign over God's creation. It was the seat of power, the seat of honor, the seat of royal authority. It is also called the Throne of Glory.

God gave Ezekiel a vision of this throne. It is recorded in Ezekiel 43:7 (NKJV), "Son of man, this is the place of My throne and the place of the soles of My feet, where I will dwell in the midst of the children of Israel forever." Jeremiah confirms for us this throne was present at creation. Jeremiah 17:12 (AMP) says, "A glorious throne, set on high from the beginning, Is the place of our sanctuary (the temple)." Jeremiah also proves he is referring to a location here on earth and not in heaven when he wrote Jeremiah 3:17 (NKJV), "At that time Jerusalem shall be called The Throne of the LORD, and all the nations shall be gathered to it."

God's creation of the earth was strategic. Can you imagine the kingdom of God on earth and what such a place would have been like in the beginning? Imagine a place that is more beautiful than any place you have ever seen. A diverse landscape with rolling hills, majestic mountains, scenic lakes, and rivers, living waterfalls, forests, and meadows. A place where luscious gardens of every beautiful flower is grown. A place with abundant orchards and every imaginable fruit. No fruit is withering on the tree or vine, and there are no worm holes or bruises on fruit that has fallen to the ground. Every leaf, stem, and flower are perfectly formed with no sign of imperfection. Every blade of grass has the richest green colors. No animal or insect has died. There is no trace of death or decomposition, and everything is alive and full of life.

With such an abundance of life, colors abound. The human eye can see millions of colors, but the infinite number of colors in this place are beyond anything we have seen. It is a place that has no darkness and no shadows because darkness does not exist. God's light is in every place and from every direction. Because of that, every location is a vista to behold the beauty of ultra-high-definition living color that cannot be expressed in words. The trees are so big our biggest redwoods and sequoias today dwarf next to them. Everywhere you look you see something new, and it leaves you breathless and in awe.

This place has an abundance of diverse sounds, all crisp and clear. The faintest of sounds travels with precision and is tuned to the environment of its surroundings. Every living thing has been created with such precise detail that the simple ratios of length, width, and height combined with its material composition, results in a precise mathematical relationship to produce cords of sound with divine quality. It invites you to pause and just enjoy. As you hear the immersive surround sound of the symphony of life, it creates instant peace and tranquility.

The molecular arrangement of every particle in this place has been arranged in such a way that it has created a cornucopia of different textures; all inviting the beholder to touch and feel its uniqueness. The by-passer pauses what they are doing just to reach out and feel what things are made of. Fields are covered with the softest of grass and laced with precious stones, yet they are soft to the touch and soft as cotton to walk upon. The leaves of certain plants feel like silk and the bark of trees are diverse and multi-dimensional. As nature is embraced, it causes a sensation of comfort and enhances rest while at the same time exhilarating and satisfying the desire for adventure.

The air is crisp, and fresh, and filled with the fragrance of its surroundings. Every plant and spice emanate an aroma that is meant to be enjoyed. There is no foul smell or unpleasant odor. Instead, everything is pleasing and complimentary to the other senses. The smells of fruit and vegetation, combined with the perfection of their design, produce a variety of tastes from the simple to the complex. While some taste spicy, sweet, or complex, others are plain and simple. All are mouth-watering and leave you wanting more. Some are just to be viewed, and the aromas enjoyed as they add to the ambiance of nature.

There is no crime or evil to contend with in this place. The inhabitants speak no ill word and have no evil thought. There is no corruption of any kind. Can you imagine what that would be like? The land is filled with the host of heaven and angelic beings are so beautiful you can't help but stare at them. Their size, strength and appearance are mesmerizing. Every inhabitant in this land has purpose. They are rich in talents and abilities and complement one another in precision and harmony. It is a place where the inhabitants are busy while at the same time experiencing rest, peace, order, and unity, and always filled with the anticipation of what's next.

This place far exceeds any Pandora the human mind can dream of today. It is a place not only akin to being over the rainbow but a place from where all rainbows proceed. As you walk through the countryside, you walk on streets paved with gold and every precious stone. Common place riches include precious stones of jasper, sapphire, turquoise, emerald, onyx, sardius, diamond, beryl, topaz, agate, jacinth, and amethyst. Gold is in abundance and the beauty of each city reflect the glory of the surroundings. The appearance of everything displays richness, abundance, and plenty. There is no shortage or want in this place.

In the center of this magnificent kingdom is a mountain, and on the mountain the most beautiful city you have ever seen. At the top and center of the city is a throne, and from the throne proceeds a pure river of water of life, clear as crystal. The river of life flows down the mountain and branches out to water the land in all directions. It is a river of living waters, liquid life, and each drink brings with it a fountain of youth. On each side of the river are trees of life that bear twelve types of fruit, each unique and in abundance in its own season. The leaves of the trees are for perpetual health. There is no sickness of any kind. There are no doctors, no nurses, or healthcare concerns because everyone is in perfect health, without flaw or blemish. All this, a paradise of perfection.

Although this sounds familiar to the breathtaking descriptions of views found in heaven, such a place once existed here on earth, in a kingdom and a land called Eden. Before there were humans, there was a paradise on earth, created and modeled after heaven itself. It existed long ago when everything was perfect and good. It was all part of God's master plan that would eventually include a family with whom He would live with and be one with just as the Father, Son, and Holy Spirit are one. This was the beginning stages of Heaven on Earth, the kingdom of God, and the unfolding of the greatest mystery of the ages. It was the beginning of God's plan for what should be natural and normal.

Reflections of Who I Am

1. Who/What is the Ancient of Days?
2. According to Jewish sages, where did God begin the Earth's creation?
3. Did Eden exist prior to the creation of Adam and Eve, and what are the implications of this truth for the future?
4. What are some of your greatest questions about creation and the story of humanity?
5. Jesus said, "I AM the bread of life" (John 6:35 NKJV). How can the information discussed in this Chapter help you apply the fullness of that truth in your daily life?

Prayer of Activation

Our Father in heaven, I thank you for planning a kingdom and a family before the foundations of the world. Thank you for loving me so much you included me in those plans. You are the same yesterday, today, and forever and your plans for my life do not change because of my circumstances. Open my spirit and soul to dream again and to know your eternal truth. Help me to not covet or become envious of others. Instead, help my heart rejoice over the things that make you rejoice and my heart break over the things that make your heart break. I pray for peace upon this earth, especially your beloved city Jerusalem, the focal point of history. Help our leaders turn to you and seek your favor rather than the favor of others. My life is in your hands to turn whichever way you will. Lead me into all truth. I pray this in the name of Jesus, Amen.

CHAPTER 5

The Fall of Satan and the Desolation of Earth

"The earth was without form and an empty waste, and darkness was upon the very great deep" (Genesis 1:2 AMPC).

When it comes to the story of planet Earth, many have wondered how sin and evil began and how creation became flawed? God's amazing and wonderful masterpiece somehow became blemished and disfigured. The context of our story is incomplete without an understanding of what took place in Eden and the Earth after Genesis 1:1. It is important that you understand Eden is not a fairy tale or an allegory of what could be or might have been. It was a real place with a history that impacted our story in a dramatic way.

As the first geographical area and most ancient place on Earth, the mountainous region of Eden was the headquarters of God's paradise. It showcased the abundance and luxury of creation and soon became a distraction to Lucifer. While the angelic host of heaven continued their oohs and aahs, Lucifer began to focus his attention on the crown jewel of creation. Eden became the pièce de résistance and the stage upon which the origins of evil would be played out.

Within the heart of Lucifer, a rebellion began to stir, and soon an abominable act that had never existed would threaten to abort the fledgling kingdom. According to Revelation 12:4, Lucifer and one-third of the angelic host conspired together and rebelled against the kingdom of God. In this chapter, we will investigate issues that have been debated by academics for ages. We will begin with an examination of the descriptions of Earth in Genesis 1:2 and explore questions relating to the fall of Lucifer, when it took place, and the impact upon creation.

The Gap

To the casual reader, Genesis 1:2 appears to be a description of the original creation and a picture of what Earth looked like in its infancy. However, a deep dig into the text raises many sobering questions. To begin our analysis, let's scrutinize this text more thoroughly by studying the meaning of the Hebrew words used in this passage.

- Was (*Hayah*[33]) – "come to pass, become, be."
- Without Form (*tou*[34]) – "that which is wasted, laid waste," "destruction," "emptiness, vanity," "in vain."
- Void (*bou*[35]) – "something void and empty," "an undistinguishable ruin."
- Darkness (*hosek*[36]) – "a dark place, as of Hades," "misery, adversity," "wickedness." The root of the word means "to be dark as withholding light."
- Face (*panim*[37]) – "face." It comes from a root word that means to "turn," "pass away," or "banish."
- Deep (*tehom*[38]) – "wave," "a great quantity of waters," "abyss, even used of the deep hollows of the earth." It is one of the names for hell. This is the first reference to hell in the Bible. In the Greek, the *abyssos*[39] is the "bottomless," "the pit."

This text describes the earth as a land that had been laid waste, a place of destruction and chaos. It is empty, void, and filled with chaos. If that's not bad enough, God's light has been withheld and the earth is covered in darkness, wickedness, and death. Even the most novice of scholars quickly concludes something is amiss.

While these descriptions of Earth are upsetting, the question becomes what happened in the gap between Genesis 1:1 and Genesis 1:2 to cause the Earth to become a barren dark wasteland? The answer to this question is alarmingly clear. This was the period Lucifer and one-third of the angelic host rebelled against God. To prove this assertion, let's consider the following:

1. When Satan (the serpent) presents himself to Adam and Eve in Genesis Chapter 3, he had already fallen and taken on the role of tempter. Therefore, his fall had to have occurred after Genesis 1:1 but before God created humans and their encounter with the serpent in the Garden.
2. Genesis 1:1 says the Earth became (*Hayah*) without form and void. There has been much debate over the word *Hayah* among Hebrew scholars. Some argue it should be translated "was" while others argue it should be translated "to become" or "come to pass." To me, the argument for translating *Hayah* as "come to pass" is settled when considering the description of the Earth. The context of this verse is indisputable when examining the condition of creation at this point. As a side note, hold on to the meaning of this word as we will discuss it in later chapters. We will see this one Hebrew word gives us tremendous insight to the nature of God and his name.
3. Genesis 1:2 is the first reference to darkness. As we have previously noted, I John 1:5 (KJV) says, "God is light, and in him is no darkness at all." James 1:17 tells us that God does not even cause a shadow when he turns. All of creation was filled with light and light was the natural state of creation until darkness was born. Sin, darkness, and the kingdom of darkness began when the first sin was committed by the original sinner, Lucifer. The fact that darkness was upon the face of the deep confirms to us that Lucifer's fall occurred prior to Genesis 1:2.

4. Genesis 1:2 gives us the first reference to wickedness and destruction. This is a clear reference to the teachings of Romans 6:23 (KJV), "the wages of sin is death."
5. Genesis 1:2 gives us the first reference to the abyss or hell. Jesus taught his disciples that hell was created as a result of Satan's fall. Matthew 25:41 (NKJV), "Then He will also say to those on the left hand, Depart from Me, you cursed, into the everlasting fire prepared for the devil and his angels."
6. Scripture tells us God did not originally create the earth as a place of chaos or vanity. Isaiah 45:18 (KJV) says, "For thus saith the Lord that created the heavens; God himself that formed the earth and made it; he hath established it, he created it not in vain, he formed it to be inhabited." That same verse in the Orthodox Jewish Bible (OJB) reads, "He created it not tohu (chaos), he formed it to be inhabited." These are not contradictory verses to the Genesis account. Instead, Genesis 1:2 describes the aftermath of an existential event.
7. Genesis 1:2 mentions the face of the earth. The original text gives reference to presence or surface and means to turn away. What caused God to turn away from his creation and withhold his light. Habakkuk 1:13 (NKJV) says, "You are of purer eyes than to behold evil, And cannot look on wickedness."

The evidence is overwhelmingly clear. The fall of Lucifer occurred in the gap between Genesis 1:1 and Genesis 1:2. Understanding these events is relevant to the mysteries of God that have been hidden from the foundation of the world. Consider this. We are living in the 21st Century; and if this is the end of days, we are born at the end of our story. It's like going to a bookstore, picking up a book, and opening it towards the end. While the pages you read may seem fascinating, you have no context of what happened in the first three-fourths of the book. The truth of our beginning supplies context to the creation of humanity, gives us key insight to our purpose, and shows us God's plan for the kingdom.

Lucifer's Fall – The Original Sin

Many Christians mistakenly point to Adam and Eve as the origins of sin; however, the author and originator of sin is Satan. I John 3:8 (KJV) says, "He who sins is of the devil, for the devil has sinned from the beginning." There are two questions we must answer. First, why did Lucifer fall? Secondly, what exactly was his sin?

In the gap between Genesis 1:1 and Genesis 1:2, the seeds of corruption began as Lucifer focused his attention upon Eden and particularly the sides of the north and seat of authority. We know from scripture that angels had access to both heaven and earth. At some point, Lucifer began to wonder what role the angels would play, and what position he would hold. Perhaps he thought God was preparing all this for him. Maybe this would be another jewel for his covering as a reward for his acts of service. He walked upon Mount Zion and saw the cornerstone in Eden. He saw the beauty of planet Earth. What a prize and honor it would be to exercise dominion over such a place. No doubt, his excitement and anticipation grew.

Lucifer's mindset began to change as he learned more of God's plans. As a member of the Divine Counsel and one of the angels that covered the throne of God, it is entirely possible this is where he learned of God's design for the kingdom. There was talk of a progeny, a called-out assembly, and the elect of numerous brothers that would be gathered at the Mount of Congregation on Mount Zion. But who were these brothers? Who were the progeny?

Lucifer's disappointment was solidified when he learned of God's plan for a new creation, a race of humans in the image and likeness of God. Humans would carry God's presence, anointing, and glory, and they would be given dominion and authority over the earth. From this progeny, a King would be named to sit upon the throne. No doubt Lucifer watched as the Father, Son, and Holy spirit planned the kingdom and prepared the Book of Life. In this Book names were given to all who would be part of the kingdom. He watched as the plans and purposes of God were written out in their Books. Each one had a divine destiny and purpose.

With each act of service, Lucifer received a covering stone of reward.

With each stone, his beauty grew along with his pride. The tipping point occurred when he learned of the creation of man. We are given some insight to this in an incident that occurred in the courts of heaven. It is recorded in Hebrews 2:5-6 (NKJV), "For He has not put the world to come, of which we speak, in subjection to angels. But one testified in a certain place, saying: What is man that You are mindful of him…" While the writer is quoting one of the Psalms of David, it is a picture of a scene occurring before the creation of man when the angels learned that God was going to put the world to come in subjection to man. Imagine if you will Lucifer confronting God and saying, "What is man that You are mindful of him." The writer goes on to say that man was created a little lower than God. The world to come speaks of the future state of planet earth inhabited by humanity. Ask yourself this question, of all of creation, who was created in the image and likeness of God. The answer is man. As we shall discuss in a few moments, Lucifer said in Isaiah 14:14 (KJV), "I will be like the most High." Lucifer wanted to be like the man God was going to create. He wanted to be the one created in the image and likeness of God.

His disappointment became ingrained. He did not want to share authority or have anyone be placed in a position above him. His pride and jealousy became a lethal combination. Therefore, he decided to conspire with the angelic host to destroy the plans of God and seize control.

Now that we have looked at the reasons for Lucifer's fall, let's examine his sin. What exactly was Lucifer's sin and what insight can we gain from his horrible actions? It is recorded for us in the following scriptures:

> "You are the anointed cherub that covers; and I have set you so: you were upon the holy mountain of God; you have walked up and down in the midst of the stones of fire. You were perfect in your ways from the day that you were created, till iniquity was found in you" (Ezekiel 28:14-15 AKJV).

> "How are you fallen from heaven, O Lucifer, son of the morning! How are you cut down to the ground, which

> did weaken the nations! For you have said in your heart, I will ascend into heaven, I will exalt my throne above the stars of God: I will sit also upon the mount of the congregation, in the sides of the north: I will ascend above the heights of the clouds; I will be like the Most High. Yet you shall be brought down to hell, to the sides of the pit" (Isaiah 14:15-20 AKJV).

Ezekiel tells us from the moment he was created, Lucifer was perfect in all his ways until iniquity was found in him. It refers to wickedness and injustice. It is a turning aside from what is right to commit an injustice. He felt within his heart he had been treated unjustly and unfairly and in turn committed an act of iniquity. He wanted to take matters in his own hands and make right what he thought was an inequity through an act of iniquity. Isaiah 14:13-14 (KJV) lists a series of five "I will" statements made by Lucifer when he conspired to rebel.

1. "I will ascend into heaven."
2. "I will exalt my throne."
3. "I will sit also upon the mount of the congregation."
4. "I will ascend above the heights of the clouds."
5. "I will be like the Most High."

According to Isaiah, Lucifer was on the Earth and said he would ascend into heaven. He had illegally seized the throne of authority in Eden and said he would exalt his throne. He disclosed his plans to take over and sit upon the mount of the congregation. In other words, he wanted to be in the image and likeness of God so he could sit upon the mount of the congregation. And finally, he said he would be like the Most High. He wanted to be like man. He wanted to be like God and be worshiped.

The origin of Lucifer's fall was because of his focus on himself, his desires, and his will. The condition of his heart is verified in Ezekiel 28:17-18 (NKJV), "Your heart was lifted up because of your beauty; You corrupted your wisdom for the sake of your splendor." Lucifer's sin was pride and narcissism. Think for a moment about Greek Mythology and the man named Narcissus. He saw his reflection in a pool of water and fell in love with himself. Although the term narcissism may have been coined from that story, its origin was from Lucifer's fall.

Before the fall of Lucifer, sin did not exist. There was no ill thought, word, or deed. No one tempted Lucifer with these ambitions. They all originated within himself after he learned of God's plans to create humanity. He authored the rebellion, and his fall was purely selfish. It was about his power, pride, ego, and desire for admiration. It all began when he took his eyes off the heart of God and placed his own desires and wants above God's plan.

The First Abomination That Made Desolate

It is important to understand God's plan to create humanity was the catalyst to Lucifer's rebellion and the birth of darkness. Lucifer's pride and narcissism became the seeds of all sin. This original motive is confirmed to us in John 8:44 (NKJV), "You are of your father the devil, and the desires of your father you want to do. He was a murderer from the beginning, and does not stand in the truth, because there is no truth in him. When he speaks a lie, he speaks from his own resources, for he is a liar and the father of it." Notice the text says he was a murderer from the beginning. The Greek word for "murderer" is *anthrōpoktonos*[40] and it means "a manslayer."

From the beginning, Lucifer's fall was connected to destroying the race of humanity and overthrowing God's kingdom. This is confirmed to us in Isaiah 45:13 (KJV), "I will exalt my throne above the stars of God." What are the stars of God? The Hebrew word is *kowkab*[41] and its usage refers to the "Messiah, brothers, youth, numerous progeny." That's us. It includes Jesus as the Son of Man and the sons and daughters of God.

It is also important to note Lucifer was not alone, one-third of the angelic host joined this rebellion. These were not haphazard acts. They were conscious decisions made by Lucifer and the Angels that sided with him. We can only surmise they disagreed with God's plan and decided to take it upon themselves to not only put a halt to them but to also overthrow God himself. For some reason they were convinced this was possible as Lucifer himself said his desire was to exalt his throne above God. It's hard to imagine they thought they could succeed.

The impact of this rebellion was complete devastation. Lucifer's rebellion was an abominable act and the original abomination of desolation. The Bible records three separate abominations that make desolate. The first was the fall of Lucifer. The second was at the flood and the last will be at the end of days during the tribulation period. Jesus speaks of this future event in Matthew 24:15 (KJV), "When ye therefore shall see the **abomination of desolation**, spoken of by Daniel the prophet, stand in the holy place, (whoso readeth, let him understand)."

It's interesting to note the final abomination of desolation is referenced by Jesus himself. In the Book of Daniel Chapter 1, Nebuchadnezzar, king of Babylon, invaded Jerusalem and took the holy vessels from the temple of God and carried them away to a foreign land. He placed them in the house of his god. The Bible says these were abominations before God. During the tribulation period, the antichrist will seize the rebuilt third temple in Jerusalem, set upon the throne, and proclaim himself to be God. His original goal has not changed. Lucifer's desire is to destroy the race of humanity and make himself God. These cycles of abominations will continue to repeat themselves until his ultimate demise in the last days.

Lucifer's first and original abomination resulted in the desolation of Eden and the Earth. It is authenticated for us in Jeremiah 4:23-27 (KJV):

> "I beheld the earth, and, lo, it was without form, and void; and the heavens, and they had no light. I beheld the mountains, and, lo, they trembled, and all the hills moved lightly. I beheld, and, lo, there was no man, and all the birds of the heavens were fled. I beheld, and, lo, the fruitful place was a wilderness, and all the cities thereof were broken down at the presence of the Lord, and by his fierce anger. For thus hath the Lord said, the whole land shall be **desolate**; yet will I not make a full end."

As a side note, the desolation of the earth was so catastrophic, it caused the Earth's ice age. The warmth of the earth is generated from the light of the sun. Prior to the sun's creation, God's light was the warmth upon the Earth. When Lucifer fell, the light was withheld or blocked, and it caused the warmth to be withheld.

When Genesis 1:2 (KJV) uses the phrase "face of the deep," it indicates not only the abyss but also the primeval oceans. This same Hebrew word is used again in Job 38:29-30 (KJV) which says, "Out of whose womb came the ice? and the hoary frost of heaven, who hath gendered it? The waters are hid as with a stone, and the face of the deep is frozen." From this verse, we learn that the waters covering the earth were frozen and it provides for us a perfect description of the ice age. This verse also asks the question "who hath gendered it?" In other words, who caused this to happen? Who gave birth to this? The frozen waters covering the earth was the direct result of an event that happened. We understand given the chronology of events in scripture that this was the direct result of the separation of God's light at the fall of Lucifer. The result was the ice age in earth's early history.

Satan's fall was so catastrophic, it affected all of creation. The Earth was marked with the results of the original sin. Yet, God would not let this rebellion stand. These events set the stage for God's response to create time and begin the six days of recreation.

Reflections of Who I AM

1. What evidence supports the gap between Genesis 1:1 and Genesis 1:2?
2. What was the root cause of Lucifer's rebellion, and what did he want?
3. What was Lucifer's sin (the original sin)?
4. How did Lucifer's fall affect the Earth?
5. Is there a connection between Lucifer's fall and the Ice Age?
6. Jesus said, "I AM the bread of life" (John 6:35 NKJV). How can the information discussed in this Chapter help you apply the fullness of that truth in your daily life?

Prayer of Activation

Our Father in heaven, you are the source of light for humanity and the world. There is no darkness in you. I recognize the source of all sin and darkness is the enemy of my soul and the enemy of God. My battles are not against flesh and blood or anyone I meet on this earth. My battles are against the kingdom of darkness. I am thankful that I am more than a conqueror through Christ. I pray you will search my heart and expose any sin of selfishness, pride, or rebellion. I choose to partner with you God and walk in the fullness of who you created me to be. I pray this in the name of Jesus, Amen.

SECTION II
I AM the Light of the World

"Then Jesus spoke to them again, saying, I AM the light of the world" (John 8:12 NKJV)

God is light and the true light comes from him. The light of God is his fire, his glory, his understanding, and his truth that shines upon all of creation. In this section, we will discover God's response to the original sin. He pierced the darkness to refashion the earth. He created the firmament and time. He formed humanity in his image and likeness to be his light bearers. As the Son of God, Jesus is the light of the world bringing his ferocious love to whosoever will. In the end, light will prevail, darkness will cease to exist, and God will restore all things to his original design. As we learn to *Walk in the fullness of I AM*, we come to understand we have been commissioned by God to bring his light to the world. As the world sees our good works, they will give glory to God.

GOD'S RESPONSE – THE SIX DAY CREATION

CHAPTER 6

Piercing the Darkness – Day 1

"And the Spirit of God moved upon the face of the waters. And God said, Let there be light: and there was light. And God saw the light, that it was good: and God divided the light from the darkness. And God called the light Day, and the darkness he called Night. And the evening and the morning were the first day" (Genesis 1:2-5 KJV).

The story of creation looked dismal at this point. Before Adam had opportunity to draw his first breath, the rebellion of Lucifer appeared to have aborted the plans of God. The insightful reader quickly realizes Satan has been in the abortion business from the beginning. He hates God, humanity, babies, and new beginnings. In his sin of pride and narcissism, Lucifer thought he could prevail against God. He wanted to be like God and set upon the throne of Eden. He was not about to be upstaged by humans.

After his rebellion and the subsequent war in heaven, Satan thought he outwitted God. But like a master chess player, God knew his next move before the opponent made his. It's proof Lucifer never really knew the heart of God. It is reminiscent of God speaking to the prophet in Jeremiah Chapter 18. Jeremiah went to a potter's house and found him turning a piece of clay upon a wheel. After the work become flawed, the potter crushed the clay. Instead of ending his work, he began anew and continued to turn the wheel to refashion its intended design. God has shown himself to be the potter and the earth and humanity the clay in his hands.

We do not know how long the earth laid dormant in darkness; however, at the appointed time, God had a resounding response. The Father sent the Holy Spirit, who began to move over the face of the deep. The Hebrew word for "moved" is *rachaph*[42] and it has two meanings. The first is to be moved "with the feeling of tender love, hence to cherish." The second is to be moved "with fear, tremor, hence to tremble." The meaning is clear. The Holy Spirit was softly and tenderly fluttering or hovering over the earth. It's the picture of a mother bird brooding over her young as she sooths her child. God was moved with compassion and love for his cherished creation. However, to the fallen angelic host, the tender love and compassion of God towards creation caused them to fear and tremble. They were horrified at what was about to happen. Their worst fears were about to be realized. At that moment, the Father turned to the Son and said in Genesis 1:3 (KJV), "let there be light."

God did not sit idly by and watch the destruction of creation. He saw the brokenness of earth and the destruction and chaos that followed. His wrath was not against the earth; rather, it was against the kingdom of darkness. In fact, when God said "let there be light," he was speaking to the fallen Titans of the Angelic Host, speaking forth his light and their future demise.

As God spoke light into darkness, we see the nature and character of God on display. The Hebrew word for "let there be" is *hayah*. As you recall, we discussed this word in Genesis 1:2 (KJV), "And the earth was (hayah) without form, and void." It means "come to pass." In this verse, God is saying let my light come upon the earth, let my will and plans come to pass just as I intended.

The response of God was not haphazard or the result of him being in a good mood that day. God is forever the same and does not change. Let every reader take note, God will never give up on you or his plans for your life. No matter how chaotic or dark your situation appears, at the appointed time, he will speak light into your world and bring to pass his plans.

God began the process of healing and restoration through his spoken word. The first recorded healing in scripture was when God said in Genesis 1:3 (KJV), "Let there be light." In the presence of God, all his attributes are present. Light will always prevail against darkness. It reminds us of Psalm 107:20 (NKJV), "He sent His word and healed them, And delivered them from their destructions." When God spoke, he wanted all creation to hear his voice. God desires to be heard! Sometimes, we try to figure things out through logic and understanding which can cloud our ability to hear from God. While our ears may be dull and our eyes dim, it does not mean God is not speaking. God wants to be known, but we must seek him out to discover his ways.

In Genesis 1:2-5, God describes the first of six days to refashion the earth. It is a monumental task of making all things new. For those having difficulty grasping the concept of God refashioning the earth, understand that God repeats this task two more times in scripture. He repeated this task a second time after the flood in the days of Noah, and he will complete the task a third and final time at the end of days. On that final day, he will usher in his ultimate solution to the problem of sin and the angelic rebellion with a new heaven and a new earth as recorded in Revelation 21.

To summarize God's actions, on this first day he spoke light into darkness and declared the following truths. First, God called the light good. Light speaks of God's blessings, favor, and healing. It speaks of the joy and satisfaction he brings to all who receive him. Secondly, God divided the light from the darkness. As you research the word "divided," you will discover something fascinating. There are two Hebrew words associated with this word. The first is *badal*[43] and it means "to separate, to disjoin," "to distinguish," "to shut out," "to be secluded," "to depart." In other words, God made a distinction between light and dark. Darkness was to be distinguished and separated. It should be secluded from our lives. The second word is *beyn*[44] and it means "interval, space between." When God created time, he declared that in the interval between the first day and the last day, he stands between light and dark, good, and evil. He will be our shield and protector of all that is good. We will continue to see this theme throughout scripture as God sets in motion his decree for righteousness and justice in the earth. Third, God called the light day and the darkness he called night. The word used for day is *yowm*[45] and it means a "division of time." This is the first reference to time. It includes the meaning of warmth, and heat, and refers to a time period or a specific time. The Hebrew word for night is *layil*[46] and it means "opposed to day," and "calamity." It comes from a root word that means "to fold back, a spiral step, winding stair." This gives us insight to the nature of light and darkness. The light of God is good. The nature of darkness and evil is to twist that which is good. It also implies a winding down and an unfolding.

On the first day of creation, God spoke light into darkness and created time. The implications of this truth are far reaching. It raises many questions in the realms of the scientific and faith communities. We are going to discuss some of these implications in the next chapter. The hidden meaning and revelation may come down to a single question, why did God create time?

Reflections of Who I AM

1. Why did Lucifer naively think he aborted God's plan for creation?
2. What is the first recorded miracle of healing in the Bible?
3. Besides the six days of creation, are there other examples in scripture of God refashioning the earth?
4. Are there other references in the Bible of God restoring the earth after destruction?
5. How did God distinguish light from dark?
6. Jesus said, "I AM the light of the world" (John 8:12 NKJV). How can the information discussed in this Chapter help you apply the fullness of that truth in your daily life?

Prayer of Activation

Our Father in heaven, I celebrate you and who you are. I thank you for your light and that you will always stand between me and darkness. Help me to look to you and submit myself to you in all things. Help me to rightly discern your ways from the ways of darkness. Since the beginning of time you have been speaking. Help me have ears to hear what you are saying that I may know you more. I pray this in the name of Jesus, Amen.

CHAPTER 7

The Firmament and Time – Days 2 & 4

"And God said, Let there be a firmament in the midst of the waters, and let it divide the waters from the waters.... And God called the firmament Heaven. And the evening and the morning were the second day.... And God said, Let there be lights in the firmament of the heaven to divide the day from the night; and let them be for signs, and for seasons, and for days, and years.... And the evening and the morning were the fourth day" (Genesis 1:6, 8, 14, 19 KJV).

Have you ever looked up and wondered at the magnificence of creation? On a clear night, you can see thousands of stars, and their beginning is traced back to Genesis. In this chapter, we are going to look at days two and four of creation and discover some amazing secrets hidden from many since the beginning of time.

Day Two

On day two, God created the firmament, which he called heaven. The careful reader soon realizes this heaven is different than the creation of heaven in Genesis 1:1. When creating the firmament, God set up the boundaries of darkness and confined it to the second heavens. Heaven is now divided into thirds, consisting of the first, second, and third heaven. As simple as it may sound, this is the reason outer space is a place of darkness.

Let's turn our attention to science and what we can learn about the second heaven. The universe consists primarily of dark matter that is so dense it does not interact with the electromagnetic field. Because of that, it does not reflect, emit, or absorb light. This is noteworthy when we consider the words of John 1:5 (NKJV), "And the light shines in the darkness, and the darkness did not comprehend it." Just as God declared, dark matter cannot grab hold of or make itself a part of light.

When we consider the natural laws of science and the spiritual laws of God, we begin to see the formation of a principle. Paul discussed this principle in I Thessalonians 5:5 (NKJV), "for you are all sons of light and sons of day. We are not of night nor of darkness." The principle we should all learn is that the kingdom of light is distinct from the kingdom of darkness, and it is impossible to separate activity in the spiritual realm from the physical. The actions in one realm will always affect the other.

Knowing this spiritual law, Satan conspired to tempt Adam and Eve so he could gain legal dominion over the earth. With humanity's fall, the doors would be opened to allow the spirits of sin and death to enter the realm of humans. This is why Ephesians 6:12 (NKJV) says, "For we do not wrestle against flesh and blood, but against principalities, against powers, against the rulers of the darkness of this age, against spiritual hosts of wickedness in the heavenly places."

Fire and Water in the Heavens

Rabbi Rashi, a highly revered medieval French Rabbi gives us this translation of Genesis 1:8, "God called the expanse heaven because it was made from fire and water. There was evening and there was morning, a second day."[47] Rashi said the Hebrew word for heaven is a contraction of a word that means carrying water. He said it was a combination of two Hebrew words *esh*,[48] which means "fire" and *mayim*, which means "waters." In other words, God mingled and blended fire and water to create the expanse of heaven. His interpretation says when the spirit of God moved upon the hard surface (face) of the waters, the fire of God mingled with the frozen waters to create the atmosphere of the heavens. The blending of fire and water is a perfect description of outer space. Science tells us water is an abundant substance in space. There are vapors of water surrounding some planets, other planets contain frozen water, and the stars burn with fire.

As we examine the Hebrew word *esh* a little further, we find it has a dual set of meanings. While it means fire, it is also used to describe endangering, destroying, or being consumed. In the Greek, the word is *pyr*[49] and it means "fire," "to purify," "penal torments," and "penal destruction." Both the Hebrew and Greek meaning of the heavens declare to us that the second heaven is a battle ground in the spiritual realm. No wonder God separated the light from the dark and confined it to a separate realm.

Day Four

As we move forward in our story and look at day four, a series of mysteries and questions arise. On day four, God created the sun, moon, and stars and placed them in the firmament to supply light, seasons, and days to the earth. These elements have been used to measure time and distance.

Science teaches us the rate of expansion in the universe can be used to calculate its age. As a side note, it's interesting that God called the heavens an expanse, which corresponds with the scientific use of the expanding universe. However, without an understanding of God, science has misunderstood the age of the universe. By measuring the distance between the velocity of stars and calculating age based upon the speed of light, Science has concluded the universe is approximately fourteen plus billion years old. However, when the age of the earth is calculated using carbon dating, the conclusion is the earth is about 4.5 billion years old. Because of the differences, science theorize a big bang in the universe caused the earth to evolve and is therefore younger than the universe. But what does God say?

According to the Bible, the earth existed long before the universe and may very well be 4.5 billion years old considering the gap between Genesis 1:1 and Genesis 1:2. However, when God created the expanse of the heavens, he spoke it into existence at the speed of his word as he spread it across the empty space. I believe Science is observing God's creation of the second heaven, which did not begin to expand until after he spoke it into existence. This explains the incorrect calculation that the universe is older than the earth. It also explains the existence of matter at the beginning of time since heaven and earth were already in existence. While science has learned much, their theories and conclusions contain many unexplained questions. This gives credence to the words of II Timothy 3:7 (NIV) which says they are "always learning but never able to come to a knowledge of the truth."

The Creation of Time

On the fourth day of creation God does something so amazing the greatest minds in history are still puzzled over it. Before this moment, there was no sun, moon, or stars. The earth did not revolve around the sun to give us seasons and a 365-day year. Therefore the question arises did God actually create time on day four? If not, how could there have been a day one, two and three? The mystery is recorded in Genesis 1:14-16 (KJV):

> "And God said, Let there be lights in the firmament of the heaven to divide the day from the night; and let them be for signs, and for seasons, and for days, and years: And let them be for lights in the firmament of the heaven to give light upon the earth: and it was so. And God made two great lights; the greater light to rule the day, and the lesser light to rule the night: he made the stars also."

Imagine if you will, God's desire to create time. Can we begin to fathom what that means? What is time? Time has been described as a measurement of the past, present, and future, and all the spatial points between. It is expressed in hours and minutes in relationship to the earth's revolution around the sun and gives us time and seasons.

Sir Isaac Newton described time as a fundamental part of the universe that was not dependent on events and occurs in a sequence. In his view, time is linear, and we move forward through time. Others theorize time is not a measurement at all and cannot be traveled through or measured. It is merely something we humans use to order and compare events. Einstein theorized time could be traveled through, forwards or backwards.

Scientists, physicists, mathematicians, and theologians have been grappling with the concept of time and space, creation, and evolution for thousands of years. Some theorize we have four dimensions consisting of length, height, depth, and time. Others theorize there are ten dimensions, with the other six dimensions of string theory describing the existence and possibility of all things. In recent history, the Hadron Collider was built to perform complex experiments to discover how everything began. Their experiments are in search of the God particle that holds all matter together and what happened after the so-called big bang. But with all their knowledge they continue to reach wrong conclusions or just scratch the surface of the events of God's creation.

Many scientists teach a young earth theory and believe the earth is younger than 10,000 years old. Others say the earth is much older and point to carbon dating, the dinosaurs, and other such findings. Those scientists find it hard to believe in an intelligent design and have argued the theory of evolution and random events occurring over time. However, these theories contradict the scientific laws of entropy. The laws of entropy argue over time chaos is increased, and order is decreased. For life to evolve over time into order, it had to violate the laws of entropy. Also, the second law of thermodynamics says all energy will wind down over time. If true, how could the earth have increased its evolution development from chaos to order. Even with the explanation of a big bang, science still theorizes life and humanity must have evolved, even though it violates known scientific laws. Eventually, one must realize that all matter had a beginning. Logic dictates there had to be nothing before there was something. Such is the case with the concept of time.

While God created the sun, moon, and stars for seasons, days, and years, does this mean time did not exist before day four? This appears problematic to many theologians to their chagrin as they try to answer the scientific community. To solve this mystery, some theologians argue the 1st, 2nd, and 3rd days were merely a way of describing a starting point and an ending point of a set of events and was not describing a 24-hour period. In this view, creation could have taken millions of years and seems to provide an answer to scientific discovery. The problem with this theory is that it is contradicted by the Bible itself. God tells us plainly he created the heavens and the earth in six days. Exodus 31:16-17 (KJV) says, "Wherefore the children of Israel shall keep the Sabbath, to observe the Sabbath throughout their generations, for a perpetual covenant. It is a sign between me and the children of Israel for ever: for in six days the LORD made heaven and earth, and on the seventh day he rested, and was refreshed."

What if God's word is true and he created time on day one, just like he said? If true, how do we explain day and night, and evening and morning, if there was no sun until day four? The answer is quite simple and disclosed to us by the Bible itself, even though theologians and scientists have argued this point for years. Let's examine this question, where did the light come from to give us a 24-hour period? Genesis 1:4-5 (KJV) says, "And God saw the light, that it was good: and God divided the light from the darkness. And God called the light Day, and the darkness he called Night. And the evening and the morning were the first day."

On day one, God spoke light into darkness and separated daytime from nighttime. He plainly tells us there was evening and morning, day, and night. But how could this be if there was no sun to supply light? As you recall, we discussed the location of heaven being true north and the rotation of the heavens around that point. In addition, the earth began revolving around its axis the moment it was created. When God spoke his light into the darkness, the earth would experience God's light coming from true north where heaven is located. Half the earth would be in darkness while the other half would experience the light of God as the earth rotated around its axis. God is light and his light exists separately from the sun, moon, and stars. Let's unpack this truth to understand what occurred.

Day one began in the darkness that covered the earth and concluded when God spoke light into darkness, giving the earth evening and morning. On day two, God confined the darkness to the firmament of the second heaven. Therefore, day two began in the morning when God spoke light into darkness and concluded when God confined the darkness to the second heaven. At that point, the second heaven once again blocked the light from heaven, and the earth experienced night. On day three, God created the vegetation of the earth. It began in the night and did not conclude until the dawn of day four when God created the sun, moon, and stars. Once again, there was evening and morning, a full day. At this point, not only did the earth continue to rotate around its axis but it also rotated around the sun to continue the cycle of evening and morning. Therefore, on day four, the lunar day was created along with the seasons we now enjoy, which were established by the 365-day revolution of the earth around the sun.

To conclude, from the first day of creation, there was a 24-hour period for the earth to revolve around its axis and receive light. At first, the light was from God, true north, and after the creation of the firmament, sun, moon, and stars, the earth continued a 24-hour cycle of days and nights through our lunar calendar. Mystery solved! Or is there more?

Why did God Create Time?

Before we go ahead, I want to take a moment and ask another important question. Many have wondered when time began, how old is the earth, and what is eternity; however, have you ever wondered why God created time? As I was researching scripture, I gained insight to one of the reasons God created time. It was an insight that I had never thought about.

As I was researching the mystery surrounding when time began, day one or day four, I couldn't find a definitive answer. I decided to pause and ask the author of creation for the answer. After praying, I suddenly understood and just knew the answer as I have described above. God allowed me to see the simplicity of the truth just as God had recorded. Afterwards, I began to rejoice in my spirit. It felt like God allowed me to uncover one of the greatest secrets about time that has been debated by scholars and theologians for years. As I began to thank God for the answer, something unexpected happened. In my spirit, I saw the Father sitting on his throne laughing and celebrating with me. As I was thanking the Father for his goodness and truth, the demeanor of his face changed. Instead of laughing with pleasure, the countenance of his face became serious and stern. Suddenly, I heard in my spirit the Father say, "*I created time to number Satan's days.*" I was taken aback in awe as I realized one of the reasons God created time. As I thought on this revelation, it made perfect sense and it opened a treasure trove of insight.

God is eternal and stands outside of time. He is timeless. When he initially created heaven and earth, there was no need for time. After Lucifer and the angels rebelled, darkness and destruction began. When God refashioned the earth by speaking his light into darkness, time began. Prophetically, the Father was declaring the days of darkness have been measured and numbered. From that moment, the clock began to tick down on the influence of Lucifer's fall.

One day, this age will end, and eternity will begin. Satan's reign of terror is approaching the moment of "time's up." This truth is horrifying and frightening to Satan and his cohorts. Revelation 12:12 (KJV) says, "Therefore rejoice, your heavens and you who dwell in them! But woe to the earth and the sea because the devil has gone down to you! He is filled with fury, because he knows that his time is short."

God has dealt with the problems of sin and darkness and is in the process of bringing forth the fulfillment of his kingdom.

Reflections of Who I AM

1. Why did God create the firmament?
2. What is the principle that discusses the actions of the spiritual realm impacting the physical?
3. When did time begin?
4. Why did God create time?
5. Does Satan know his time is short? If so, what has been his reaction?

6. Jesus said, "I AM the light of the world" (John 8:12 NKJV). How can the information discussed in this Chapter help you apply the fullness of that truth in your daily life?

Prayer of Activation

Our Father in heaven, you are the source of all light. I am so thankful you have seen all my days and every difficulty I will ever face. I am thankful that you have executed your plans to address the darkness and evil in this world and those days have been numbered. Just as you separated the darkness from the light, help me to walk in your ways and the light of your truth. Fill me with the fire of your Holy Spirit and let the actions of my life impact the spiritual realms around me in a positive way. I pray this in the name of Jesus, Amen.

CHAPTER 8

Mirror Image of God – Day 6

"And God said, Let us make man in our image, after our likeness: and let them have dominion over the fish of the sea, and over the fowl of the air, and over the cattle, and over all the earth" (Genesis 1:26 KJV).

To all who have encountered the goodness of God, you have learned that he always saves the best for last. Day six was the crescendo of creation. All of God's planning and preparation was for this one moment. Before the first act of creation, God knew every person that would ever be born and recorded their names in the registry of heaven. It would all begin with the creation of one man and one woman, the birthing moment of the family of God. Like an expecting parent whose first child was about to be born, God anticipated with enthusiasm this moment.

As a hush fell over heaven, the trinity announced to all of creation and eternity, "Let us make man in our image, after our likeness" (Genesis 1:26 KJV). This was a holy moment and a startling statement. In the earlier acts of creation, God did not make a declaration ahead of time about what He was going to do. However, the creation of humans was unique. In this proclamation, God spoke the greatest of his mysteries, the revelation of the design and purpose of humankind. Humans would not be like the angels, plants, or animal life. Instead, humans would be created in the image and likeness of God. For the first time, the invisible creator would see the visible image of himself on display in human form. The documented, eye witnessed account of humanity's creation forever establishes who I AM, my heritage, and identity; and it is much more than we imagined.

Created to be the Mirror Image of God

Jewish scholars teach the creation of man took place upon the foundation stone of the Temple Mount. Upon this stone, God formed Adam's body. But what did these actions look like? How did God form man in his mirror image and likeness?

The mystery unfolds as we examine the language of the text. The Hebrew word for "image" is *selem*[50] and it means "something cut out," "resemblance," or "a representative figure, especially an idol." It is the same word used in Ezekiel 16:17 when they took gold and silver and formed graven images of men. It is comparable to the Hebrew word *pesel*[51] which also means "an idol - carved (graven) image;" however, this word deepens the meaning and explains how the image is made. The root of the word means "to cut, "hew out," "quary," "to carve, whether wood, or stone - grave." In other words, it means to cut or carve out a cast or mold of wood or stone to make an exact replica. Paul confirms the creator's original design when he writes II Corinthians 3:18 (NKJV), "But we all, with unveiled face, beholding as in a mirror the glory of the Lord, are being transformed into the same image from glory to glory, just as by the Spirit of the Lord."

Adam was created in both the image of God and his likeness. The Hebrew word for "likeness" is *demut*[52] and it means "similitude," "model, shape." The root of the word means to "be like, resemble," "external appearance," or "think." In other words, Adam was to look like, be like, think like, and act like his creator. He would house the treasures of heaven and the mind of God. There would be no distance between himself and his creator. He would be the genesis of God's family and they would be one.

The detailed account of God's creation of Adam is recorded for us in Genesis 2:7 (KJV), "And the Lord God formed man of the dust of the ground, and breathed into his nostrils the breath of life; and man became a living soul." The Hebrew word for "formed" is *yasar*[53] and it means "the squeezing into shape," "to mould into a form." The root of the word means "to lay, spread out," and is "used of a marriage bed." Let's fill in the gaps of the process by examining the rest of the language used in the text:

> Dust – The Hebrew word is *apar*[54] and it means "clay or loam," "dust, dry earth."
>
> Breathed – The Hebrew word is *napah*[55] and it means "to inflate, blow hard."
>
> Breath – The Hebrew word is *nsama*[56] and it means "breath of God," "breath of man," or "spirit of man."
>
> Life and Living – The Hebrew word is *hay*[57] and it means "alive, living." In the feminine it is singular, but in the masculine it is plural and speaks of kinsfolks and families.
>
> Man – The Hebrew word is *adam*[58] and it means "man, human being," or "ruddy."
>
> Soul – The Hebrew word is *nepes*[59] and it means "living being, life, self, person, desire, appetite, emotion, and passion." It also means, "a living being whose life resides in the blood."

With this information, the picture of Adam's creation begins to come into focus, and we understand the process God used to create man. God created Adam by stretching himself out upon the foundation stone and hewing out a cast of himself. He filled the cast with dry red earth and squeezed into shape the body of the man. As he laid upon the man, face to face, he blew into his nostrils a part of his own spirit and Adam arose a living being in the image and likeness of God. With the life of God in him, Adam had desire, emotion, passion, and the ability to think and commune with his creator. When God looked at him, he saw the visible image of the invisible, a man created in the mirror image and likeness of himself. When the man arose, filled with life, it was a veiled prophetic announcement of the future resurrection.

I don't know about you, but the revelation of how we were created in God's image and likeness changes how I look at myself. Let's explore these amazing events a little further for some added truths God wants to make known.

The Life of Every Human was Breathed into Adam

The Hebrew word for life in the masculine form in Genesis 2:7 (KJV) is plural. When God breathed into Adam the breath of life, he breathed into him the life of every man or woman that would ever be born. A correct reading is "breathed into his nostrils the breath of lives." When you were born and took your first breath, the breath you took originated from God himself back in the Garden when he breathed a part of himself into Adam. You were created by God himself as much as Adam was. Your origin, heritage, and DNA came directly from God. Leviticus 11:17 (KJV) says, "For the life of the flesh is in the blood." Every drop of blood in your body carries in it the breath and DNA of God.

All Humanity's Beginning is in God

While each of us has a birth father and mother, your beginning was planned by God. James 1:18 (NIV) says, "He chose to give us birth through the word of truth." God chose you to be born. It does not matter the circumstances surrounding your birth, before you were a twinkle in your parent's eyes, God chose you. He chose the time, place, and parents you would be born to. While many parents have made mistakes and have not lived up to their calling, every child was designed by God and their beginning is in him.

The timing of your birth was not random? Ephesians 1:4 (NKJV) says, "He chose us in Him before the foundation of the world, that we should be holy and without blame before Him in love." Every person's beginning is important. You may have been born with a birth defect, in impoverished conditions, abandoned by your parents, or dearly loved. Regardless of the circumstances of your birth, where you were born, or when you were born, your beginning was foreordained. This trumps any circumstance you may find yourself in.

Since your life was preordained by God, this means he has a plan, purpose, and destiny for your life and an answer for every question you have or problem you face. Acts 17:28 (KJV) says, "For in him we live, and move, and have our being." As a child of God, everything we face in life is already in him. That means no problem is insurmountable, no miracle impossible, and no mountain uncrossable. You are in him and that makes you special.

God Wants You to Know Who He is and Who You are

One of the greatest revelations you will ever receive is a knowledge and understanding of who God is and who you are. Have you considered the significance of being created in the image and likeness of God and the message that shouts out to the world?

Jesus did not come to earth to only redeem us from sin, he also came to reveal to us who we are and the mystery of our relationship in him. Ephesians 3:9 (NKJV) says, "to make all see what is the fellowship of the mystery, which from the beginning of the ages has been hidden in God who created all things through Jesus Christ." The Father earnestly wants to reveal to all of creation his sons and daughters. This sounds too good to be true; however, it is one of the greatest mysteries to be discovered in this present age. We are in the beginning stages of a great awakening.

You may look at yourself in a mirror and wonder what all the fuss is about, but God sees you very differently. The Father sent Jesus to introduce us to himself and ourselves. God has always fully known you. While we have at best a cloudy view of who we are, one day, we will fully see ourselves. I Corinthians 13:12 (NIV) says, "For now we see only a reflection as in a mirror; then we shall see face to face. Now I know in part; then I shall know fully, even as I am fully known."

Think about the mirror spoken of in this text. Mirrors can become cloudy with age and not give a clear picture of the person looking in it.

But this text declares something totally unexpected. It says one day we shall see ourselves face to face. Since it is impossible to see yourself face to face, who was Paul talking about? One day, we will see Christ face to face and realize the man in the mirror we were looking at was not only ourselves but also Christ. One day, we will see ourselves just as God sees us, the mirror image of who he created us to be. Our image has become cloudy, but one day it will become clear. Consider the words of I John 3:1-3 (THE MIRROR Bible):

> "Consider the amazing love the Father lavished upon us; this is our defining moment: we began in the agape of God – the engineer of the universe is our Father! So, it's no wonder that the performance-based systems of this world just cannot see this! Because they do not recognize their origin in God, they feel indifferent towards anyone who does! Beloved, we know that we are children of God to begin with, which means that there can be no future surprises; his manifest likeness is already mirrored in us! Our sameness cannot be compromised or contradicted; our gaze will confirm exactly who he is – and who we are. And every individual in whom his expectation echoes also determines to realize their own flawless innocence mirrored in him whose image they bear."[60]

You were created to look like and act like Jesus. He is the revelation of who I AM and the blueprint and pattern for life. John 14:20 (NKJV) says, "At that day you will know that I am in my Father, and you in Me, and I in you." We are our Father's child.

The Race of All Humanity was in Adam

Let's consider for a moment the red soil from which God formed Adam. As we have already noted, the angelic rebellion led to the destruction of earth as described in Genesis 1:2. That verse describes the earth as a wasteland. It is interesting to note the Hebrew word for dust also means powder, dry earth, ashes, or rubbish. Did God use the debris and ashes left in the wake of earth's destruction to create man? This is an interesting question with two possibilities. One possibility is the creation of man was like a phoenix arising from the ashes of destruction. It is a beautiful picture of restoration and redemption. The other possibility is that God did not use the rubbish and ashes to create man but used the original untainted earth to form man. This view is supported by the Jewish historian Josephus in Antiquities of the Jews Book 1 Chapter 1 verse 2, "This man was called Adam, which in the Hebrew tongue signifies one that is red, because he was forced out of red earth, compounded together; for of that kind is virgin and true earth."[61] Josephus said Adam was formed out of virgin earth and implies God used the original earth that had not been contaminated by the fall. It's a picture of God using his hands to brush aside the rubbish and ashes of destruction until he reached virgin earth that was uncontaminated. This is also a beautiful picture of God creating humanity from his original design, destined to walk without spot or blemish.

Regardless of the correct interpretation, God formed Adam from the red soil of the earth. Why is this significant? The red color in Adam's DNA explains the genetic makeup of every race. Our skin color is determined by the amount of melanin in our skin. There are two types of melanin, eumelanin and pheomelanin. The more eumelanin you have, the darker the skin color. Those with more pheomelanin than eumelanin has lighter skin. This explains the different color of races we see on the earth today. God is a God of diversity, and all the races came from Adam.

Humanity was Designed to Act Like God

You were designed to be like God. The knowledge of this truth is a key to walking in the fullness of I AM. Think about the things Jesus did on earth. John 5:19 (NIV) says, "Jesus gave them this answer: Very truly I tell you, the Son can do nothing by himself; he can do only what he sees his Father doing, because whatever the Father does the Son also does." Everywhere Jesus went, he preached the kingdom of God, performed miracles, healed the sick, delivered those possessed by demonic spirits, and raised the dead. In turn, Jesus taught his disciples to do exactly what he did. Matthew 10:7-8 (NKJV), "And as you go, preach, saying, 'The kingdom of heaven is at hand.' Heal the sick, cleanse the lepers, raise the dead, cast out demons. Freely you have received, freely give." Just like the disciples, our blueprint for life is to be like Jesus.

Humanity will Live Forever

The last concept I want to discuss is God's design for humanity to live forever. This is a deeply mysterious subject and filled with questions and complications. Many believe life is finite and at death we cease to exist; however, the world's concept of death is a lie. The Bible speaks about both death and eternal life. While this seems contradictory, it isn't. James 2:26 (KJV) says, "the body without the spirit is dead." Therefore, the death of the body occurs when it is separated from the spirit and the soul. But while the body may die, the soul and spirit are eternal. Paul says this in II Corinthians 5:1-2,4-5 (NIV), "For we know that if the earthly tent we live in is destroyed, we have a building from God, an eternal house in heaven, not built by human hands. Meanwhile we groan, longing to be clothed instead with our heavenly dwelling.... so that what is mortal may be swallowed up by life. Now the one who has fashioned us for this very purpose is God, who has given us the Spirit as a deposit, guaranteeing what is to come."

The question isn't will we live forever; rather, it is where will we be living? By accepting Christ, we are promised eternal life with God. Those who do not accept Christ will face eternal punishment as described by Matthew 25:46 (KJV), "And these shall go away into everlasting punishment: but the righteous into life eternal." In the end, death is separation from God.

Reflections of Who I AM

1. What was God's greatest act of creation?
2. Who is the man in the mirror Paul describes in I Corinthians 13:12, and what does that say about the design of humanity?
3. Does the Bible give clues to explain the different races on earth?
4. Describe how Adam was created in the image and likeness of God?

5. Will the righteous and unrighteous live forever? If so, how are they different?
6. Jesus said, "I AM the light of the world" (John 8:12 NKJV). How can the information discussed in this Chapter help you apply the fullness of that truth in your daily life?

Prayer of Activation

Our Father in heaven, I am amazed that you knew me and designed me even before the beginning of time. Your love for me began before I was born, and it will never cease. Since I was created in your image and likeness, help me to live like you and act like you. Help me to not be distracted by the obstacles in life or limit my potential with earthly boundaries. Rather, help me to come to the knowledge and truth of the unique way you have designed me and the purposes you have for my life. Because I have accepted Jesus as my Lord and Savior, I have the promise of eternal life. Help me live each day living and acting like Jesus the blueprint of my design. I pray this in the name of Jesus, Amen.

CHAPTER 9

The Birthright and First Commission

"So God created man in His own image; in the image of God He created him; male and female He created them. Then God blessed them, and God said to them, be fruitful and multiply; fill the earth and subdue it; have dominion" (Genesis 1:27-28 NKJV).

With the creation of Adam as his mirror image, God continued his establishment of the family with the creation of Eve. During his initial encounters with the first family, God established the promises and birthright of his blessings and gave them a commission and calling to pass down to each generation.

I invite you to set back with an open mind and plunge into the conversations between God and humanity and discover his great plans for us all.

Creation of Eve

After the six days of creation, Genesis 2:8 (NKJV) says, "The Lord God planted a garden eastward in Eden, and there He put the man whom

He had formed." There was no better place for the kingdom to begin than Eden. It was the original seat of power in the ancient of days and God's Garden of luxury and finery. It would be a reminder to all their starting point was in God and all blessings flowed from him. Built upon the wreckage of destruction, Eden was a picture of things past and a foreshadow of things to come.

After placing Adam in the garden, God had another announcement to make to the world. Genesis 2:18 (KJV) says, "And the Lord God said, it is not good that the man should be alone; I will make him a help meet for him." One day, the world and the church will wake up to the significance of God's creation of woman. Eve was not an afterthought because Adam could not find a companion among the rest of creation. God knew all along he was going to create Eve; however, Adam needed to realize his need for a companion and partner. As Adam observed and named every animal, he came to the realization that the multiplication of every species was dependent upon a male and female. The concept of family was designed into nature with every living creature having the ability to produce after its own kind. I imagine Adam had some interesting conversations with God around that topic when he began to realize he had no female companion. This became one of the first revelations to humanity. The earth was a massive planet and Adam soon realized it was not designed for one person.

With that in mind, do you think God created Eve just so Adam would have a reproductive partner? Absolutely not! The world has greatly misinterpreted Genesis 2:18 (KJV) when God said Adam needed a "help meet." The Hebrew word for "meet" is *ezer*[62] and it means "one who helps," "aid." Many societies and even churches have taught the wife's role is to help and aid her husband and view her as being less than the man, a type of servant. Many churches limit the role of women in the duties they can perform and have mistakenly taken scripture out of context to support that view. For example, Ephesians 5:23-24 discusses wives being in subjection to their husbands and I Corinthians 14:34 discusses women keeping silent in church. By misunderstanding the context of these scriptures, many have taken these isolated words that were given to address specific situations and rationalized their mindset of man's superiority over woman. These misguided beliefs are an affront to the design of God and foreign to his view of humanity as both male and female.

God designed Adam and Eve to co-partner together as a unified team of equal importance. In fact, God made that principle very clear when he said, "it is not good that man should be alone" (Genesis 2:18 NKJV). For those wondering, that same declaration applies to women just as it does to men. When God says man in this instance, he is speaking of humanity. We were not created to isolate ourselves from others.

If God saves the best for last, wouldn't Eve be the Grand Finale of God's masterpiece of creation, to display the essential part and completion of his design? When God said in Genesis 2:18 (KJV) Adam needed a "help meet," what was he saying? The Hebrew word *ezer* is used twenty-one times in scripture and in most cases speaks of God's help and aid to humanity. In each of these instances, the help and aid supplied was essential for survival, deliverance, and protection. In fact, the root of this word is *azar*[63] and it means "to surround, i.e. protect or aid." It is a type of the Holy Spirit as one who comes alongside.

The marriage of a man and a woman as a family unit is sacred to God. Ephesians 5:25 (KJV) says, "Husbands, love your wives, even as Christ also loved the church, and gave himself for it." Jesus laid down his life in every way for his church. In Galatians 3:28 (NIV), God says, "There is neither Jew nor Gentile, neither slave nor free, nor is there male and female, for you are all one in Christ Jesus." Scripture makes it clear; God shows no partiality or favoritism of one sex above the other. Can you imagine God having two classes of humans in heaven? Ridiculous! While it is perfectly fine to view the responsibilities of men and women differently, it is an offence to the design of God to view one as subservient to the other. While some Christians and churches quote Ephesians 5:22 (KJV) which says, "Wives, submit yourselves unto your own husbands," they conveniently overlook the preceding verse of Ephesians 5:21 (KJV) which says, "submitting yourselves one to another in the fear of God."

If husbands and wives are to submit themselves one to another, you may wonder why Adam called Eve woman? The answer is found in Genesis 2:23 (NKJV), "And Adam said: "This is now bone of my bones

And flesh of my flesh; She shall be called Woman, Because she was taken out of Man." This explains the reason men have both an x and y chromosome and women have two x chromosomes. The woman was taken out of man (two x chromosomes), leaving Adam with both the x and y. Do you want to know another startling revelation? God didn't call the female Eve, Adam did. Adam was the one to name her Eve and that was after the fall and the resultant curse upon humanity.

The revelation of the union between a man and a woman gives us a picture of the relationship between humanity and God. Genesis 1:27 (KJV) says, "So God created man in his own image, in the image of God created he him; male and female created he them." Since God created both male and female in his own image and likeness, we must have an understanding and appreciation of the dynamics, nature, and differences between man and woman to fully understand the nature of God. A husband joined to his wife portrays the mystery and revelation of marriage and the church. Ephesians 5:31-32 (NKJV), "For this reason a man shall leave his father and mother and be joined to his wife, and the two shall become one flesh. This is a great mystery, but I speak concerning Christ and the church."

For societies or churches to advocate the submission of wives to their husbands is a distortion of God's original design and advances the concepts of division and confusion. Since woman was taken out of man and the breath of life in every human is taken from God, why would the creator want us divided against ourselves. The husband and wife are one just as God and his church are one. This revelation is central to understanding the topics of birthright and blessing.

The Birthright and Blessing

After the creation of Adam and Eve, God's first official action was to bless them. While many casually read Genesis 1:28 as a general blessing and best wishes, it was much more than that. When God blessed Adam and Eve, he instituted a ceremony that would be repeated from generation to generation. To fully grasp its significance, we need to understand the blessing God pronounced upon Abraham when he established his covenant with him. A study of Genesis 12, 13, 15, 17, and 22 establishes the promises and birthright of that blessing. In the blessing, God gave ten promises to Abraham:

1. God will make you a great nation,
2. God will bless you,
3. God will make your name great,
4. You will be a blessing,
5. God will bless those who bless you and curse those who curse you,
6. In you, all the families of the earth will be blessed,
7. God will give you and your descendants the land,
8. God will multiply you and your descendants,
9. God will make you exceedingly fruitful, and finally,
10. God will establish his covenant with you and your descendants.

Once God established his covenant with Abraham and proclaimed his blessings upon him, each successive generation performed the same ceremony. Before the Father of each family died, he gathered his children, placed his hands upon them, and pronounced his blessing. While each child received a blessing from the Father, the responsibility of leading the family was usually passed down to the firstborn son; however, provision was made that a younger son could be selected. The child that received this blessing also received a double portion of the inheritance, called the birthright. The birthright included the following responsibilities:

- The receiving of authority to become the head of the family, charged with their care.
- The responsibility of being the priest of the family.
- The receiving of a double portion of inheritance.
- The responsibility of judicial authority.

While the blessing and birthright became an established practice from Abraham onward, the origins of that ceremony began in the Garden of Eden when God pronounced upon Adam and Eve his blessing. It's recorded for us in Genesis 1:27-28 (NKJV):

"So God created man in His own image; in the image of God He created him; male and female He created them. Then God blessed them, and God said to them, Be fruitful and multiply; fill the earth and subdue it; have dominion over the fish of the sea, over the birds of the air, and over every living thing that moves on the earth."

The Hebrew word for "bless" is *barak*[64] and it means "to bend the knee, to kneel." It carries with it the meaning of invoking and declaring a blessing, to adore, to invoke divine favor, to cause to prosper with abundance, and to make one's name great. The full meaning of this word provides an amazing insight to God and reflects the same blessing God pronounced upon Abraham.

Since the word "bless" means to "to bend the knee," who do you think was kneeling, Adam and Eve, or God? The Bible clearly says, "God blessed them" (Genesis 1:28 KJV). Can you see the image in your mind? God knelt down in front of Adam and Eve, laid his hands upon them, and blessed them. What do you think that looked like? Imagine for a moment Dr. Spock in Star Track. Leonard Nimoy would hold up his hand and spread apart his first and middle finger from his last two fingers forming a V. His thumb would also be spaced apart from his first two fingers. As he held up his hand, he uttered the phrase, "live long and prosper." Leonard Nimoy chose this sign for the TV series based on his Jewish upbringing from a synagogue in Boston when the Rabbi blessed the congregation. The tradition of this blessing goes all the way back to Abraham and even further to the Garden of Eden. A Rabbinical priest pronouncing a blessing holds up both hands, each one forming this "V" sign. This sign is also the form of the 21st letter of the Hebrew Alphabet, Shin, which represents the name of God, "Shaddai." God as El Shaddai is all powerful and the supplier of every need.

When God knelt down before Adam and Eve and blessed them, it portrayed a kind loving father putting his hands upon his children to bless them with all that he has. God displayed his love and commitment to Adam and Eve when he knelt before them and placed his hands upon their heads; and with his shekinah glory shining upon them, he gave them his name, blessing, and birthright inheritance of all his fullness.

This is the first example of humans walking in the fullness of I AM. God the Father wanted his children to know he would be the supplier of their every need, all that he had was theirs, and they could walk in the fullness of God's blessings, power, and authority upon this earth as they fulfilled their commission. You will also notice, God did not bless just Adam; rather, he blessed each of them equally and made no distinction in the blessing or birthright being conferred upon them.

When God pronounced his blessing and birthright upon Adam and Eve, who was given the double portion of inheritance? While there are differences in the sexes, it's interesting to note that it was Eve who received a double portion of the x chromosome. Most of the distinctions between men and women came after the fall and became the norm because of the curse of sin. Originally, the blessing and birthright was placed on the heads of the family, which consisted of both the man and woman, and together they operated in the blessings and authority of God.

This practice of conferring a blessing has been repeated throughout history and is even practiced today in churches and synagogues. The practice has been referred to as the Priestly Blessing and is recorded for us in Numbers 6:24-27 (NKJV), "The Lord bless you and keep you; The Lord make His face shine upon you and be gracious to you; The Lord lift up His countenance upon you and give you peace. So, they shall put My name on the children of Israel, and I will bless them." If you were to perform a study of the Hebrew words and their meaning in this prayer, it could be interpreted as follows:

> *May the Lord (the self-existing one) kneel-down as your father before you, place his hands upon you and proclaim this blessing. The self-existing one will put a hedge of protection around you and keep watch over you. He will guard, protect, and save you from all enemies. He will keep his eyes upon you and celebrate and treasure you as he preserves and takes care of you. The self-existing one will cause his face, his fire, and his presence to be before you, behind you and surround you to give you light and illuminate his glory and entire being. The self-existing one will bend down, encamp about, and dwell*

with you and show you his favor, grace, and mercy. The self-existing one will bring the fullness of who he is upon you. The self-existing one will establish, appoint, and give you completeness, safety and soundness of body, welfare, health, and prosperity, peace, quiet, tranquility and contentment, friendship with others and with God, and give you peace from your enemies. Finally, the self-existing one will lay his hands upon you and establish, ordain, appoint, constitute, and place upon you his name, his reputation, his fame, and his glory.

The First Great Commission

When God blessed Adam and Eve, it was more than a blessing, it was also a commission. It was the first Great Commission. The Great Commission Jesus gave to the disciples was not new; rather, it began with Adam and Eve. With that in mind, let's examine the original and First Great Commission given to both Adam and Eve in Genesis 1:28 (KJV), "And God blessed them, and God said unto them, Be fruitful, and multiply, and replenish the earth, and subdue it: and have dominion over the fish of the sea, and over the fowl of the air, and over every living thing that moveth upon the earth."

Prior to the creation of Adam and Eve, the Father, Son, and Holy Spirit planned this moment. Their conversation between each other is recorded in Genesis 1:26 (KJV), "Let us make man in our image, after our likeness: and let them have dominion." In other words, humanity is to subdue, rule over, and have dominion over creation. Even before this commissioning ceremony, prior to the creation of humanity, God planned for man and woman to have dominion over the earth. For those who doubt the fall of Lucifer between Genesis 1:1 and Genesis 1:2, ask yourself why was there the need for Adam and Eve to take dominion? Who were they to subdue? Why was there a need for anything to be subjugated to God? The answer is obvious.

With the angelic rebellion, the earth suffered a catastrophic destruction. After the creation of man and woman, God called them together and pronounced upon them his blessing, birthright, and commission. This ceremony took place on top the foundation stone of the earth, in the garden of new beginnings, and future site of the temple mount. The solemnness of this moment shouted its significance. The whole race of humanity would have their origins in one couple who were made in the image and likeness of God. As God's children and first born, the fate of the world rested in their hands and God entrusted to them the task of taking authority over the earth and subduing it for the kingdom. From this moment, Adam and Eve were on Satan's hit list and in the crosshairs of the kingdom of darkness.

Reflections of Who I AM

1. Why do you think God began the first family on Earth in the location of Eden?
2. What is the significance of the creation of woman as man's *ezer*?
3. When did the concept of the blessing and birthright begin, and what does it mean?
4. Describe the First Great Commission.
5. Jesus said, "I AM the light of the world" (John 8:12 NKJV). How can the information discussed in this Chapter help you apply the fullness of that truth in your daily life?

Prayer of Activation

Our Father in heaven, I am amazed at how much you love me and how committed you are to my life and my family. From the very beginning, you proved to us your heart for restoring what was lost no matter how dark our situation may seem. I shake off all doubt and all brokenness that has affected my life and I receive your restoration. Let your face shine upon me and your light and presence fill my life. Help me discover my place in this world and the callings and giftings you have designed for me. I receive the blessings you want to pour out over my life. Help me to be the man/woman/husband/wife you have called me to be. I am your child, and from this day forward, I will face each day from a place of hope, a place of confidence, a place of peace, and a place of rest knowing that you are with me. I pray this in the name of Jesus, Amen.

SECTION III

I AM the Way, the Truth, and the Life

"Jesus said to him, I am the way, the truth, and the life. No one comes to the Father except through me" (John 14:6 NKJV).

The Greek word for "way" is *hodos*[65] and it means a "road," "traveler's way, journey." The Greek word for "truth" is *aletheia*[66] and it means "what is true in any matter under consideration," "in reality, in fact." The Greek word for "life" is *zoe* and as we previously discussed, it means "the absolute fullness of life, both essential and ethical, which belongs to God." In this section, we will look at the choices made by Adam and Eve and a band of Angels known as the Watchers. Their bad choices resulted in immediate consequences and a sudden realization that God's word is true in all circumstances. Adam and Eve realized there were snakes in the garden of God's paradise, and the Watchers were drawn away by their desire to overthrow God. The consequence of humanity's fall was the entrance of sin and death to the world, and the fall of the Watchers led to a flood and the second desolation of Earth. But through it all, God's word was true, and he never abandoned his plans. As God's plan for the kingdom continued to unfold, he revealed himself to Moses as I AM and gave humanity the law and pathway to righteousness. As we learn to *Walk in the fullness of I AM*, we come to realize God's word is absolute truth and is our roadmap for life. While Jesus is the way and the truth, he is also the bridge to life. It takes the quickening life of the spirit and a relationship with the creator to make us complete and whole. We are commissioned to share this good news.

ADAM'S FAMILY

CHAPTER 10

Snakes in the Garden

"And [in that garden] the LORD God caused to grow from the ground every tree that is desirable and pleasing to the sight and good (suitable, pleasant) for food; the tree of life was also in the midst of the garden, and the tree of the [experiential] knowledge (recognition) of [the difference between] good and evil" (Genesis 2:9 AMP).

"And the LORD God commanded the man, saying, Of every tree of the garden thou mayest freely eat: But of the tree of the knowledge of good and evil, thou shalt not eat of it: for in the day that thou eatest thereof thou shalt surely die" (Genesis 2:16-17 KJV).

While the creation of humanity caused a holy hush in heaven followed by rejoicing and celebration, it struck fear in the heart of Satan. God not only created Adam and Eve in his mirror image and likeness, but he also bestowed upon them his name and blessed them with his authority, favor, and inheritance. Commissioned by God, they would have dominion and authority over the earth and subdue it for the kingdom of God. To begin their journey, God placed them in Eden, a land of plenty where there was no shortage of anything they needed.

While Eden was a paradise of perfection, there were snakes in the

Garden. Specifically, there was a particular serpent which Revelation 20:2 (KJV) identifies as "that old serpent, which is the Devil, and Satan." As we go back to the beginning of our story, we discover the entry point of death and sin in this earth.

From the moment God planned the creation of humanity, Satan conspired their murder and demise. Satan's problem was how could he bring it all down. How could he destroy God's plans, the humans he created, and gain dominion over the earth? What strategy would he use? A direct frontal assault would be easily recognized, so he used deceit and trickery. The unfolding of these events reminds us of the true nature of our enemy. As a child of God walking in the fullness of your creator, you are a threat to the enemy; however, if you become blinded or deceived, the wrong choices you make can lead to your downfall. With this in mind, let's look at the first environment of humanity.

Did God Create the Tree of the Knowledge of Good and Evil?

The Garden of Eden had two very important trees, the Tree of Life and the Tree of the Knowledge of Good and Evil (henceforth referred to as the Tree of Knowledge). As wonderful as the descriptions of Eden are, a perplexing question comes to mind when we consider humanity's first environment. How did the Tree of Knowledge get there? Did God plant it along with the Tree of Life? Why was it there? While the Bible offers no direct answer to these questions, there are clues to the answer.

Our first observation is the Genesis account gives no reference to God creating either of these two trees. God did not say, "let there be" when he created the trees on the earth. Instead, scripture says it had not yet rained, and God caused a mist to rise up to water the ground, which in turn caused the growth of vegetation and trees. Before Genesis 1:2 and prior to the fall of Lucifer, the earth had already been created as God's paradise on Earth. Therefore, God was causing to grow again what had already been created in Genesis 1:1. But what about these two trees? After God planted a variety of trees, the Bible simply says in

Genesis 2:9 (NIV), "In the middle of the garden were the tree of life and the tree of the knowledge of good and evil."

Our second observation is since all of creation on the earth was patterned after heaven, the Tree of Life must have had its origins from heaven itself. This is supported by Revelation Chapter 2 and Chapter 22 which tells us the Tree of Life will be in the New Jerusalem throughout eternity and all overcomers will have access to it. But what about the Tree of Knowledge? There is no reference of this tree being in the New Jerusalem nor is it mentioned as being in existence in eternity.

I propose the possibility that God did NOT plant or create the Tree of Knowledge? Like most people, you may have assumed God created this tree since it is mentioned in the context of the creation story. However, consider the words of Acts 3:21 (NKJV), "whom heaven must receive until the times of restoration of all things, which God has spoken by the mouth of all His holy prophets since the world began." At the end of the age, God will restore all things to his original design and complete his plans for the beginning of eternity and the kingdom. Therefore, if the Tree of Knowledge was part of God's original design it would be in the New Jerusalem and eternity. However, there is no mention of this tree being present in eternity.

After the conclusion of this age, there will be no vestige of evil, nor will the Saints of God have the option to partake of evil and rebellion. Instead, I Corinthians 15:53 (KJV) says, "For this corruptible must put on incorruption." In eternity, there will be no temptation, no evil, and no experiential knowledge of sin or corruption in any form. For these reasons, I believe the earth as created in Genesis 1:1 had the Tree of Life but did not have the Tree of Knowledge.

Lucifer did not fall because he partook of the Tree of Knowledge. He fell because of his pride and rebellion against God. In addition, the Tree of Knowledge is not mentioned until day six of the creation account. Where did this tree come from? I believe the tree was planted by the original deceiver, Satan, after his fall. There is one hint in scripture that may allude to this assertion. Matthew 13:24-25 (NKJV) says, "Another parable He put forth to them, saying: The kingdom of heaven is like a man who sowed good seed in his field; but while men slept, his enemy came and sowed tares among the wheat and went his way."

Why do you suppose the Tree of Knowledge was located near the Tree of Life? Satan had access to the Garden of Eden and tempted Adam and Eve to sin. It would be completely in the character of Satan to present a counterfeit to the things of God; however, it would be completely outside the character of God to create a tree that brings forth death. God offered Adam and Eve the Tree of Life and Satan offered them death. John 10:10 (NKJV) says, "The thief does not come except to steal, and to kill, and to destroy. I have come that they may have life, and that they may have it more abundantly." To me, the only logical conclusion is that the originator of the Tree of the Knowledge of Good and Evil had to be Lucifer.

What was the Tree of Knowledge? There is a mystery surrounding this tree that reveals to us the truth of the gospel, our identity in Christ, and who we are created to be. To explore this mystery, I want you to think outside the box of traditional thinking for a moment. Ask yourself two important questions. Why was partaking of this tree bad? What was the choice placed before Adam and Eve?

Most people have an idea of what sin is or is not. Most people think of sin in terms of doing something they should not be doing, or not doing something they should be doing. In fact, the meaning of sin is to miss the mark, to miss the goal, to lose oneself, or to wander away. This sounds self-explanatory. In other words, if we do something God said we should not do, then it is sin, or if we do not do something God says we should do, that is also sin.

While this sounds simple, the mystery and key to understanding the significance of this tree is centered in the full definition of sin. The true nature of sin is more than just missing the mark, it is losing yourself or wandering away from who you are. The significance of this tree is understood more fully when you consider the meaning of the word "knowledge." The Hebrew word for "knowledge" is *da'at*[67]and it means "perception," "creative skill," "prophetic knowledge," and "knowledge of God." Notice how the Hebrew word closely resembles our English word death. The root of the word is *yada*,[68] and it means to "learn to know," to "know by experience." Interestingly, it is the same word used in Genesis 4:1 (KJV), "And Adam knew (*yada*) Eve his wife; and she conceived, and bare Caine." This gives new meaning to the words of

James 1:15 (NKJV), "Then, when desire has conceived, it gives birth to sin; and sin, when it is full-grown, brings forth death." By partaking of the Tree of Knowledge, Adam and Eve wandered away from who they were and gained first-hand experiential knowledge of evil. Their choice was rebellion against God's command.

As a side note, some have wrongly concluded that the Tree of Knowledge is a metaphor and warning to Adam and Eve against having a sexual relationship. However, this is not true since God blessed them, and commanded them to be fruitful and multiply. Instead, God warned them to not partake of the tree that would give them experiential knowledge of evil and bring about their destruction, death, and loss of innocence.

Think about the deception Satan used. When the serpent tempted Adam and Eve, he questioned their identity. Genesis 3:4-5 (NKJV) says, "Then the serpent said to the woman, "You will not surely die. For God knows that in the day you eat of it your eyes will be opened, and you will be like God, knowing good and evil." Adam and Eve were already created in the image and likeness of God. The serpent caused them to doubt who they were and their true identity. By partaking of the Tree of Knowledge, they wandered away from who God said they were and lost what they already had.

Who/What was the Snake in the Garden?

Some have wondered if the serpent in the Garden was a snake or Satan? Genesis 3:1 (AMP) says, "Now the serpent was more crafty (subtle, skilled in deceit) than any living creature of the field which the Lord God had made. And the serpent (Satan) said to the woman, "Can it really be that God has said, 'You shall not eat from any tree of the garden'?"

While the Amplified translation indicates the serpent was Satan, lets dig deeper into the meaning of the word. The Hebrew word for serpent is *nahas*,[69] a noun, and can be translated as either snake or serpent and the root of the word means to "practice divination," "observe the signs or omens," "whisper a (magic) spell," an "enchanter." These practices were used by soothsayers and fortunetellers in the observation of signs or omens. The *nahas* was not a holy creature and was referring to someone or something that was evil.

Revelation 12:9 (NKJV) positively identifies who this serpent was, "So the great dragon was cast out, that serpent of old, called the Devil and Satan, who deceives the whole world; he was cast to the earth, and his angels were cast out with him." It is interesting to note the Greek word for "Devil" is *diabolos*[70] and means "false accuser, slanderer." In other words, his name speaks to his nature, and it is exactly what he did to Eve when he deceived her.

When Adam and Eve choose to partake of the Tree of Knowledge, they experienced separation from God and death just like God said to them in Genesis 2:17. Instead of walking in their identity, they choose a path of trying to earn through works who they already were. Their disobedience opened a Pandora's Box that resulted in every man and woman drifting farther and farther away from God.

Where was Adam?

Prior to their fall, Adam and Eve did not have a sin nature and were pure before God. Nevertheless, the presence of the Tree of Life and the Tree of Knowledge gave them a choice to make. Their daily life consisted of partaking of the other trees and fruits in the garden and communicating with each other and God. It must have been amazing to walk and talk with God each day. For them, this was routine and normal.

The Book of Jubilees says Adam and Eve lived in the garden seven years before they sinned. For seven years, they lived life as God intended. No doubt, they were in the process of walking in their authority with dominion over God's creation. This had to be troubling to Lucifer who continued to advance his plans for their demise.

It is interesting to me there is no reference in the Bible of Adam and Eve partaking of the Tree of Life. I find this fascinating. They are in God's Garden of perfection and was given permission by God to eat the fruit of the Tree of Life, yet they did not. Maybe they saw no need to partake of its fruit, maybe it was a mystery to them, or maybe they stayed clear of it because it was close to the Tree of Knowledge.

Eventually, Lucifer manipulated their circumstances and presented them with a choice to make.

Many people reading the story of the fall falsely believe Eve was alone when she was tempted. They surmise Satan isolated Eve, tempted her to sin, and subsequently she gave the fruit to Adam. But this is not the case. Look closely at Genesis 3:6 (NKJV), "So when the woman saw that the tree was good for food, that it was pleasant to the eyes, and a tree desirable to make one wise, she took of its fruit and ate. She also gave to her husband **with her**, and he ate." Genesis 3:6 (NIV) makes it even clearer, "She also gave some to her husband, **who was with her**, and he ate it."

The Apostle Paul takes this truth a step further in I Timothy 2:14 (NKJV), "And Adam was not deceived, but the woman being deceived, fell into transgression." In other words, Eve fell into transgression because she was deceived. Adam transgressed with eyes wide open, knowing what he was doing. Both sinned but Adam's transgression was greater. He should have stood between Eve and the serpent. He should have given pause to the situation before it progressed. He should have taken a stand and exposed the deception. Instead, he stood there and not only watched but also partook of the same sin, knowing the actions were forbidden.

When we read Genesis 3:6 (NKJV), we conclude that Eve ate of the fruit first; however, does scripture confirm this to be true. It says "she took of its fruit and ate. She also gave to her husband with her, and he ate." Does this verse definitively conclude she ate first? She could have given the fruit to her husband who ate first and then she ate as well. The reason I raise this possibility is the language of Romans 5:12 (KJV), "Wherefore, as by one man sin entered into the world." The language does not say two people, the man, and the woman. It says by one man. Therefore, the possibility exists that it was Adam who partook of the fruit first before Eve who followed closely behind him.

The Fall and Cover Up

When Adam and Eve partook of the fruit, their eyes were opened, and they knew they were naked. At that moment, they gained experiential knowledge of evil. I can only imagine the conversation they had with each other after their actions. No doubt they experienced tremendous guilt and shame and began to blame each other for their bad choices. At some point they decided to sew fig leaves together to cover their nakedness.

Later that day, they heard God walking in the garden and hid from his presence. Isn't it foolish to think we can hide from God? Genesis 3:9 (NKJV) says, "the Lord God called to Adam and said to him, Where are you?" God did not ask Adam where he was because he did not know; instead, he wanted Adam to know where he was and what he had done. Adam's response revealed the torment he was feeling. Genesis 3:10 (NKJV) says, "I heard Your voice in the garden, and I was afraid because I was naked; and I hid myself." Sin will always lead to fear and their response was to cover up and hide. When God asked them how they knew they were naked, Adam said in Genesis 3:12 (NKJV), "The woman whom You gave to be with me, she gave me of the tree, and I ate." And when God asked Eve what she had done, she said in Genesis 3:13 (NKJV), "The serpent deceived me, and I ate." They each blamed someone else. The fallen nature will always blame someone or something else instead of taking responsibility.

The Consequences of the Fall

Humanity's fall had consequences. It is recorded in Genesis 3:14-19 (KJV):

> "And the Lord God said unto the serpent, Because thou hast done this, thou art cursed above all cattle, and above every beast of the field; upon thy belly shalt thou go, and dust shalt thou eat all the days of thy life: And I will put enmity between thee and the woman, and between thy seed and her seed; it shall bruise thy head, and thou shalt bruise his heel. Unto the woman he said, I will greatly multiply thy sorrow and thy conception; in sorrow thou shalt bring forth children; and thy desire shall be to thy husband, and he shall rule over thee. And unto Adam he said, Because thou hast hearkened

> unto the voice of thy wife, and hast eaten of the tree, of which I commanded thee, saying, Thou shalt not eat of it: cursed is the ground for thy sake; in sorrow shalt thou eat of it all the days of thy life; Thorns also and thistles shall it bring forth to thee; and thou shalt eat the herb of the field; In the sweat of thy face shalt thou eat bread, till thou return unto the ground; for out of it wast thou taken: for dust thou art, and unto dust shalt thou return."

The Serpent - God declared the serpent was cursed above every other creature and said he would put enmity between his seed and the woman's seed. This is a curious statement because a woman does not produce seed, only the man produces seed. God was speaking prophetically of the day the seed of the word of God would enter a virgin, that virgin would conceive and bare the only begotten of the Father, and there would be enmity between the Son of Man and the Serpent. He foretells of a day when the Son of Man would put his heel on the neck of the serpent (Lucifer) and defeat him in death. His heel would be bruised through crucifixion, but the results would be the defeat of Satan and the kingdom of darkness.

The Woman - Eve and every woman after her would experience pain in childbirth, and her desire would be to her husband, and he would rule over her. Notice this is a result of the fall and not the original design of God.

The Man - Adam would now have to work hard and provide for his family by the sweat of his brow. God declared that all humanity upon their death would return to the dust of the earth from which they were created.

The earth - The ground would yield thorns and thistles, and the harvest would not be as bountiful. No wonder, the bible declares the earth groans for the revealing of the sons of God.

When Adam and Eve sinned, God expelled them from the Garden (Genesis 3:22-24) to prevent them from partaking of the Tree of Life and living forever in a permanent state of sin. God had an eternal solution to sin and death through his son, Jesus Christ, and he did not want light and darkness coexisting together. The coming of Jesus and the new birth would restore humanity to their original design, and in a future period they would once again have access to the Tree of Life.

When Adam and Eve disobeyed God, the impact was far reaching and touched more than just their lives. Romans 5:12 (KJV) says, "Wherefore, as by one man sin entered into the world, and death by sin; and so death passed upon all men, for that all have sinned." Through one human's disobedience, sin gained legal access to the earth and all of creation.

When God created Adam and Eve, he gave them dominion over the earth and the legal right to rule and reign. Through their disobedience, their dominion was given up, and the kingdom of darkness gained access to earth. Two entities of the kingdom of darkness were sin and death.

It is interesting to note the words for sin and death are both nouns with the root of the words being verbs. This means sin and death are entities and their names describe their nature and the results of their actions. When sin and death entered the world, they were not just repercussions of humanity's fall. They were spiritual entities that gained access to the world of humans.

Proof of this assertion is provided for us in II Thessalonians 2:3 (KJV), "Let no man deceive you by any means: for that day shall not come, except there come a falling away first, and that man of sin be revealed, the son of perdition." Paul refers to this person as the man of sin and the son of perdition. Similarly, in John 17:12 (KJV), Jesus referred to Judas as the "son of perdition." Obviously, these two scriptures are not referring to the same person. Instead, they refer to the spirit behind these individuals. In other words, sin is a spirit, an entity.

Likewise, consider I Corinthians 15:25-26 (NKJV), "For He must reign till He has put all enemies under His feet. The last enemy that will be destroyed is death." Paul refers to death as an enemy, an entity, which will be destroyed. This is also confirmed to us in Revelation 6:8 (KJV), "And I looked, and behold a pale horse: and his name that sat on him was Death, and Hell followed with him." And finally, in Revelation 20:14 (KJV), John says, "death and hell were cast into the lake of fire." Sin and death were spiritual entities that fell with Lucifer and gained access to earth with the fall of humanity.

This same spirit of Sin is also the spirit of the Antichrist. Remember II Thessalonians 2:3 (KJV) refers to the Man of Sin as the son of perdition. The son of perdition is another name for the antichrist or adversary of the Messiah. I John 4:3 (NKJV) says, "every spirit that does not confess that Jesus Christ has come in the flesh is not of God. And this is the spirit of the Antichrist, which you have heard was coming, and is now already in the world." John tells us the spirit of the Antichrist is already in the world.

The Spirit of Suicide and Genocide

From the moment sin and death entered the world, two of the horrific sins humanity has faced is suicide and genocide. Suicide is the intentional act of taking your own life. Genocide is the intentional act of taking the lives of a group of people or even a nation.

Each year, many people die from suicide and it's a leading cause of death among young people. The numbers are shocking and many of you know someone who has taken their life or struggle with the aftermath of those actions. Within the religious community there is debate over whether a person who has committed suicide can go to heaven or if they are doomed to hell. While God is the judge of all things, I want you to consider this subject in the context of the fall of Adam and Eve.

Since God told Adam and Eve they would die if they partook of the Tree of Knowledge, was their decision to eat the fruit an action of suicide? Remember, Adam ate the fruit with eyes wide open to what he was doing. I realize this is a hard question, and we can't fully know what was going on in their minds; however, we also do not know what is going on in the minds of individuals today who take their lives. Are they deceived? Are they in pain and see no way out? Are there contributing factors?

I raise this question because I want to bring hope to those who know someone who might have taken their life and you are now struggling with the question of their eternity. When Adam and Eve sinned, God could have ended his plans for humanity and start over. However, the gospel of Luke recounts the genealogy of Jesus and refers to Adam as being the son of God. In other words, Adam was still considered in Jesus' day a child of God.

God foresaw all things. He saw the end from the beginning and everything in the middle. He sent his son to die for our heartaches and sins. If you are struggling with the pressures of life, I want to encourage you to take hope, and realize your identity is in Christ and not what others think or the circumstances you find yourself in. God is a restorer, a healer, and has the answer for all of life's problems. Taking your life is not the answer. Instead, go to the giver of life. Go to God with all your questions and disappointments. Deuteronomy 30:19 (NKJV) says, "I have set before you life and death, blessing and cursing; therefore choose life, that both you and your descendants may live."

The sin of Adam and Eve caused their death and the death of every person that would ever be born. When they ate the forbidden fruit, it was a mass extinction of the human race. Did their sin equate to the sin of genocide? It's an interesting question for consideration. While God holds the answers to all our questions, he also holds the solution to every sin and problem you will ever face.

The Birth of Racism and Governmental Responsibilities

As we think about the sin problem, let's consider for a moment the topics of racism and governmental responsibilities. Racism is directly related to Satan's desire to subjugate humanity. Satan was the first murderer and the original racist. He wanted to rob, kill, and destroy the human race. Humans were different than angels. Satan wanted to be like us, to be in the image of God. Since he wasn't, he hated us and wanted us to be divided against each other.

The truth is that all of humanity is made in the image and likeness of God. We are all his children. The racial tensions in our world have at their root a spirit of division and strife that goes back to Satan's original desire to destroy the human race. Unfortunately, sin will continue, and the tempter will run rampant until the Prince of Peace returns to set up his kingdom. As Christians, we should be against all forms of hatred, racial division, and all forms of misjudging the actions and intentions of others.

If you have experienced injustices, I want to encourage you to embrace the truth that we are all one in the eyes of God. Instead of dividing humanity into racial groups, we should celebrate ourselves and others. Every lineage is traced back to Adam and Eve, and the Father of us all is God. As we turn to the healer, let's lay aside the wounds of division, ask for forgiveness, and let the healer bring peace to our hearts. We can do this without being naive enough to think that all will repent of their sins. We are each responsible for our actions.

For our government leaders, I encourage you to embrace laws and policies that promote unity and the benefit of all. It is not the responsibility of Government to guarantee equal outcomes. We are all different, and each of us should pursue our dreams. Some will work harder than others and be subject to different influences and dreams. God did not create only one flavor, vanilla. We each have a responsibility for our own lives and should be accountable for our own actions. There are natural consequences written in the laws of nature, and our leaders should not try to supersede those laws. Instead, I would like to see our government promote healthy and strong families that give each man, woman, boy and girl the opportunity to succeed. Many will, but others will not.

In my opinion, our governmental leaders have grossly failed in the area of promoting unity. In their attempts to regulate bad behavior, they have inadvertently created and perpetuated more divisions, hurts, and inequalities. Humanity's performance is not based on our different skin color. Therefore dividing humanity into racial groups as a means to guarantee the same outcomes can lead to more division, favoritism, or celebrating one race or gender to the exclusion of others. Rewriting history or ignoring our past is also not the answer. The truth is some people do not seek equality. Some people perpetuate division, and some seek revenge or retribution as a way of dealing with their wounds. Government leaders should legislate Godly laws that treat each person with dignity and respect while promoting freedom and liberty within the strict boundaries of the constitution. Isaiah 10:1 (NKJV) warns our leaders of straying from their responsibilities, "Woe to those who decree unrighteous decrees, Who write misfortune, which they have prescribed."

Reflections of Who I AM

1. Did Adam and Eve eat the fruit of the Tree of Life?
2. How long were Adam and Eve in the Garden before they ate from the Tree of Knowledge of Good and Evil, and who/what tempted them?
3. Who ate the forbidden fruit via temptation, and who ate the fruit with eyes wide open?
4. What was Adam and Eve's initial response to their sin, and how did they answer God when he questioned them about their disobedience?
5. Name some of the consequences of Adam and Eve's sin?
6. Jesus said, "I AM the way, the truth, and the life" (John 14:6 NKJV). How can the information discussed in this Chapter help you apply the fullness of that truth in your daily life?

Prayer of Activation

Our Father in heaven, I am thankful that you did not give up on humanity even after the fall. I thank you for the gift of life and the forgiveness you offer for all. I ask that you help me to discern the times and circumstances I face in life each day. When I don't know why or how, let me look to you with trust and hope. I pray for healing in my soul for all the tragedies that have touched my life and I choose to look to you as the author and finisher of my faith. Help me to choose life over death in every circumstance. Give me the courage to stand firm in my trust of you and encourage others who are struggling with their choices.

A Prayer for Families

Father, I pray for your protection and blessings on my family and all the families in my community. Help us to stand together as one and live in peace and harmony with each other. Give us wisdom for when to take a stand and when to keep silent. Let us always speak your truth in love and show your compassion and mercy to others. I pray for your favor and blessings upon my family and community and that you will raise up godly leaders that will promote your will and kingdom values.

A Prayer for those Impacted by Racism

Father, I forgive all those who have mistreated me based on my race, gender, or any other reason. I break the chains of unforgiveness, and ask that you heal me of the torments those injustices have caused. I choose to walk in love, forgiveness, and encouragement to those around me. I choose to be an example for others to follow.

A Prayer for those Impacted by Suicide/Murder

Father, I forgive the person who affected my life because of suicide or murder. I not only forgive them, but I ask that you heal me of the impact it has had on my life and heart. Let me walk in hope, and restore my joy and peace. Their lives are in your hands, and you are the judge of us all. Restore to me what has been taken away, and renew my life each day.

A Prayer for Government Leaders

Father help me to lead my community with the same love and values you have. Help me to only legislate laws and guidelines pleasing to you. Give me wisdom to lead well and encourage others. Help me model your love and compassion without trying to impose my will on others. As we follow you, bless our community, and let your favor rest on us.

All these things I ask in the name of Jesus, Amen.

CHAPTER 11

The Second Desolation and Prelude to the End of Days

"There were giants in the earth in those days; and also after that, when the sons of God came in unto the daughters of men, and they bare children to them, the same became mighty men which were of old, men of renown" (Genesis 6:4 KJV).

Have you ever wondered why there is so much evil in the world? Many people struggle with this question and wonder why God allows so many bad things to take place if he is all powerful and loving. The answer is God has given us free will. When God placed Adam and Eve in the Garden, they had the choice to partake of the Tree of Life, or the Tree of Knowledge of Good and Evil. When they fell, sin and death entered the world. From that moment, the horrors of sin have ravaged the world. The good news is Satan's days are numbered and God's timing isn't always aligned with ours. The next question many ask is why hasn't God already acted to put an end to evil? I think the best answer is found in 2 Peter 3:8-10 (NIV):

> "But, beloved, do not forget this one thing, that with the Lord one day is as a thousand years, and a thousand years as one day. The Lord is not slack concerning His promise, as some count slackness, but is longsuffering toward us, not willing that any should perish but that all should come to repentance. But the day of the Lord will come as a thief in the night, in which the heavens will pass away with a great noise, and the elements will melt with fervent heat; both the earth and the works that are in it will be burned up."

For every reader who struggles with the question of why evil continues to grow, I hope this chapter provides you with some of the answers you are looking for.

The Unthinkable Happened

After being expelled from the garden, the story of humanity continued with Adam and his family facing the consequences of sin. It took only ten generations, just over 1,600 years, for the sins of humanity and the activities of the kingdom of darkness to reach a tipping point that moved the hand of God to act. These were some of the darkest years of humanity's history.

Much of the darkness of those days was seen by Adam, who remained alive through the ninth generation when Lamech was born. He was Adam's great, great, great, great, great, great grandson. Adam died during his lifetime at the age of 930. Lamech's first born was Noah. At the age of five hundred, Noah began to have children, Shem, Ham, and Japheth. Talk about a late starter. During the first ten generations after Adam and Eve, the youngest age of a father when he began to have children was 65 years old. What were those guys waiting on? A possible explanation is that the Bible focuses primarily on the birth of sons to track the lineage of the Messiah; therefore, these men may have been younger when daughters were born to them.

What was the condition of the world just 1,556 years after the creation of Adam? It was so horrible, it reads like something out of a science fiction horror movie and the conditions led to the flood of Noah's day, or as I call it, the second abomination that made desolate. The condition of the world is recorded in Genesis 6:1-8 (KJV):

> "And it came to pass, when men began to multiply on the face of the earth, and daughters were born unto them, That the sons of God saw the daughters of men that they were fair; and they took them wives of all which they chose. And the Lord said, My spirit shall not always strive with man, for that he also is flesh: yet his days shall be an hundred and twenty years. There were giants in the earth in those days; and also after that, when the sons of God came in unto the daughters of men, and they bare children to them, the same became mighty men which were of old, men of renown. And God saw that the wickedness of man was great in the earth, and that every imagination of the thoughts of his heart was only evil continually. And it repented the Lord that he had made man on the earth, and it grieved him at his heart. And the Lord said, I will destroy man whom I have created from the face of the earth; both man, and beast, and the creeping thing, and the fowls of the air; for it repenteth me that I have made them. But Noah found grace in the eyes of the Lord."

This passage of scripture raises a lot of questions. To gain a better understanding of what took place, let's turn to the Book of Enoch, which describes these same events. Enoch 6:1-8:

> "And it came to pass when the children of men had multiplied that in those days were born unto them beautiful and comely daughters. And the angels, the children of the heaven, saw and lusted after them, and said to one another: 'Come, let us choose us wives from among the children of men and beget us children.' And Semjaza, who was their leader, said unto them: 'I fear

> ye will not indeed agree to do this deed, and I alone shall have to pay the penalty of a great sin.' And they all answered him and said: 'Let us all swear an oath, and all bind ourselves by mutual imprecations not to abandon this plan but to do this thing.' Then sware they all together and bound themselves by mutual imprecations upon it. And they were in all two hundred; who descended in the days of Jared on the summit of Mount Hermon, and they called it Mount Hermon, because they had sworn and bound themselves by mutual imprecations upon it. And these are the names of their leaders: Samlazaz, their leader, Araklba, Rameel, Kokablel, Tamlel, Ramlel, Danel, Ezeqeel, Baraqijal, Asael, Armaros, Batarel, Ananel, Zaqiel, Samsapeel, Satarel, Turel, Jomjael, Sariel. These are their chiefs of tens."[71]

As horrific as it sounds, a group of two hundred angels known as the Watchers made a pact with each other to leave their habitation in heaven and take wives from the human race. Their offspring were giants or demigods, and the DNA of humans became corrupted. Their children were no longer in the image and likeness of God; instead, they were part human and part angel. For those that doubt the reliability of Enoch's words, remember, these same events are recorded in Genesis 6 as well as other portions of the Cannon of scripture. For example, Jude 1:6 (NKJV) says, "And the angels who did not keep their proper domain, but left their own abode, He has reserved in everlasting chains under darkness for the judgment of the great day." Also, 2 Peter 2:4 (KJV) says, "For if God spared not the angels that sinned, but cast them down to hell, and delivered them into chains of darkness, to be reserved unto judgment."

The Sons of God and Giants

To gain a better understanding of what took place we need to answer a few questions. When did this occur? What and where did this happen? Who were the sons of God? And who were the giants?

When did this occur?

According to Enoch 6:6, this wickedness began during the days of Jared. From the creation of Adam until the birth of Jared was 460 years. When Jared was 162 years old, his son Enoch was born. Jared lived another 800 years before he died at the age of 962. Based on this genealogy and the Book of Enoch, we can conclude that somewhere between the year 460 (birth of Jared) and 1,422 (death of Jared) this group of Angels began to have children with the daughters of men. Therefore, it is probable Adam lived long enough to see these tragic events.

What/Where did this happened?

Enoch 6:6 says two hundred angels descended upon Mount Hermon and bound themselves together with an oath to commit these abominable acts. The children born of these unions was a hybrid race that grew to become giants and mighty men of valor. The Jewish historian Josephus tells us they were the same demigods written about in Greek mythology. For those who thought Greek mythology was made up stories, according to ancient text, they were real people and were in fact the offspring of angels and men. They were known for their superhuman strength and became the source of mythology because of their mighty deeds. From this point forward, these children and every child born from them were no longer fully human. Eventually, as these children grew older and took spouses, the DNA of much of the human race became corrupted.

Who were the Sons of God?

As we have already noted, the parents of these children were the "sons of God," or sons of *Elohim*. This phrase is used eleven times in the Bible, five times in the Old Testament and six times in the New Testament. In the Old Testament, it always refers to Angels. In the New Testament, it always refers to believers in Christ. Therefore, the parents of these children were without question fallen angels.

Who were the Giants?

The offspring of the angels and daughters of men were giants. There are two Hebrew words for giants in the Bible, *napil*[72] and *rpaim*.[73] The word *napil* is sometimes translated as Nephalim and means "giants," "fallers, rebels, apostates." The word *rpaim* is sometimes translated as Rephaim and means "casting down, throwing down," or "of an ancient giant, whose descendants, who were also giants." While some theologians have debated this subject and have tried to explain away the Nephilim and Rephaim as being wicked men, or children born from the lineage of Seth, there interpretation does not agree with the context of scripture or archeological evidence. There are many scripture accounts of giants including Goliath who was killed by David. When the twelve men of Israel spied out the land of Canaan, they saw a race of giants and saw themselves as grasshoppers in their eyes. In Deuteronomy Chapter 3, we read about King Og whose bed was thirteen ½ feet long and six feet wide. There are also other ancient texts in addition to Enoch and the Bible that speaks of these giants. For example, the Book of Jubilees Chapter 5 and the Genesis Apocryphon found amongst the Dead Sea Scrolls also speak of the giants. In addition, modern Archeologists have found the skeletal remains of some of these giants measuring up to thirty-six feet tall. Therefore, there is archeological evidence, biblical text, and ancient manuscripts that describe and confirm the giants of that day.

What Was Satan's Motive for Corrupting Humanity?

Now that we have answered the basic questions of what took place in Genesis Chapter 6, let's look at the motives behind their deeds. Why did Satan want angels to procreate with women? I believe there were several reasons. First, as we have already mentioned, corrupting the seed of humanity would result in a race that was no longer in the image and likeness of God. This was one of Lucifer's original grievances that prompted him to rebel. Secondly, Satan was fearful of God's promise in the Garden of Eden. In Genesis 3:15 (KJV), God said to Satan "And I will put enmity between thee and the woman, and between thy seed and her seed." Notice God foretold of Satan's seed. It is a foreshadowing of the Nephilim and Rephaim that were to come. Since the seed of the woman was a reference to the coming Messiah, Satan was trying to stop God's prophecy. That leads us to the third reason, which I believe to be the main reason Satan wanted the seed of humanity corrupted. By comingling the DNA of humans with the fallen angels, their children became the seed of Satan, the children of fallen angels. It would be a way to not only destroy the plan of God but also a way to ensure these children would be eternally lost. There would be no possibility of salvation for these children or their offspring. This is confirmed for us in Isaiah 26:14 (KJV), "They are dead, they shall not live; they are deceased, they shall not rise: therefore hast thou visited and destroyed them, and made all their memory to perish." The Hebrew word used in this text for "deceased" refers to the *rpaim*. This is the spirits of the dead, the Rephaim. Isaiah tells us when they die, they shall not raise from the dead or take part in the resurrection. These spirits are eternally lost. This would be a way to stop the plan of salvation for humanity and aid them in their desire to overthrow God and take his place.

A key to their decision making is given to us in the Book of Enoch 6:3-5, "And Semjaza, who was their leader, said unto them: 'I fear ye will not indeed agree to do this deed, and I alone shall have to pay the penalty of a great sin.' And they all answered him and said: 'Let us all swear an oath, and all bind ourselves by mutual imprecations not to abandon this plan but to do this thing."[74] This passage tells us they knew there would be a penalty to pay for their decision to fall. It was a suicide pact they made with each other. The implication is only if they succeeded was there hope for them; otherwise, their fate was sealed. They must have thought they had a chance to prevail and therefore escape the judgment of their rebellion. In the end, their actions were not successful and Jude verse 6 (NKJV) says, "And the angels who did not keep their proper domain, but left their own abode, He has reserved in everlasting chains under darkness for the judgment of the great day."

The Second Abomination that Made Desolate

The sins of the fallen were great and abominable and led to the second destruction of the earth. Genesis tells us the wickedness of humanity was great and their thoughts were continually evil. From ancient texts and historians, we learn that the acts of the Nephilim and Rephaim became horrific. They developed an unquenchable blood thirst and began to ravage the earth and humanity. It was like something out of a living dead movie where zombies terrorized people.

They not only corrupted the DNA of humans, but their wickedness led to acts of cannibalism and bestiality. Even the DNA of the animal kingdom became corrupted. Think about Greek Mythology that includes stories of beasts that are part animal and part human. For example, Isaiah 13:21 references the Satyr, a part human and part goat or horse creature. Another ancient text called the Book of Jasher describes the corruption of the animal kingdom. Jasher 4:18:

> "And their judges and rulers [the Watchers] went to the daughters of men and took their wives by force from their husbands according to their choice, and the sons of men in those days took from the cattle of the earth, the beasts of the field and the fowls of the air, and taught the mixture of animals of one species with the other in order therewith to provoke the Lord; and God saw the whole earth and it was corrupt, for all flesh had corrupted its ways upon earth, all men and all animals."[75]

But Noah found grace in the eyes of the Lord. Genesis 6:9 (KJV) says, "Noah was a just man and perfect in his generations, and Noah walked with God." Notice that Noah was perfect or pure, and walked upright before God. He and his family were perhaps the only humans whose DNA had not been defiled by the Nephilim and Rephaim. Since Noah and his family was saved, they could re-start the human race and their offspring would not be corrupted with tainted DNA.

To save the world, God asked Noah to build an ark (Genesis 6:14). The ark was three stories tall, made of gopher wood, and took one hundred years to complete. In total, eight people (including Noah, his wife, his sons, and his son's wives) entered the ark and was saved. Also boarding the ark was seven pair of every clean beast and one pair of every unclean beast, male and female.

When Noah was six hundred years old, the rain began. Some have speculated that 40 days of rain would not be enough to cover the earth with a flood. But in addition to the rain, the fountains of the deep were broken up from the subterranean to help flood the earth.

After the flood waters abated, Noah and his family left the ark. After making an offering to the Lord, Genesis 9:1 (KJV) says, "And God blessed Noah and his sons, and said unto them, Be fruitful, and multiply, and replenish the earth." From this point forward, humans began to eat meat and were no longer vegetarian. As a sign of his covenant with them, God set his bow (rainbow) in the sky and promised to never again destroy the earth by water (Genesis 9:12-15).

Birth of Demons

The destruction and death of the Nephilim and Rephaim had repercussions many have not given much thought to, namely the birth of demons. Have you ever wondered where demons came from? The Bible says allot about the demonic, especially in the New Testament during the ministry of Jesus. According to the Book of Enoch, when the giants (Nephilim and Rephaim) died, the spirits that left their bodies became demons. Enoch 15:8-9 says, "And now, the giants, who are produced from the spirits and flesh, shall be called evil spirits upon the earth, and on the earth shall be their dwelling. Evil spirits have proceeded from their bodies; because they are born from men and from the holy Watchers is their beginning and primal origin."[76]

One more unbelievable note about the demonic. As astonishing as it may sound, scripture tells us that after the flood, the race of giants continued. Genesis 6:4 (KJV) says, "There were giants in the earth in those days; **and also after that**, when the sons of God came in unto the daughters of men." It appears from scripture, it happened again. As previously noted, giants are mentioned in scripture as being present in the land of Canaan and in the story of David and Goliath. Even after their destruction during the flood, somehow, the race of giants started again.

Demons, Sickness, and Disease

The influence of the kingdom of darkness, the fallen angels, and the demonic upon the earth is apparent when we consider the amount of evil present in our world. Specifically, there is a connection between sickness, disease, and the demonic. I'm not suggesting people who are sick are demon possessed; however, since God created everything good and perfect, and humans were created to live forever, something went wrong to introduce sickness and disease to humanity.

As we look at the ministry of Jesus, he often associated the sickness or disability of the individual with demonic spirits. Consider the following examples:

- "And He was casting out a demon, and it was mute. So it was, when the demon had gone out, that the mute spoke" (Luke 11:4 NKJV).
- "When evening had come, they brought to him many who were demon-possessed. And He cast out the spirits with a word, and healed all who were sick" (Matthew 8:16 NKJV).
- "And He healed many who were sick with various diseases, and cast out many demons" (Mark 1:34 NKJV).

Since Jesus connected sickness with the demonic, it is possible that the corrupted DNA of humans, because of the fallen angels, unleashed viruses and other mutated cells that are still with us today to cause sickness and disease? In Exodus 15:26 (KJV), God says, "for I am the Lord that healeth thee." Isn't it interesting that one of the names of God is Jehovah Rapha, the Lord that heals? The same Hebrew word used for Rapha in the name of God is the same Hebrew word used for Rephaim. Does this provide another piece of evidence that sickness and disease are associated with the demonic realm, and as Lord, Jesus is able to heal all?

Different Type of Demonic Spirits

There are different types of demonic spirits just like there are different types of angels:

- Familiar Spirits - Leviticus 19:31 (KJV), "Regard not them that have familiar spirits, neither seek after wizards, to be defiled by them: I am the Lord your God." These are the types of spirits channeled by psychics. It is the practice of a necromancer or one who evokes the dead. They are referred to as familiar spirits because they are familiar with the things they speak of.
- Unclean Spirits – "And when he had called unto him his twelve disciples, he gave them power against unclean spirits, to cast them out, and to heal all manner of sickness and all manner of disease" (Matthew 10:1 KJV). The term unclean means they are morally unclean, foul, or demonic.
- Seducing Spirits – "Now the Spirit speaketh expressly, that in the latter times some shall depart from the faith, giving heed to seducing spirits, and doctrines of devils" (I Timothy 4:1 KJV). These spirits try to mislead people and draw them away from the truth.
- Tormenting Spirits - "But the Spirit of the Lord departed from Saul, and an evil spirit from the Lord troubled him" (I Samuel 16:14 KJV). These spirits trouble or torment people.

We could go on and on with different types of demonic spirits spoken of in the Bible. They include deaf and dumb spirits, foul spirits, lying spirits, perverse spirits, spirits of bondage, spirits of divination, spirits of error, spirits of haughtiness, spirits of heaviness, spirits of infirmity, spirits of jealousy, spirits of slumber, and spirits of whoredom. Every sin, wickedness, sickness, and disease imaginable can be associated with one of these types of demonic spirits. The origins of all sin and everything that is bad goes back to its originator and author. Satan is the father of all sin. The rebellion of Lucifer, the fallen angels, and the demonic host have unleashed the characteristics and nature of their fall upon the world and humanity.

I believe every sin can be linked to one of these cohorts. Every sickness and disease can be associated with the twisting, perverting, and mutating of what was created as natural and normal. All wars and sinful behavior can be associated with a twisting of the truth and a desire for something that was not intended, and the oppressive forces of darkness continue to seek the subversion of God's plans. I am not suggesting that you are innocent of all bad behavior, but I am saying that the origins of all bad behavior, sin, sickness, disease, and death originated with the fall of Satan, the angelic host, and the myriad of demonic forces propagating their rebellion. In contrast, everything that is good comes from God.

A Prelude to the End of Days and Mark of the Beast

As we conclude our discussion on the spread of evil in the world, there is one final topic we need to visit. Specifically, the horrors of evil experienced during the days of Noah was a prelude to the end of days and a clue to the Mark of the Beast mentioned in the Book of Revelation. Time had a beginning, and the works of darkness will ultimately come to an end. But before that day, there will be a period of tribulation referred to in the Bible as the time of Jacob's trouble (Jeremiah 30:7). Jesus described this time in Matthew 24:21 (NKJV), "For then there will be great tribulation, such as has not been since the beginning of the world until this time, no, nor ever shall be." In addition, Jesus said the last days would be like the days of Noah. Matthew 24:37-39 (KJV) says, "But as the days of Noah were, so shall also the coming of the Son of man be. For as in the days that were before the flood they were eating and drinking, marrying and giving in marriage, until the day that Noe entered into the ark, And knew not until the flood came, and took them all away; so shall also the coming of the Son of man be."

What was Jesus telling us in this passage? Some have concluded that before Jesus returns, people will not be expecting his appearing. While I certainly believe this is true, there are deeper revelations to be learned from this scripture. Why did Jesus single out the days of Noah, and what were the distinguishable activities of those days? It had to be more than just eating, drinking, marrying, and giving your children in marriage. These activities have always occurred, and God blessed the family and sanctioned marriage. The one distinguishing factor during the days prior to the flood were the activities involving the Nephilim and Rephaim. Jesus wasn't expressing concern over people marrying. His concern was related to who they were comingling with and the offspring of those unions. The sins of Noah's day were related to the corruption of human DNA. Was Jesus suggesting this will happen again?

In the Book of Daniel, there is a prophetic dream suggesting the corruption of the seed of humanity in the last days. In a description of the final kingdom upon earth, Daniel 2:43-44 (NKJV) says:

> "As you saw iron mixed with ceramic clay, they will mingle with the seed of men; but they will not adhere to one another, just as iron does not mix with clay. And in the days of these kings the God of heaven will set up a kingdom which shall never be destroyed; and the kingdom shall not be left to other people; it shall break in pieces and consume all these kingdoms, and it shall stand forever."

Notice Daniel's reverence to "they." In other words, there will be something other than human that will comingle with the seed of men. In addition to the prophecy in Daniel, Jesus gave us another clue to these events in Matthew 24:15-16 (NKJV), "When ye therefore shall see the abomination of desolation, spoken of by Daniel the prophet, stand in the holy place, (whoso readeth, let him understand:) Then let them which be in Judaea flee into the mountains." Jesus declared that in the end of days, there would be another event that would lead to desolation. To date, there have been two prior abominable events that led to earth's destruction. In both instances, they involved fallen angels. The first was the fall of Lucifer and the angelic host and the second was when the Watchers fell.

Jesus referenced the abomination of desolation spoken of by Daniel. That passage is recorded in Daniel 12:11 (NKJV), "And from the time that the daily sacrifice is taken away, and the abomination of desolation is set up, there shall be one thousand two hundred and ninety days." Notice Daniel's use of the phrase "set up." According to this text, a system will be set up or placed into the hands of a foe that will cause people to give in to their power. Their actions will lead to the final desolation of the earth. What kind of system will be set up that could be so abominable?

The abominable system referenced by Daniel is described in the Book of Revelation. There will arise an antichrist who will implement a system that requires people to participate if they want to buy or sell or participate in commerce. The system is called the mark of the beast and those that refuse will be beheaded for their stance against the antichrist kingdom. This system is described for us in Revelation 13:15-18 (KJV):

> "And he had power to give life unto the image of the beast, that the image of the beast should both speak, and cause that as many as would not worship the image of the beast should be killed. And he causeth all, both small and great, rich and poor, free and bond, to receive a mark in their right hand, or in their foreheads: And that no man might buy or sell, save he that had the mark, or the name of the beast, or the number of his name. Here is wisdom. Let him that hath understanding count the number of the beast: for it is the number of a man; and his number is Six hundred threescore and six."

Let's examine the key words used in this passage:

- Image - Greek word is *eikon*[77] and it means "figure, likeness."
- Beast - Greek word is *therion*[78] and it means "an animal; a wild animal, wild beast."
- Mark - Greek word *charagma*[79] and it means "a scratch or etching, stamp, or sculptured figure," "stamp (as a badge of servitude)." The root of the word is *charax*[80] which means "to sharpen to a point."
- Number - Greek word *arithmos*[81] and it can mean "a fixed and definite number," "an indefinite number, equivalent to a multitude," or "a number whose letters indicate a certain man."

- Man – Greek word *anthropos*[82] and it means "a human being, whether male or female" and "generically, so as to include all human individuals."
- Six hundred threescore and six – Greek word *chx.*[83] The meaning of 666 is "a mysteical number whose meaning is unclear." The word is composed of the "22nd, 14th, and an obsolete letter as a cross." The obsolete letter is *stigma*,[84] which means "to stick, prick." To mystify the word even further, the obsolete letter of stigma is an intermediate between two Greek words one of which is a reference to God the Father as *abba* and the other is a reference to Abel who was killed by his brother Cain.

This passage of scripture has been written about for ages and theologians and scholars have debated what the mark of the beast could be and what it could look like. Given the meaning of the words used in this scripture, let's speculate on a possible meaning. The system to be set up will involve a mark of a beast involving the number of humanity and 666. Since this will be an abominable action and it is related to the period of time before the flood, it's reasonable to assume this system will somehow involve the comingling of the seed of humans with something that is other than human. This system may also involve sticking or pricking the skin to impact the number, or could we say the sequence, of humans that represents all of humankind, our DNA. The intent is to come between us and God much like Cain killed Abel. If we were to speculate, we could ask if this mark may be a computer chip or an injection into the skin to alter humanity's DNA, which would make them a hybrid and no longer human? This would explain why those that receive the mark are eternally lost. Remember the Nephilim and Rephaim could not take part in the resurrection because they were no longer human, their DNA had been corrupted. Revelation 14:9-10 says anyone receiving this mark will suffer eternal damnation and could not be saved.

What could precipitate the setting up of such a system? When we saw the outbreak of the Covid-19 virus, we saw the introduction of vaccines to ward off the sickness. People were lining up to take the shot and some could not keep their jobs unless they received the vaccine.

Some stores and restaurants would not allow people to enter without the shot. Was this a trial run for the days ahead? Will something similar take place that will lead to the development of another vaccine or mark that will alter humanity's DNA?

As a side note, are you aware that archeologist have uncovered the skeletal remains of some of the giants referenced in the Bible and have been working to discover the genetic makeup or DNA of those bones? Will there ever be a temptation to use that DNA for nefarious purposes, thus fulfilling scripture.

Perhaps science will seek to mix or alter humanity's DNA for medical reasons. There have been scenarios where some have suggested the mixing of human and animal DNA to develop cures for diseases. Many have discussed the need for Transhumanism. In fact, our own Department of Defense has conducted research on hybrid insects, part robotics and part insect for military purposes. Experiments have been conducted by defense agencies from multiple countries in their search for the elite soldier.

Genetic research and gene therapy known as CRISPR Cas9 allows gene manipulation to target diseases and/or prolong life. Could this along with other technologies result in a hybrid human or a super-human? What if scientific and technological advances in robotics, bionics, artificial intelligence, genetics, gene therapy, and digital implants result in the ability to develop a system such as the Mark of the Beast that could dramatically affect the life of humanity. Are all these the beginning stages and prelude of the mark of the beast and end of days? Does this sound eerily familiar to Revelation 9:6 (KJV), "And in those days shall men seek death, and shall not find it; and shall desire to die, and death shall flee from them."

The Mark of the Beast has been speculated about and debated for centuries and we don't know exactly what it will be. What is clear from scripture is that in the end of days, a system will be set up that will accomplish the goals we have just discussed. It will be the system of the antichrist and will produce results similar in motive to the days of Noah.

Reflections of Who I AM

1. Who were the Sons of God and Giants spoken of in Genesis Chapter 6?
2. What was Satan's motive for corrupting the human race?
3. Discuss the different types of demons and how they differ from fallen angels?
4. In Matthew 24:37 (KJV) Jesus said, "But as the days of Noah were, so shall also the coming of the Son of man be." What did Jesus mean by this prophecy?
5. What will be the fate of all who partake of the mark of the beast?
6. Jesus said, "I AM the way, the truth, and the life" (John 14:6 NKJV). How can the information discussed in this Chapter help you apply the fullness of that truth in your daily life?

Prayer of Activation

Our Father in heaven, thank you for loving me so much that you sent your son Jesus to destroy the works of darkness. I thank you for your mercy, grace, and forgiveness when I fail. Help me to be mindful of my actions and behaviors and the unseen forces of darkness that would try to lead me astray. Help me to always know that because of Christ, I have victory over all sin, sickness, and disease. Father, I come to you in the name of Jesus and break all forces of darkness that would work against me or my family. I pray for healing and deliverance in my life and the lives of those in my family. While the kingdom of darkness continues to operate in this world, I now live by faith in the Son of God. Give me wisdom and discernment to walk as your child and represent you to all the world. I pray this in the name of Jesus, Amen.

CHAPTER 12

I AM that I AM

"And God said unto Moses, I AM That I AM: and he said, Thus shalt thou say unto the children of Israel, I AM hath sent me unto you" (Exodus 3:14 KJV).

After the flood, Noah's descendants began to populate the earth and God sought someone with whom he could establish his covenant and produce the lineage for the Messiah to be born. Through the filters of our modern eyes, Abraham did not appear to be the best candidate for the job. His one debilitating factor was his age. In fact, I believe it was by design God waited until Abraham was 99 years old before he established his covenant with him. Genesis 17:1-2 (NKJV) says, "When Abram was ninety-nine years old, the LORD appeared to Abram and said to him, "I am Almighty God; walk before Me and be blameless. And I will make My covenant between Me and you and will multiply you exceedingly."

This wasn't only an awe-inspiring moment for Abraham, it was also a shock and awe moment. The problem with God's promise was Abraham did not have any children. He was 99 years old and his wife, Sarah, was 90 years old and well past the age to bear children. But James 2:22 (NKJV) says, "Abraham believed God, and it was accounted to him for righteousness. And he was called the friend of God." No wonder Abraham has been called the Father of Faith. But this was not his only qualifying credential. In Genesis 18:19 (KJV), God said this about Abraham: "For I know him, that he will command his children and his household after him, and they shall keep the way of the Lord, to do justice and judgment; that the Lord may bring upon Abraham that which he hath spoken of him." Isn't it comforting to know that despite all our shortcomings, God knows who we are?

Approximately 450 years after the flood, God established his covenant with a 99-year-old man and introduced the sign of circumcision. Perhaps you or I would say, "you're kidding me," I'm 99 years old. Abraham and every male child born through him would need to submit to the rite of circumcision on the eighth day after their birth.

The Hebrew word for "circumcise" is *mul*[85] and it means "to cut off." It signified cutting for blood to flow and provided a seal of the covenant. It was a foreshadow of the sacrifice for sin and the circumcision of the heart. It also established the consummation of the marriage ceremony when a man and woman came together for the first time and the skin was broken and blood flowed. The seed of man would pass through the sign of the covenant. It's one of the reasons sex outside of marriage is prohibited. It creates a soul-tie between partners and was established as part of the marriage covenant.

God made good on his promises. Abraham fathered Isaac, and Isaac fathered Jacob. Jacob's name was changed to Israel, and he fathered twelve children. Through his son Joseph, the tribes of Israel ended up in Egypt to be cared for during a time of severe drought. But over time, a new Pharoah arose that did not know Joseph and the land of blessing became a land of enslavement. It was during those years of harsh taskmasters the children of Israel began to cry out to God for a deliverer.

This brings us to our introduction of Moses, the man God would use for the exodus of Israel and the next step in his plan, namely the giving of the law. As Paul records in Romans 5:13 (NIV), "To be sure, sin was in the world before the law was given, but sin is not charged against anyone's account where there is no law."

Through Moses, God introduced the law and with it the knowledge of sin. The law showed the way, the truth, and the life promised by God.

However, Moses was much more to the world than the man through whom God would give the ten commandments. In a close encounter of the first, second, third, fourth, and fifth kind, Moses had a divine encounter with God himself.

God Reveals Himself as I AM

Moses' encounter began on an ordinary day when he was tending the sheep of Jethro, his father-in-law, a Midianite priest. He moved the sheep to the backside of the desert near Mount Horeb and noticed a burning bush. When he decided to explore the bush to see why it was on fire but not consumed, he experienced a lifechanging event. Exodus 3:4-8 (NKJV):

> "So when the Lord saw that he turned aside to look, God called to him from the midst of the bush and said, "Moses, Moses!" And he said, "Here I am." Then He said, "Do not draw near this place. Take your sandals off your feet, for the place where you stand is holy ground." Moreover He said, "I am the God of your father—the God of Abraham, the God of Isaac, and the God of Jacob." And Moses hid his face, for he was afraid to look upon God. And the Lord said: "I have surely seen the oppression of My people who are in Egypt, and have heard their cry because of their taskmasters, for I know their sorrows. So I have come down to deliver them out of the hand of the Egyptians, and to bring them up from that land to a good and large land, to a land flowing with milk and honey."

Can you imagine what was going through the mind of Moses? This encounter was no coincidence. While in the presence of God, Moses was instructed to go to Egypt and deliver his people. How would you feel if you were given a task that big? This was one of those situations where Moses felt small compared to the enormity of the task. Therefore, Moses asked God in Exodus 3:11 (NIV), "Who am I that I should go to Pharaoh and bring the Israelites out of Egypt?" He realized he would be going against the most powerful kingdom and army in the world and seeking to set their workforce free. This was an impossible task for one person to perform. When Moses asked God in Exodus 3:11 (KJV), "Who am I?" God's response was both surprising and revealing. God said in Exodus 3:12 (NIV), "I will be with you."

Some may wonder if God's response was adequate. God's message was to not worry about going against the most powerful nation and army on the face of the earth all by himself, because he was going to be with him. What's even more astonishing is that Moses was completely satisfied with God's answer. Why? How many of us would have given a thousand reasons why it would not work? But you must remember; when Moses encountered the glory of God and saw the enormity of his power, every fear and question he had about the impossibility of the task in front of him melted away. Can I share with you a secret? God has given you the same promise he gave Moses, I will be with you and will never leave you. It's recorded in Hebrews 13:5 (AMP), "I WILL NEVER [under any circumstances] DESERT YOU [nor give you up nor leave you without support, nor will I in any degree leave you helpless], NOR WILL I FORSAKE OR LET YOU DOWN OR RELAX MY HOLD ON YOU [assuredly not]!"

While Moses knew in his heart nothing was too big for God, how could he convince the Israelites, who did not have this encounter. Therefore, he asks God the climactic question in Exodus 3:13-15 (KJV):

> "When I come unto the children of Israel, and shall say unto them, The God of your fathers hath sent me unto you; and they shall say to me, What is his name? what shall I say unto them? And God said unto Moses, I AM THAT I AM: and he said, Thus shalt thou say unto the children of Israel, I AM hath sent me unto you. And God said moreover unto Moses, Thus shalt thou say unto the children of Israel, the LORD God of your fathers, the God of Abraham, the God of Isaac, and the God of Jacob, hath sent me unto you: this is my name for ever, and this is my memorial unto all generations."

God's answer changed history and revealed to us the holy, eternal, and unpronounceable name of God and a mystery that has been discussed for ages. In the Hebrew tradition, the name of God is considered holy and revered. In the Hebrew, it is *YHVH*. It is composed of 4 Hebrew letters, *Yod*, *Hey*, *Vav*, and *Hey*. In Judaism, the vowels are removed to prevent the mispronunciation of God's name for fear of taking his name in vain. When the vowels are added, it is Yehovah, Yahweh, or Jehovah and it means the self-existing one.

What is the mystery surrounding God's response to Moses when he said in Exodus 3:14 (KJV), "I AM that I AM," and what does it mean? It is the Hebrew phrase *ehyeh-asher-ehyeh* (pronounced - eh-heh-YEH ah-SHAIR eh-heh-YEH). *Ehyeh* comes from the Hebrew verb *Hayah*. It is the first-person form of the word. Do you recall when we first came across this word back in Genesis 1:2 (KJV), "And the earth was (*Hayah*) without form and void." As you recall, the word was significant to our discussion because it means to become or come to pass. It revealed to us the gap between Genesis 1:1 and Genesis 1:2.

If we pause but for a moment, we immediately see the mystery. As *YHVH*, God is the self-existing one. He is eternal. He does not change (Malachi 3:6). The Hebrew root of the word is *Hayah*, which is also the first-person form of the phrase "I AM that I AM" (Exodus 3:14 – KJV) and the same word used back in Genesis 1:2. How can this word be the name of God that means he does not change, he is the self-existing one, while at the same time meaning something that is coming to pass or coming into existence? And to make this even more puzzling, he said to Moses in Exodus 3:15 (KJV), "this is my name for ever, and this is my memorial unto all generations."

The answer to the mystery is shrouded in the character and nature of God. "I AM that I AM" literally means "I AM Jehovah, I do not change, and I AM bringing to pass my word into existence." This was exactly what Moses and the children of Israel needed to hear. It did not matter that Moses and Israel was facing the largest most powerful nation on the earth, once God declared his promise, it was irrevocable. His word forever settled the matter. Though Satan and the gates of hell attempted to bring destruction and change everything God has planned, those attempts were futile.

As you learn to *Walk in the fullness of I AM*, you will come to understand that God will bring to pass who you are uniquely designed and destined to be before the worlds were formed. Remember Psalm 139:16 (NIV), "Your eyes saw my unformed body; all the days ordained for me were written in your book before one of them came to be." God has a purpose for your life, and it is backed by God's design for you and his eternal word that does not change. As a child of I AM, you have the capacity to walk in the fullness of God's promises, his presence, his power, and all the revelation of who he is and who you are as his son or daughter.

It is no wonder, God's response to Moses settled his questions. God was with him, and he would be used by God to bring Israel to a land flowing with milk and honey and no obstacle was big enough to prevail against that promise.

Lessons learned from Moses

As we close this chapter, let's reflect on some important lessons from Moses' encounter.

1. Moses experienced self-doubt - When God told Moses what he wanted of him, he was filled with self-doubt and fear, a response traced back to the fall of Adam. When Moses replied, "Who am I" in Exodus 3:11 (KJV) he knew the task was monumental and he was incapable of leading the nation to their freedom. God was asking Moses to look beyond his circumstances and see himself the way he saw him. God would be with him, and he could walk in the fullness of that identity as the one God chose. This is what God designed Moses to be (*Hayah*). The enormity of your doubt is not as important as knowing you are in the center of God's will.
2. Moses was the first person to know God as I AM - Exodus 6:2-3 (KJV) says, "And God spake unto Moses, and said unto him, I am the LORD: And I appeared unto Abraham, unto Isaac, and unto Jacob, by the name of God Almighty, but by my name JEHOVAH was I not known to them." The nation of Israel had

only known God as El Shaddai, the Almighty all-powerful God, but they did not know him by his eternal name, *YHVH*. The Hebrew word for "known" is *Yada*. As we previously discussed, it means to intimately know God by experience.

3. Moses was the first person to Walk in a measure of the Fullness of I AM – This was the first time in scripture God introduced himself as I AM. The law of first reference says the first time something is mentioned in scripture, it reveals the fundamental meaning of the doctrine. Here are some of the principles we learn from Moses' encounter with God:
    A. God our Father Sees All – In Exodus 3:16 (KJV) God said, "Go, and gather the elders of Israel together, and say unto them, The Lord God of your fathers, the God of Abraham, of Isaac, and of Jacob, appeared unto me, saying, I have surely visited you, and seen that which is done to you in Egypt." Moses stepped into the knowledge that God was his father and he sees everything. He sees every obstacle, heartache, and trouble. As your Father, Yahweh loves and cares for you. He wants you to walk in the revelation that he sees everything and will supply the resources you need.
    B. Freedom from All Bondage – Exodus 3:17 (KJV) says, "And I have said, I will bring you up out of the affliction of Egypt." God promised Israel freedom and deliverance. Whatever the bondage and affliction you may be dealing with (sin, sickness, addictions, finances, persecution, oppression, etc.), God is your deliverer. It doesn't always happen immediately. Wait for the change.
    C. Defeat of All Enemies – In Exodus 3:17 (KJV) God said, "unto the land of the Canaanites, and the Hittites, and the Amorites, and the Perizzites, and the Hivites, and the Jebusites." Before Israel could inherit the promise land, they had to drive out their enemies. Who do you suppose took up habitation in their land of promise? It was the Canaanites, Hittites, Amorites, Perizzites, Hivites, and Jebusites. It doesn't take much research to realize that these "ites" were the Rephaim. Remember, the Nephilim and Rephaim

occurred before and after the flood. This was the reason God instructed them in Deuteronomy 20:16-18 to utterly destroy them, every man, woman, child, and animal. Many have wondered why God gave instruction to kill them all, even down to the children and livestock. It is because their DNA had been corrupted by the fallen angels and God was protecting the human race. The implication is that Moses and Israel could step into the role of victor, and defeat all their enemies, even the demonic forces of hell.

D. All the Inheritance from God – God said in Exodus 3:17 (KJV) he would bring them, "unto a land flowing with milk and honey." God wanted Moses and Israel to receive their birthright and inheritance promised to Abraham, Isaac, and Jacob. God has not forgotten you, your inheritance, or destiny designed for your life.
E. All his Miraculous Wonders – God said in Exodus 3:20 (KJV), "And I will stretch out my hand, and smite Egypt with all my wonders." There were ten miraculous and symbolic plagues God brought against Egypt. His mighty powers did not cease with the Old Testament or with the death of the last Apostle. His mighty hand and miracle working power is with you today through the power of the Holy Spirit. As his child, it should be natural for you to experience the supernatural power of God in your life.
F. All his Favor and Increase – God said in Exodus 3:21-22 (KJV), "And I will give this people favour in the sight of the Egyptians: and it shall come to pass, that, when ye go, ye shall not go empty…ye shall spoil the Egyptians." Israel lived in a state of slavery and bondage for four hundred years and had nothing; however, God gave them the spoils and riches of the enemy. As you live in covenant with him, the I AM that I AM can and will supply all your needs. Philippians 4:17 (KJV) says, "But my God shall supply all your need according to his riches in glory by Christ Jesus."

Moses was the first person in history to walk in a measure of the fullness of I AM, but Jesus came that we might walk in the fullness of this revelation. We may all be part of Adam's family, but Jesus came to restore us to our original family and who we really are. Jesus is the way, the truth, and the life and in the next section, we are going to see the progression of our story and how Jesus shepherds us into the life of who he has called us to be.

Reflections of Who I AM

1. Who was the Father of faith that God established his covenant with?
2. What happened to Moses' doubts when he encountered the glory of God?
3. What is the hidden meaning of "I AM that I AM"?
4. Who was the first person to walk in a measure of the fullness of I AM?
5. Using the law of first reference, what are the principles Moses learned about God as I AM?
6. Jesus said, "I AM the way, the truth, and the life" (John 14:6 NKJV). How can the information discussed in this Chapter help you apply the fullness of that truth in your daily life?

Prayer of Activation

Our Father in heaven, I am so thankful for your Son Jesus. He is the way, the truth, and the life and the entirety of scripture points to this great truth. Help me to always look beyond my circumstances, no matter how difficult they may be, and know in my heart you are bringing to pass your will for my life. Help me to experience for myself what it means to know you as I AM. Every need and circumstance I face in life, I yield to you. Let your glory go before me and supply every need and lead me into the paths you have designed for my life. I pray this in the name of Jesus, Amen.

SECTION IV
I AM the Good Shepherd

"I am the good shepherd. The good shepherd gives his life for the sheep" (John 10:11 NKJV).

The Greek word for "shepherd" is *poimen*[86] and it means "a herdsman, especially a shepherd." It also means "the presiding officer, manager, director, of an assembly." In this section, we will discover God's brilliant plan to send his son to pay the price for sin, redeem his children, and restore us to our original design. As Emanuel, God is not only with us, but he became one of us. At the birth of Jesus, the angel of the lord appeared to shepherds watching over their flocks at night and the glory of God shined around them. It was only fitting the angel would appear to shepherds to announce the birth of the Good Shepherd. As the Good Shepherd, Jesus gave his life for us. As our elder brother, he became our kinsman redeemer. After fulfilling all that was written of him, Jesus ascended to heaven and sent the promise of the Father. Through him, we can be born again to our original family. This new birth is the restoration of who I AM, a child and offspring of the living God, and a king and priest of the kingdom. As we learn to *Walk in the fullness of I AM*, we learn through experiential knowledge the revelation of what it means to be a natural child of God, all the benefits of that relationship, and how to live and experience life in its fullness.

THE UNVEILING/ REVEALING

CHAPTER 13

The Birthing

"Upon this rock I will build my church; and the gates of hell shall not prevail against it" (Matthew 16:18 KJV).

After Moses, the story of humanity continued until the fullness of time had come for Jesus to be born. His life and ministry turned the world upside down and revealed to all the love of the Father. Jesus is the truth of God's love for us, his eternal commitment to his promises, the revelation of who I AM, the restoration of God's plan for our lives, and the unveiling of the mysteries of God concealed since the foundation of the world.

The revelation of truth is sometimes difficult for people to receive, especially religious folks who have become comfortable in their traditions. When God begins to unveil his mysteries to you, it can be scary because it can shake the foundations of your beliefs you once thought were unshakable. This was certainly the case for the religious people of Jesus' day.

As an example, the Jewish people revered the sabbath to the point they developed laws and customs so they would not dishonor the day. In doing so, they lost their way and did not see the heart of God. Jesus' ministry challenged those traditions and shattered their way of thinking.

After healing a man on the Sabbath and thereby breaking one of their rules, the religious leaders were so offended, they confronted Jesus about his actions, and in their heart, they wanted to put him to death. Think about it, in their desire to honor the sabbath day, they did not recognize the God of the sabbath in their presence. In response, Jesus said to them in John 5:39 (NIV), "You study the Scriptures diligently because you think that in them you have eternal life. These are the very Scriptures that testify about me."

When Jesus came, everything changed. The conversation changed. Old thoughts, ideas, and beliefs were questioned. The covers were pulled back and the essence of who God is and who we are began to be exposed. Through Jesus Christ, all things would be fulfilled and restored to God's original design of what is normal and natural.

As we begin this Chapter, we will begin transitioning from the historical context of our family life story to what it means to *Walk in the fullness of I AM* in a personal way. The truth of God's design for our lives was revealed in Christ. The Apostle Paul wrote about Jesus being the man in the mirror and the image of God in whom we were all created to be like (I Corinthians 13:12). Jesus is the fullness of the Godhead bodily (Colossians 2:9), and we are the fullness of Christ (Ephesians 1:23). Let's begin the unveiling.

A New and Better Covenant

Through Moses, God introduced the ten commandments and the law. It showed us the standards of righteousness and pointed the way to life. The problem was our heart, sinful nature, and inability to measure up to those standards. Romans 3:19-20 (NKJV) says, "Now we know that whatever the law says, it says to those who are under the law, that every mouth may be stopped, and all the world may become guilty before God. Therefore by the deeds of the law no flesh will be justified in His sight, for by the law is the knowledge of sin." While all men before the law are guilty, it served an important purpose in fulfilling the plans of God. Galatians 3:24 (KJV) says, "Wherefore the law was our schoolmaster to bring us unto Christ, that we might be justified by faith."

To emphasize this point, we must ask ourselves an important

question, did the law change the hearts of men? The answer is self-evident. Have you ever tried to do what is right, only to find yourself failing repeatedly? Why does this happen? Trying hard can never produce the results that can be achieved through a heart and life changed and filled with the Spirit of God.

While the covenant rooted in the law was good, God planned a better way. In Jeremiah 31:31-34 (NKJV), the Prophet foretells this new covenant:

> "Behold, the days are coming, says the Lord, when I will make a new covenant with the house of Israel and with the house of Judah - not according to the covenant that I made with their fathers in the day that I took them by the hand to lead them out of the land of Egypt, My covenant which they broke, though I was a husband to them, says the Lord. But this is the covenant that I will make with the house of Israel after those days, says the Lord: I will put My law in their minds, and write it on their hearts; and I will be their God, and they shall be My people. No more shall every man teach his neighbor, and every man his brother, saying, 'Know the Lord,' for they all shall know Me, from the least of them to the greatest of them, says the Lord. For I will forgive their iniquity, and their sin I will remember no more."

Jeremiah provides such an amazing insight to the heart of God and his desire to connect with his family. Even when God miraculously delivered Israel from their bondage and led them out by the hand, their hearts were not bound to him. You would think God's faithfulness to them in such an hour of need would invoke their gratitude and cause them to turn their minds. But for many of them, their love was far from him. God new the essence of who he is had to be infused into their heart. God would write his nature upon their hearts so they could know him. Then he would forgive their sins and remember them no more.

God was progressively unfolding his plans, and with each dispensation, he pointed more and more to the time when this new covenant would come. The advent of Christ was that pivotal point in history. Galatians 5:4-5 (NKJV), "But when the fullness of the time had come, God sent forth His Son, born of a woman, born under the law, to redeem those who were under the law, that we might receive the adoption as sons." Jesus became the Good Shepherd to bring us to God and restore us to the kingdom. Jesus fulfilled the law and introduced us to a new and better covenant. This truth is confirmed to us in Hebrews 8:6 (NKJV), "But now He has obtained a more excellent ministry, inasmuch as He is also Mediator of a better covenant, which was established on better promises." Through this new covenant, the walls of separation would be broken between Jew and Gentile and God would restore us as one new man.

The Birthing of Jesus and His Ministry

The birth of Jesus opened the veil between the spiritual and the natural. As God manifested in the flesh, Jesus represented all the plans and dreams of the Father. It was planned from the beginning. I Peter 1:19 (NKJV), "He indeed was foreordained before the foundation of the world, but was manifest in these last times for you." Even after the fall of humanity in the Garden, God spoke the prophetic word to the serpent. Genesis 3:15 (NKJV), "And I will put enmity Between you and the woman, And between your seed and her Seed; He shall bruise your head, And you shall bruise His heel." Between the seed of woman and the seed of Satan there would be enmity and hatred. God declared Satan the enemy and Jesus was the planned answer to defeat all the works of the devil.

The prophet revealed his birth in Isaiah 7:14 (KJV), "Therefore the Lord himself shall give you a sign; Behold, a virgin shall conceive, and bear a son, and shall call his name Immanuel." The insights and mysteries of this relationship between God and humanity, God with us as one of us, was concealed from the beginning of time and is still unfolding. Paul said in Ephesians 3:9 (KJV), "And to make all men see what is the fellowship of the mystery, which from the beginning of the world hath been hid in God, who created all things by Jesus Christ." Paul further expands on this theme in Colossians 1:26-27 (KJV), "Even the mystery which hath been hid from ages and from generations, but now is made manifest to his saints: To whom God would make known what is the riches of the glory of this mystery among the Gentiles; which is Christ in you, the hope of glory."

The message is clear, God wants to open your eyes so you may receive his glory and come to understand the treasures of the fellowship he has with you. This declaration cannot be emphasized enough and needs to be shouted from the rooftops till all come to know who God is and who they are. God wants a relationship with you.

Jesus' life perfectly demonstrated our relationship with the Father. As he grew in age, he continued to grow in statue, wisdom, and favor with God and man (Luke 2:52). You must remember Jesus has always been God, but he did not become the Son of Man until the virgin conception and birth. While he was fully God, he set aside his deity to live a human life. This is confirmed to us in Philippians 2:7-8 (AMP):

> "but emptied Himself [without renouncing or diminishing His deity, but only temporarily giving up the outward expression of divine equality and His rightful dignity] by assuming the form of a bond-servant, and being made in the likeness of men [He became completely human but was without sin, being fully God and fully man]. After He was found in [terms of His] outward appearance as a man [for a divinely-appointed time], He humbled Himself [still further] by becoming obedient [to the Father] to the point of death, even death on a cross."

This is a stumbling block for many Christians who have a hard time accepting Jesus operated in this earth completely as a man. However, it is such an important principle, God declared in I John 4:3 (NKJV), "and every spirit that does not confess that Jesus Christ has come in the flesh is not of God. And this is the spirit of the Antichrist." Why is this so important? It's important because Jesus is our example, the mirror image of who we really are and how we are to live. By coming in the flesh, Jesus fulfilled all the legal requirements of the law to become our sacrifice, High Priest, and example of how to live. He could only do this as a man.

After his birth and reaching the proper age, Jesus completed rabbinical school, and became a Rabbi of the highest order. These were his silent years in scripture but in agreement with the norms of the day for those becoming a Rabbi. At the age of thirty, Jesus came of age to begin his ministry and was introduced at his baptism. Upon seeing him, John the Baptist and cousin of Jesus said, "Behold! The lamb of God who takes away the sin of the world" (John 1:29 NKJV). When John baptized Jesus and he came up from the water, an important event took place. The Holy Spirit descended upon Jesus in the form of a dove and the voice of the Father thundered from heaven. Matthew 3:17 (NKJV), "And suddenly a voice came from heaven, saying, This is My beloved Son, in whom I am well pleased." Father God confirmed Jesus as Son of God and Son of Man and sanctioned his ministry that was about to begin.

Interestingly, another event in the life of Jesus has a connection to his baptism. On one occasion, Jesus took some of his disciples to a high mountain. The event is recorded in Matthew 17:1-3 (KJV), "Now after six days Jesus took Peter, James, and John his brother, led them up on a high mountain by themselves; and He was transfigured before them. His face shone like the sun, and His clothes became as white as the light. And behold, Moses and Elijah appeared to them, talking with Him." At a later date, Peter wrote about this event in 2 Peter 1:17-18 (NKJV), "For He received from God the Father honor and glory when such a voice came to Him from the Excellent Glory: "This is My beloved Son, in whom I am well pleased." And we heard this voice which came from heaven when we were with Him on the holy mountain."

The traditional site for the Mount of Transfiguration is Mount Horeb. This mountain is filled with history concerning Moses and Elijah. When Moses led Jethro's flock of sheep to the backside of the desert, he came to the mountain of God, Mount Horeb. On this mountain, Moses saw the burning bush, God introduced himself as I AM, and God declared his eternal name to be *YHVH*. On Mount Horeb, Moses struck the rock and water came out to feed the Israelites. It was on Mount Horeb, God gave Moses the ten commandments. (Note: while some scriptures reference Mt. Sinai as the place the ten commandments were given, it is believed Mount Sinai and Mount Horeb are the same mountain with different names. This is because many scriptures reference Mount Horeb as the place where the commandments were given and the covenant was established - Deuteronomy 4:10, 4:15, 5:2, 18:16, 29:1; Psalm 106:19, Malachi 4:4). In addition to Moses, Elijah had history on this mountain. This was the Mountain Elijah ran to after he was threatened by Jezebel when he defeated the Prophets of Baal on Mount Caramel. On this Mountain, Elijah came out of a cave and heard a small still voice that gave him instruction about where to go and what to do. When we fast forward to Jesus, it was upon this same mountain he took a group of disciples and was transfigured before their eyes and both Moses and Elijah appeared to them. This was no coincidence.

What was Peter trying to tell us when he connected the transfiguration event and the baptism of Jesus? Notice in Matthew's account of the transfiguration, there is no mention of God's voice speaking to them, only the voice of Moses and Elijah. However, in Peter's account of the transfiguration, he said they heard the same voice of God they heard at Jesus's baptism. Therefore, we must conclude the conversations on the Mount of Transfiguration included not only the voice of Moses and Elijah but also the voice of the Father.

What was the significance of God connecting the New Testament ministry of Jesus with Old Testament Prophets? To Moses, God revealed his eternal name of *YHVH*, the I AM that I AM. Regarding Elijah, his name means my God is *YHVH* and he walked in the supernatural power and anointing of God's spirit, defeated God's enemies, and represented the prophets foretelling the coming of the Messiah. In fact, at every Jewish Seder, an extra cup is provided at the table called Elijah's cup. At the conclusion of the seder, they open the door to look for Elijah and invite his presence. The symbolism of opening the door signifies God protected them from all their enemies and poured out his wrath upon their oppressors in Egypt. It also symbolizes one of the jobs of Elijah to herald the coming of the Messiah. By connecting the ministry of Jesus with these two Old Testament leaders, God connected the revelation these two men walked in with the revealing of Jesus as the Great I AM. But there is another revelation in this connection. I believe we are entering a dispensation of time where we will *Walk in the fullness of I AM* that includes all the intimacy of relationship between Moses and God, the supernatural power Elijah walked in, all the works of Jesus and the disciples, and greater works than they did. A time of great awakening and walking in the fullness of God is upon us in these last days.

Jesus Announces His Plan for a Church

On one occasion, Jesus took his disciples to the coast of Caesarea Philippi. It is in northern Israel in the Golan Heights at the base of Mount Hermon. While there, Jesus took them to the steps of the temple of Pan. As you recall, Mount Hermon is the location where the two hundred watchers or angels fell from heaven and later fathered the Nephilim. This location became a religious center for worshipping the Greek God Pan, one of the demigods born of the fallen angels. At this site, there is a cave or grotto, that you can still visit today. The Temple of Pan stood in front of this cave and according to the historian Josephus, the cave had a cliff or precipice that descended to a large pool of water. The precipice was so high and the pool of water so deep it could not be measured. Because of this, the pagans called it the bottomless pit and they believed it was the gateway to hell. As they worshipped their false gods in this temple, they would throw human sacrifices into the bottomless pit.

It was at this site Jesus chose to ask his disciples who people thought he was. Some answered he was John the Baptist, or Elijah, or one of the Prophets. But when Jesus asked his disciples who they thought he was, Peter professed Jesus was the Christ, the son of God. With the Temple of Pan, the bottomless pit, and the gateway to hell in the background, Jesus made this famous declaration in Matthew 16:17-18 (KJV) "And Jesus answered and said unto him, Blessed art thou, Simon Barjona: for flesh and blood hath not revealed it unto thee, but my Father which is in heaven. And I say also unto thee, That thou art Peter, and upon this rock I will build my church; and the gates of hell shall not prevail against it."

There could be no better place for Jesus to introduce to the disciples and the world his plans for the church. The Greek word for "church" is *ekklesia*[87] and it means "a gathering of citizens called out from their homes into some public place, an assembly." The church is not a building, denomination, or an organization of religious people. It is the called-out assembly of believers and citizens of the kingdom. Paul writes about the general assembly and church of the firstborn who are registered in heaven (Hebrews 12:23). When Lucifer rebelled against God, his aim was to ascend into heaven and sit on the Mount of Assembly (Isaiah 14:13).

When Jesus asked his disciples who he was, it was no coincidence this occurred at the foothills of Mount Hermon. The angels that fell wanted to corrupt the DNA of humans and wage war against the kingdom of God. They wanted to overthrow God and believed they could get away with it. Even if they were to be punished, if their rebellion succeeded, their punishment would be nullified. However, on this site, Jesus declared not only who he was but also his mission on earth. In John 3:8 (NKJV) it says, "He who sins is of the devil, for the devil has sinned from the beginning. For this purpose the Son of God was manifested, that He might destroy the works of the devil." All the works of the devil includes the fallen angels and the realm of the demonic. Jesus came not only to restore us but also to destroy the works of the kingdom of darkness.

There is a real war going on between the kingdom of darkness and the kingdom of light. God's people and his called-out ones is a central theme of the gospel of the kingdom. With us, God implemented a better covenant with better promises, and it is available to all the world.

The Mystery Hidden in the Name Golgotha

Jesus said in John 12:24 (NKJV), "Most assuredly, I say to you, unless a grain of wheat falls into the ground and dies, it remains alone; but if it dies, it produces much grain." Before the birth of the church, Jesus' crucifixion dealt a defeating blow to the kingdom of darkness. It occurred at a place called Golgotha. John 19:17-18 (NKJV) says, "And He, bearing His cross, went out to a place called the Place of a Skull, which is called in Hebrew, Golgotha, where they crucified Him, and two others with Him, one on either side, and Jesus in the center."

How much commitment and love would someone have to have to voluntarily submit themselves to be crucified for the sins of others? Even before the crucifixion, Jesus wrestled with the horrors of what was to come. After celebrating the Passover with his disciples and revealing to them he would be betrayed, Jesus spent time in the Garden of Gethsemane praying to his Father. His prayers were so intense, his sweat became as drops of blood. His heart was being prepared for perhaps the cruelest form of death known.

Death by crucifixion was torturous. It was not private, swift, or carried out in a humane way. Instead, it was slow, long and drawn out, degrading, and performed in a very public manner. The victim was usually crucified along the roadside for all could see. They were made examples and a warning to all who dared become an enemy of the state. The recipient of this horrible death was subjected to humiliation. It began with a flogging. The Romans used a short whip of several braids of leather strips with pieces of bone or metal attached to the ends. Jesus' clothes would have been removed and his hands and feet tied to a post. The soldier, or in some cases two soldiers, would alternate their strikes on his back, legs, and backside. With each whip, the small pieces of bone or metal would rip through his flesh until it exposed the tissue and muscle. The loss of blood would have been extensive, and his body would have gone into shock. The amount of blood loss determined how long a person would stay alive. After the flogging, Jesus was made to carry the crossbar that would later be attached to the upright post of the cross at the site of crucifixion. In this case, it was a place called Golgotha or the place of the skull. It was located outside the city limits, North of Jerusalem along the roadside for all to see.

After arriving at the site, his body would have been thrown to the ground and his hands nailed to the crossbar. The nails used by the Romans were iron spikes hammered through the wrists so the body could be more firmly secured. Afterwards, the crossbar would have been hoisted up the upright post to form the cross. Affixed to the upright post was a horizontal block of wood that served as a seat upon which Jesus could partially brace himself to help avoid some of the pain. In Jesus' case, he was crucified in the middle of two other victims. Under normal circumstances, the victims would survive from several hours to several days depending upon how severe the flogging. To speed up their death, the Roman soldiers would break their legs so they could no longer hold themselves up on the crossbar seat. Their lungs would fill with fluid and their death would be quickened.

Above the cross, the Roman soldiers placed a sign with the victim's charge. In Jesus' case, it simply said, "Jesus of Nazareth the King of the Jews" (John 19:19 KJV). The Roman soldiers divided his clothes and cast lots to decide the winner as the crowds looked on and mocked. This was the fulfillment of prophecy recorded in Psalm 22:18 (NKJV), "They divide My garments among them, And for My clothing they cast lots." In most instances, death would be caused by multiple reasons. The loss of blood caused weakness and organ failure. The spikes driven in the hands and feet caused severe pain and shock to the body including muscle cramps and contractions. Respiration became difficult. Victims usually died of blood loss, the inability to breath, organ failure and dehydration, or the accumulation of fluid around the heart and in the lungs.

In Jesus case, the Roman soldiers did not have to break his bones to hasten his death. This was also the fulfillment of prophecy and the ordinances of Passover recorded in Numbers 9:12 (NKJV), "They shall leave none of it until morning, nor break one of its bones. According to all the ordinances of the Passover they shall keep it." In fact, it was not the crucifixion that killed Jesus. His last moment is recorded in Luke 23:46 (NKJV), "And when Jesus had cried out with a loud voice, He said, "Father, into Your hands I commit My spirit. Having said this, He breathed His last." The crucifixion did not take Jesus' life. He laid it down for us all. Jesus himself proclaimed his own death in John 10:17-18 (NKJV), "Therefore My Father loves Me, because I lay down My life that I may take it again. No one takes it from Me, but I lay it down of Myself. I have power to lay it down, and I have power to take it again. This command I have received from My Father."

Why would Jesus do this for us? The answer is recorded in Hebrews 12:2 (KJV), "Looking unto Jesus the author and finisher of our faith; who for the joy that was set before him endured the cross, despising the shame, and is set down at the right hand of the throne of God." Jesus came to do the will of his Father, and the joy set before him was you and me. Jesus paid the price to redeem us and destroy the works of Satan. It was the greatest example of love ever displayed.

Even the place of crucifixion gives insight to what God was doing. The Greek word *Golgotha* has a Hebrew Aramaic origin, *gulgolet*,[88] and it has two meanings:

1. The first meaning is "skull" - The place was named Golgotha because the location looked like the skull of a human. There are two possible locations believed to be the original site of Golgotha. One is directly north of Jerusalem and the rock formation of the mountain side looks eerily like a skull. The second is in the Mount of Olives and the location looks like a skull cap or cranium.
2. The second meaning is "head, poll" - The word was used in Numbers 1:2 (NKJV), "Take a census of all the congregation of the children of Israel, by their families, by their fathers' houses, according to the number of names, every male individually." The word Golgotha means the inclusion of every individual man/human. When Jesus was crucified, he was crucified on Golgotha, a place that represented every person from Adam to the last person who will ever be born.

If you were the only person on the face of the earth, Golgotha represented you. Every sin, failure, sickness, disease, obstacle, and need in your life was represented on Golgotha that day. It was the ultimate price to pay, and Jesus paid it all.

The Significance of the Resurrection

Before his crucifixion, Jesus spoke of the resurrection. Mark 9:31 (NKJV) says, "For He taught His disciples and said to them, The Son of Man is being betrayed into the hands of men, and they will kill Him. And after He is killed, He will rise the third day." The resurrection of Jesus was not just the finishing touches of a magic act. It was central to the work of Christ.

We understand the wages of sin is death, and the crucifixion of Jesus and the shedding of his blood was the remission price for our sins. Why then is the resurrection so important? The Apostle Paul said if there was no resurrection, then Christ is not risen, and all their preaching was in vain, and they would be false witnesses. But Paul went even further and said in I Corinthians 15:17 (NKJV), "If Christ is not risen, your faith is futile; you are still in your sins!" Consider for a moment the importance of that statement. The conclusion is that the entirety of the gospel message of salvation hinges on the resurrection. If Christ had not risen, Jesus would be a dead savior offering no hope for eternal life. Jesus' resurrection from the dead is our guarantee of eternal life. The good news of the gospel is that Christ is indeed risen and the same resurrection power that raised Jesus from the dead is available for us.

We are thankful for the gift of eternal life; however, there is more! Jesus did much more than secure our forgiveness of sins. "For God so loved the world, that he gave his only begotten Son" (John 3:16 KJV). The kingdom of darkness has been coming after Gods creation from the beginning. After God created Adam and Eve and placed them in Eden, the serpent tried to kill Adam and Eve and separate them and their offspring from God. Their sin impacted not only the human race but all of creation and the dominion they had been given over earth. When the Watchers fell in their suicide pact on Mount Hermon, they sought to corrupt the DNA of humans so there could never be redemption and God's promise of restoration would not come to pass. However, the works of Jesus was all inclusive. I John 3:8 (NKJV) says, "For this purpose the Son of God was manifested, that He might destroy the works of the devil." The resurrection of Jesus sealed the deal for eternal restoration. Acts 3:21 (NKJV), "whom heaven must receive until the times of restoration of all things, which God has spoken by the mouth of all His holy prophets since the world began."

The Bible gives us first-hand insight to what Jesus did prior to his resurrection after his crucifixion. Jesus had previously told his disciples that like Jonah, he would be 3 days and nights in the heart of the earth. What happened during those days after his crucifixion? Ephesians 4:8-9 (NKJV) says, "Therefore He says: "When He ascended on high, He led captivity captive, And gave gifts to men." (Now this, "He ascended"— what does it mean but that He also first descended into the lower parts of the earth?"

Before the resurrection, the souls of humans were held captive by the kingdom of darkness. Hell was divided into two compartments, the abode of the righteous and the abode of the unrighteous. While those who did not follow God are forever in the clutches of darkness, even those in covenant with God were held captive because of the fall. Jesus told the thief on the cross, "today you will be with Me in Paradise" (Luke

23:43 – NKJV). The Jewish sages taught paradise was a region in Hades reserved for the righteous until the resurrection.

When Jesus descended into the heart of the earth, according to Revelation 1:18, he secured the keys to hell and death. Colossians 2:15 tells us he disarmed the principalities and powers and made a public spectacle of them and triumphed over them. In the days of old, when a king conquered an enemy, the conquered king would be striped, his dignitaries put in chains, and they would be paraded around the kingdom in an open shame displaying their defeat. The Watchers thought their suicide pact and corruption of human DNA would stop the plan of God. They planned to overthrow God's kingdom and escape their punishment. No doubt Jesus held up high the keys to hell and death proclaiming to the Watchers there would be no escape from their suicide pact and their scheming had failed.

On the third day, Jesus was resurrected and was first seen by Mary Magdalene. Upon seeing him, Jesus said to her in John 20:17 (KJV), "Touch me not; for I am not yet ascended to my Father." Why did Jesus say this? After defeating the kingdom of darkness and securing the keys of hell and death, Jesus was resurrected from the dead by the Holy Spirit, took his blood, and ascended into heaven to become our eternal High Priest. It is described for us in Hebrews 9:11 through 10:12. He took his blood and offered it up before the Father as a once and for all sacrifice. Having completed this work, he came back to the earth and was among the disciples for 40 days before his ascension.

But there's even more to the backstory. Matthew 27:52-53 tells us that when Jesus was resurrected, many of the bodies of the Old Testament Saints were also resurrected and went into Jerusalem with him and were seen by many. What a surprise that must have been to the Sadducees who did not believe in a resurrection. After ascending to heaven, the Bible tells us Jesus sat down on the right hand of the Father.

For those that wonder how was Jesus raised from the dead and how is that power made available to us? Paul answers these questions in Romans 8:11-14 (NKJV):

> "But if the Spirit of Him who raised Jesus from the dead dwells in you, He who raised Christ from the dead

> will also give life to your mortal bodies through His Spirit who dwells in you. Therefore, brethren, we are debtors—not to the flesh, to live according to the flesh. For if you live according to the flesh you will die; but if by the Spirit you put to death the deeds of the body, you will live. For as many as are led by the Spirit of God, these are sons of God."

Notice the deeper revelation Paul tells us in this passage. Namely, the Holy Spirit in us is for more than our resurrection after we die. The same Holy Spirit that brought quickening (life giving) power to raise Jesus from the dead also has life giving power for us while we are living on this earth. In fact, through the resurrection, Jesus became the "firstborn among many brethren" (Romans 8:29 KJV). What does that mean? When the Holy Spirit comes to live in you, he quickens you to life and you become a son or daughter of God and Jesus becomes your elder brother since he was the firstborn from the dead. This is big news for this life and the one to come. Again, let me emphasize this does not equate you or I to the status of God, instead, it restores us to our original design as God's children, making Jesus (as the Son of Man) our elder brother.

The Birth of the Church and the Promise of the Father

Now that we understand God's fullness is possible in this life and throughout eternity, the only thing remaining is the infilling of the power or life source to make it possible. This infusion of the Holy Spirit within humans was made possible on the Day of Pentecost. It was the reason Jesus needed to ascend to the Father. He told his disciples in John 16:7 (KJV), "Nevertheless I tell you the truth; It is expedient for you that I go away: for if I go not away, the Comforter will not come unto you; but if I depart, I will send him unto you."

After the resurrection, Jesus appeared to the disciples and instructed them to preach the good news of the gospel. But before they were to go into all the world, he told them in Luke 24:49 (NKJV), "Behold, I send the Promise of My Father upon you; but tarry in the city of Jerusalem until you are endued with power from on high." Notice Jesus said the infilling of the Holy Spirit was the promise of the Father. What promises was he speaking of?

- "For I will pour water on him who is thirsty, And floods on the dry ground; I will pour My Spirit on your descendants, And My blessing on your offspring" (Isaiah 44:3 NKJV).
- "I will put My law in their minds, and write it on their hearts; and I will be their God, and they shall be My people" (Jeremiah 31:33 NKJV).
- "I will give you a new heart and put a new spirit within you; I will take the heart of stone out of your flesh and give you a heart of flesh. I will put My Spirit within you and cause you to walk in My statutes, and you will keep My judgments and do them" (Ezekiel 36:26-27 NKJV).
- "And I will not hide My face from them anymore; for I shall have poured out My Spirit on the house of Israel,' says the Lord God" (Ezekiel 39:29 NKJV).
- "And it shall come to pass afterward That I will pour out My Spirit on all flesh; Your sons and your daughters shall prophesy, Your old men shall dream dreams, Your young men shall see visions" (Joel 2:28 NKJV).

After Jesus' ascension, 120 of his followers walked down the Mount of Olives, through the Kidron Valley, pass the Garden of Gethsemane, into Jerusalem, and up the stairs to the Upper Room where they had previously celebrated the Feast of Passover. It was now 50 days later at the Feast of First Fruits, or the day of Pentecost. The Jews celebrated this day as a thanksgiving for the first fruits of the wheat harvest and in remembrance of the law given to Moses on Mount Sinai. The event is recorded in Acts 2:1-4 (NKJV):

> "When the Day of Pentecost had fully come, they were all with one accord in one place. And suddenly there came a sound from heaven, as of a rushing mighty wind, and it filled the whole house where they were sitting.

> Then there appeared to them divided tongues, as of fire, and one sat upon each of them. And they were all filled with the Holy Spirit and began to speak with other tongues, as the Spirit gave them utterance."

As you can imagine, this caused a ruckus among the townsfolk. This was not done in secret and occurred on a Feast Day when people from many nations were gathered in Jerusalem. The Book of Acts says there were Parthians, Medes, Elamites, and people from Mesopotamia, Judea, Cappadocia, Pontus, Asia, Phrygia, Pamphylia, Egypt, Libya, Cyrene, Rome, Crete, and Arabia. After hearing the rushing wind, the people came to the upper room to see what was going on and were amazed because they heard these Galileans speaking in their native tongues. They were causing such a commotion they mocked them, thinking they were drunk. But Peter stood up and said these men are not drunk because it's only the third hour after sunrise. Instead, he said in Acts 2:16-17 (NKJV), "this is what was spoken by the Prophet Joel: And it shall come to pass in the last days, says God, That I will pour out of My Spirit on all flesh."

After sharing with the people what had happened, Peter began to show them from scripture what had taken place and how the scriptures point to Jesus who had been crucified and raised from the dead. As Peter spoke, God's word pierced their hearts and they asked what they needed to do. Acts 2:38-39, 41 (NKJV):

> "Then Peter said to them, Repent, and let every one of you be baptized in the name of Jesus Christ for the remission of sins; and you shall receive the gift of the Holy Spirit. For the promise is to you and to your children, and to all who are afar off, as many as the Lord our God will call.... Then those who gladly received his word were baptized; and that day about three thousand souls were added to them."

On the day of Pentecost, the church was born as believers were filled with God's Spirit, and after Peter's first sermon, 3,000 people were added to the church. From that day, they began to preach the gospel of the kingdom beginning with Jerusalem, Judaea, Samaria, and then to the ends of the earth.

Reflections of Who I AM

1. Where did Jesus introduce his disciples to God's plans for a church, and what is the significance of that location?
2. What is the hidden meaning contained in the name Golgotha?
3. What happened between the crucifixion and the resurrection?
4. Why is the resurrection necessary?
5. How did the infilling of the Holy Spirit fulfill the promise of the Father?
6. Jesus said, "I AM the good shepherd" (John 10:11 NKJV). How can the information discussed in this Chapter help you apply the fullness of that truth in your daily life?

Prayer of Activation

Our Father in heaven, thank you for sending your son Jesus to die on a cross for every individual person that was ever born and ever will be born. I believe Jesus is the Son of God and Son of Man. I believe he died for me and was raised again on the third day. Without you, I am lost. I repent of my sins and give you my life and declare you as my Lord and Savior. Come into my life, fill me with your Holy Spirit and make me one of your children. Jesus you are the Good Shepherd to lead me through life. Help me to be your disciple and share this good news with all the world. Help me to find the right church you want me to attend that I may celebrate who you are with likeminded believers. I ask the Holy Spirit to teach me all the things I need to know to live this new life for you. I pray this in the name of Jesus, Amen.

CHAPTER 14

The Restoration of Who I AM - Sons & Daughters of God

"Beloved, now are we the sons of God, and it doth not yet appear what we shall be: but we know that, when he shall appear, we shall be like him; for we shall see him as he is" (I John 3:2 KJV).

The truths that we discuss in this chapter will forever change your life and how you view yourself. Over the years, there have been many attempts to write about the story of humanity. In most cases, writers use the so-called scientific theory of evolution to show humans evolving over time. I'm sure you remember seeing the pictures of humans evolving from an ape like creature to standing upright and finally walking on two legs. But as the Apostle Paul wrote many years ago in II Timothy 3:7 (NKJV), men will be "always learning and never able to come to the truth." As foretold by Daniel 12:4, in the last days, knowledge will increase; however, Paul points out to Timothy that humanity will be always learning but consistently reaching the wrong conclusions.

Understanding who we are changes everything. To this point we have talked about our relationship as sons and daughters of God in terms of creation and God's plan for his kingdom. In this chapter, we will go much further and boldly declare the truth of who we are. The single greatest mystery and revelation in the Bible is that we are the natural sons and daughters of God. The truth of this statement is astonishing and hard to understand. It raises many questions. It has been brushed aside, discussed as an allegory, and watered down from the full impact of its truth.

I realize this is a mind-boggling statement. I imagine some of you reading this are taken aback and wondering if you should put this book down and go no further. This sounds blasphemous! Instead, I want to challenge you to open your heart and let God's Spirit reveal to you the greatest mystery in all of creation, who you really are.

It all began when the Father, Son, and Holy Spirit counseled together to make man. Long before the creation of heaven and earth, God planned a kingdom and a family. He planned us, loved us, and knew us by name before we were ever born. What does it mean to be a child of God and what is our relationship to the trinity? While the church has been proclaiming the message of the good news, I wonder how many people have stopped to consider the significance of this message without trying to explain it away. I want you to think for a moment about what it means to be part of a family. There are different kinds of families and different kinds of children. There are natural born children, adopted children, stepchildren, and foster children. Every child is precious and thank God for every parent in this world who care for and love children. But the heart of our discussion deals with our relationship to God. How are we, his children?

The astonishing truth is humanity was planned to be the literal and natural children of God, and as such His family. To clarify once again, we are not God and will never become gods as some teach. God exists in the person of the Father, Son, and Holy Spirit. Jesus is the only begotten of the father; however, we were created and planned by the FATHER to be his natural children. It is the reason God is called "Our Father, which art in heaven" (Matthew 6:9 KJV). The implications of this truth are far reaching.

Before you can *Walk in the fullness of I AM*, you must first answer the question who AM I? The simple answer to this divine mystery has been hidden since the beginning of time. Once grasped, it will change everything. This truth is so important, Satan has been attacking it throughout history. It is a major reason many people struggle today. Satan will always attack you in the areas of who you are, your relationship with God, your purpose in life, your usefulness and worthiness, and your place in the world. Think about the struggles around identity and the lies people have believed:

- There is no life after death.
- Humanity evolved through evolution.
- Our worth and value is determined by how others perceive us.
- Our mistakes define who we are, and our failures limit our potential.
- There are no moral boundaries, laws and customs are man-made.
- Institutions such as marriage and governments are man-made.
- Our identity as male or female should be left up to the individual.
- Masculinity and femininity are a danger.
- An unborn child is fetal tissue and not a viable life.
- The most important thing in life is to be happy.
- If God exists, he is indifferent.
- And on and on we could go.

Once we come to understand we are the natural sons and daughters of God created in the image and likeness of our Father, we can begin to understand the context of our lives in God's plan. As we begin to grasp these truths, many of the big questions in life are answered, many confusions disappear, and we are no longer subject to the whims of emotion or societal trends.

In the end, it does not matter what you or I think. Instead, what does God say about it. If we are the natural sons and daughters of God, the Bible will support this truth; otherwise, it is just a belief to make us feel good about ourselves or some new age propaganda. We are going to look at 4 teachings in the Bible that prove beyond the shadow of any doubt our identity:

1. We are God's natural sons and daughters because His DNA is in us.
2. We are God's natural sons and daughters, not stepchildren or adopted children.

3. We are God's natural sons and daughters because Jesus is our Kinsman Redeemer.
4. We are God's natural sons and daughters because the Bible declares we are.

We are God's Natural Sons and Daughters Because His DNA is in Us

When questions of paternity arise, we can prove with DNA the identity of the parents. Once proven, we know without a doubt the child was the offspring of the parents. What does the Bible say about our DNA and us being the offspring of God? Acts 17:28 (NKJV) says, "For in Him we live and move and have our being, as also some of your own poets have said, For we are also His offspring." The Greek word for "offspring" is *genos*[89] and it means "family, stock, race," "the aggregate of many individuals of the same nature, kind, sort, species."

The word *gene* was first coined in the early 1900s by William Bateson, a geneticist who coined the word from this Greek word *genos*. Scripture confirms we are the offspring of God, and his genome runs through our body. This perfectly explains the Genesis account of humanity being created in the image and likeness of God. We are his children, and we look and act like our Father. We previously discussed what the process looked like when God created Adam and breathed a part of himself into him. God breathed into Adam the breath of "lives." The breath of every life that was to be born from Adam until the end of time originated in the Garden. Since then, humanity has married and had children who were also in their own image and likeness. This is confirmed to us in Genesis 5:3 (NKJV), "And Adam lived one hundred and thirty years, and begot a son in his own likeness, after his image, and named him Seth."

Does all this mean God is flesh and blood like a human? No, of course not. John 4:24 (NKJV) says, "God is a Spirit: and they that worship him must worship him in spirit and in truth." Leviticus 17:11 (KJV) says, "For the life of the flesh is in the blood." Without blood, the fleshly body would die. But remember, we are more than flesh and blood. We are spirit, soul, and body. I Thessalonians 6:23 (KJV) says, "And the very God of peace sanctify you wholly; and I pray God your whole spirit and soul and body be preserved blameless unto the coming of our Lord Jesus Christ." Without the blood in your flesh, your body would die. Without your soul and spirit, your body would also die. Death is the separation of the soul and spirit from the body. There is the flesh part of a human created by God from the dust of the earth, and there is the spirit and soul of a human which came directly from God himself.

Adam was created in the image and likeness of God in two ways. First, his physical body was molded and formed as a mirror image of his spiritual Father. Second, Adam's soul and spirit came directly from God himself when he breathed a part of his own spirit into Adam. God's spirit fused with the fleshly body of Adam, and he was animated and brought to life with a part of God within him. Therefore, Adam looked and acted like his heavenly Father, because God's DNA was a part of his genetic makeup.

God reveals this truth to us again in Ephesians 4:6 (KJV), "One God and Father of all, who is above all, and through all, and in you all." Notice how this scripture emphasizes that God is the Father of us all and in us all. God the Father is in you and a part of you. The enemy of our soul and the unbelieving would have you think you are just an accident of nature, here by random chance, a product of evolution. But all those thoughts are untruths and go against your true identity.

This truth is further revealed to us in Psalm 8:4-5 (KJV), "What is man, that thou art mindful of him? and the son of man, that thou visitest him? For thou hast made him a little lower than the angels, and hast crowned him with glory and honour." The Hebrew word used here is not the normal word used for angels. That word is *malak* and as we previously discussed, it means a messenger or angel. Instead, the Hebrew word in this verse is *elohim* which means God, divine ones, or those of the spirit real. While it could refer to angels, it is also the same word God used for himself back in Genesis Chapter 1:3 (KJV), "And God (*elohim*) said, let there be." The original translators couldn't bring themselves to translate the language of the Psalm as God. Because of that, they used the word angels. The truth is humans were created a little lower than God. We are the crowning jewel of God's creation, and we were created in his image and likeness as one of his children. The Psalmist links man and the son of man in the same verse. While the phrase son of man speaks prophetically of Jesus, it also refers to the lineage of humanity who was made in the image and likeness of God. Since we are his offspring, and his spirit is in us, we are the natural sons and daughters of God.

The Restoration of our body

We need to pause for a moment to discuss the fall and God's plan for the restoration of our natural bodies. When Adam died, death genetically passed upon all men. Romans 5:12 (NKV), "Wherefore, as by one man sin entered into the world, and death by sin; and so death passed upon all men, for that all have sinned." Jesus paid the price for all sin to defeat death. Because of Jesus, all humans will be resurrected from the dead, believers, and unbelievers. Acts 24:15 (KJV) says, "I have hope in God, which they themselves also accept, that there will be a resurrection of the dead, both of the just and the unjust." At the final judgment (Revelation 20:11-15), the kingdom of darkness will be judged. Just like Jesus received a glorified body at his resurrection, we will experience the same metamorphous. Paul talks about this in I Corinthians 15:51-54 (NKJV):

> "Behold, I tell you a mystery: We shall not all sleep, but we shall all be changed - in a moment, in the twinkling of an eye, at the last trumpet. For the trumpet will sound, and the dead will be raised incorruptible, and we shall be changed. For this corruptible must put on incorruption, and this mortal must put on immortality. So when this corruptible has put on incorruption, and this mortal has put on immortality, then shall be brought to pass the saying that is written: "Death is swallowed up in victory."

Jesus - The Only Begotten of the Father

We also need to pause for a moment to discuss the difference between you and I as a child of God and Jesus as the only begotten of the Father. When Jesus was born, he was conceived of the Holy Spirit as recorded in Matthew 1:18 (NKJV), "Now the birth of Jesus Christ was as follows: After His mother Mary was betrothed to Joseph, before they came together, she was found with child of the Holy Spirit." While the beginning of our life started the day we were born, Jesus pre-existed before his birth and has always been God. John 1:1 (NKJV) says, "In the beginning was the Word, and the Word was with God, and the Word was God."

You and I did not pre-exist other than in the mind and plans of God prior to creation. Think of it this way. If you have a child, your child is part of you, but not you. It is the same way with us and our Heavenly Father. We are a part of him since his spirit and breath is in us, but we are not him. Jesus on the other hand has always been God and became the only begotten when he was conceived by the Holy Spirit.

It's also important to point out that many translations have done a disservice in their translations of the Bible by leaving out the word "begotten" in John 3:16. Instead of saying Jesus is the only begotten Son of God, they have changed the text to say he was the only Son of God:

- "For God so loved the world, that he gave his only begotten Son" (John 3:16 KJV).
- "For God so loved the world, that He gave His only begotten Son" (John 3:16 NASB).
- "For God so loved the world that he gave his one and only Son" (John 3:16 NIV).
- "For God so loved the world he gave his only Son" (John 3:16 ESV).
- "This is how much God loved the world: He gave his Son, his one and only Son" (John 3:16 MSG).
- "For God so loved the world that he gave his only Son" (John 3:16 NRSV).

Removing the word "begotten" from the text diminishes the importance of you and I being the sons and daughters of God. The Greek word for "only begotten" is *monogenism*[90] and it means "single of its kind, only." While the Bible plainly declares Jesus is the only begotten of the Father, it also plainly tells us we are his children. For example, in Luke 3:38 (KJV), Adam is called the "son of God." I John 3:2 (KJV) says, "Beloved, now are we the sons of God." To be clear, Jesus was not created to be a son of God as some religions teach. Rather, he is the only begotten and has always been God and present with the Father and Holy Spirit at creation. Hopefully, this explanation makes clear the distinction between Jesus, who is God, and humanity who were created by God to be his children and family.

The Mystery of being Born Again

While the body will be restored to its original design at the resurrection, what about our spirit? Jesus said in John 3:3 (KJV), "Except a man be born again, he cannot see the kingdom of God." What does it mean to be born again? After the fall of Adam and Eve, humanity experienced death just like God said. They were spiritually separated from God and the process of physical death began. In the kingdom of God, there are no naturalized citizens. We cannot earn or merit our entrance. The only way to be a part of God's family is to be born into it. When Jesus said we had to be born again, he was not using a cliché to describe salvation. NO! NO! And NO! He was talking about being born again into your original family, the family of God that you had died to because of the sin of Adam being passed on to you. When you are born again, the Holy Spirit breathes the spirit of God into your life, and you are restored to your original family. We are not born again into a new family we previously had no connection to. Instead, we are born again and placed back into our original family. Being born again is the restoration of who I AM, a son or daughter of God. Just like the prodigal son did not come home to a new family he had never known before; he came home to his original family.

II Corinthians 5:17 (KJV) says, "Therefore if any man be in Christ, he is a new creature: old things are passed away; behold, all things are become new." This verse is full of mystery. When God said we are a new creature, it speaks of a new creation, superior to what it succeeded, something that previously did not exist. Many have proclaimed that when we are born again, we become a new people group that has never existed before, a brand-new creation. While there is some truth to this, there is a deeper meaning. The mystery is hidden in the context of the verse. When Paul said, "old things are passed away" (II Corinthians 5:17 KJV), it means that which has been from the beginning. Also notice that Paul says, "all things are become new" (II Corinthians 5:17 KJV). The Greek word for "become" is *ginomai*[91] and it means "to become, to come into existence." As we have noted, it is where we get our English word *genome*. In other words, when you are born again, it places you back into the original position as Adam and Eve before the fall when humans were made in the image and likeness of God.

This is the gospel of the kingdom! As Romans 6:23 (KJV) says, "For the wages of sin is death; but the gift of God is eternal life through Jesus Christ our Lord." The gospel of the kingdom is not only that we can be born again and have eternal live, but also that we are restored to our original family as the natural children of God and part of his kingdom. As Matthew 25:34 (NKJV) says, "Then the King will say to those on His right hand, Come, you blessed of My Father, inherit the kingdom prepared for you from the foundation of the world." Being born again restores us to our original design and the resurrection of Jesus secured the restoration of our eternal spiritual and physical life. God reemphasized this point in Ephesians 1:4 (KJV), "According as he hath chosen us in him before the foundation of the world, that we should be holy and without blame before him in love." God choose you to be part of his family (to be in him) from the beginning.

We are God's natural sons and daughters, not stepchildren or adopted children

The next concept I want us to explore is that we are God's natural sons and daughters, not stepchildren or adopted children as many teach. Stepchildren and adopted children are wonderful and become part of a family through marriage or adoption. Each is a blessing and thank

God for families and all children. However, over the years, two concepts made their way into the church that brought with them confusion. The first is that God's chosen people were the Jews and because of their rejection of God, gentiles have been grafted into God's family and are therefore his stepchildren/grafted in children. The second is that believers have been adopted into God's family. Where then did these misconceptions come from?

Stepchildren

Let's first discuss the concept of stepchildren. A stepchild is a child by marriage. For example, a woman through an earlier marriage has a child and at a later date and time that marriage is ended through death or divorce and the woman remarries. Her child then becomes the stepchild of her new husband. Some have described this relationship in similar ways to Jews and Gentiles. The belief is that the Jews were God's original called out ones, God's children, and it was only because of the disbelief of the Jews that the Gentiles were grafted in the family of God. Therefore, gentiles are viewed as the stepchildren/grafted in children and not the natural children of God. This belief comes from Romans 11:17-21 (NIV) where Paul says:

> "If some of the branches have been broken off, and you, though a wild olive shoot, have been grafted in among the others and now share in the nourishing sap from the olive root, do not consider yourself to be superior to those other branches. If you do, consider this: You do not support the root, but the root supports you. You will say then, "Branches were broken off so that I could be grafted in." Granted. But they were broken off because of unbelief, and you stand by faith. Do not be arrogant, but tremble. For if God did not spare the natural branches, he will not spare you either."

Because of this scripture and the fact that God's covenant was with Abraham, Isaac, and Jacob, who became the nation of Israel, some have incorrectly believed Gentiles are only God's children because of the unbelief of the Jews, which allowed the grafting in of the Gentiles. But here the Bible is speaking about the covenant relationship between humanity and God and not whether gentiles are the children of God. To understand what Paul was saying, we need to understand the context of Paul's writings. Paul wrote these verses to deal with an arrogance that had made its way into the church. Paul compares Israel to the natural branches of an olive tree and the Gentiles as branches of a wild olive tree. It is important to remember that the church at Rome started out consisting of Jewish believers. As the church grew and believers evangelized the area, many gentiles became believers and part of the church at Rome. During this time, the Roman Emperor Claudius expelled the Jews from Rome, leaving the church to consist primarily of gentiles. After a period of time, Nero allowed the Jews back; however, the gentiles had become arrogant regarding their position in the church. They concluded that Claudius' rejection of the Jews was symbolic of God's rejection of the Jews.

Even to this day, there are those who believe in a Replacement Theology. This theology teaches that the church replaced Israel in God's plan and the Jewish people are no longer the chosen people of God. Many in this camp go throughout the Bible and everywhere it mentions God's promise to the Jews or nation of Israel, they replace it with the church who has taken over as God's chosen people. This teaching; however, is false and does not hold up to scripture. There are prophetic promises that God has given to the Nation of Israel alone. This, however, does not mean that gentiles are not God's children as well.

In Paul's writing to the Romans, he discusses Gentiles being grafted in the covenant as a wild olive branch is grafted into and becomes part of an olive tree. His purpose was not to diminish the position of the Jews or the Gentiles but to allow the Gentiles to understand they had been grafted into God's covenant with the Jews as a wild olive branch is grafted into an olive tree. Notice how Paul makes this clear in Galatians 3:26-29 (NKJV) where he discusses the promise or covenant given to Abraham: "For you are all sons of God through faith in Christ Jesus. For as many of you as were baptized into Christ have put on Christ. There is neither Jew nor Greek, there is neither slave nor free, there is neither male nor female; for you are all one in Christ Jesus. And if you are Christ's, then you are Abraham's seed, and heirs according to the promise." This is further made clear in Ephesians 2:11-16 (NKJV):

> "Therefore remember that you, once Gentiles in the flesh—who are called Uncircumcision by what is called the Circumcision made in the flesh by hands - that at that time you were without Christ, being aliens from the commonwealth of Israel and strangers from the covenants of promise, having no hope and without God in the world. But now in Christ Jesus you who once were far off have been brought near by the blood of Christ. For He Himself is our peace, who has made both one, and has broken down the middle wall of separation, having abolished in His flesh the enmity, that is, the law of commandments contained in ordinances, so as to create in Himself one new man from the two, thus making peace, and that He might reconcile them both to God in one body through the cross, thereby putting to death the enmity."

These scriptures make it crystal clear that both Jew and Gentile are the children of God. God established his covenant with the Jewish people as a door into the human race through which one day he would take on the form of flesh as Jesus the Messiah. It was through this Old Covenant that God entered the human race to make a New Covenant with all of humanity that we might be one new man/woman in Christ. Therefore, we are all the natural children of God.

Adopted Children

The concept of adopted children comes from Galatians 4:1-6 (KJV):

> "Now I say that the heir, as long as he is a child, does not differ at all from a slave, though he is master of all, but is under guardians and stewards until the time appointed

> by the father. Even so we, when we were children, were in bondage under the elements of the world. But when the fullness of the time had come, God sent forth His Son, born of a woman, born under the law, to redeem those who were under the law, that we might receive the adoption as sons. And because you are sons, God has sent forth the Spirit of His Son into your hearts, crying out, "Abba, Father!"

For centuries, the church has taught that Christians are the children of God through adoption. However, those teachings generally do not advocate the concept of a natural child. Some may even consider this blasphemous because of a misunderstanding of our relationship with God. However, our present-day concept of adoption misrepresents the original intent of scripture and overlooks the truth of our relationship with the Father.

The Greek word for "adoption" is a compound of two words. The first is *yhios*,[92] which means "a son," or "a descendant." The second is *tithemi*,[93] which means "to set, put, place." In other words, Paul said when the fullness of time came, the Father sent Jesus to redeem us from the results of sin so that we might be put in, placed in, made a descendant of the father as his child. This goes back to the concept of being born again. We were created the sons and daughters of God but were separated from him because of sin. When Jesus redeemed us, we were placed back into our original family and rightful position as God's sons and daughters. We aren't placed into a new family. For us to be adopted into the family of God, it would mean we would have no prior connection with that family. There is no such thing as being adopted into your original family. Therefore, if we are adopted children, it would mean humanity would not have originally been God's family. But we were and still are. When we are born again, we are placed back into our original family!

We have a kinship with the Father and because of that, Paul said our heats cry out Abba Father or Daddy. It signifies a close and intimate relationship of a child to their Father. It is this kinsman relationship that brings us to the next concept of us being God's natural children.

We are God's natural sons and daughters because Jesus is our kinsman redeemer

God himself established the law of the kinsman redeemer. In the Old Testament, the Hebrew word "kinsman" is *gaal*[94] and it means to "redeem," "act as kinsman, do the part of next of kin." Under the Old Testament law, a kinsman redeemer was obligated to intervene for their family under 5 circumstances: 1) To redeem the land. 2) To provide an heir. 3) To redeem the enslaved. 4) To avenge death. 5) To be a trustee.

To qualify as a kinsman redeemer, the person had to be the nearest blood relative such as a brother, an uncle, or near relative. No one except the nearest male relative, and no one outside the family could perform these obligations. To make matters more difficult, the law of God required a sacrifice without blemish to fully redeem from sin. This is the reason the sacrifices of animals under the Old Covenant could only cover humanity's sin but not fully restore.

When Adam and Eve sinned, they lost their dominion over the earth. As a result, the earth was cursed, and every person born was subjected to sin and death, sickness, and disease. Humanity and the earth were in bondage. Therefore, to redeem humanity under the law, only the nearest relative to Adam and Eve and all humanity would be qualified to perform this task. On top of that, to be fully redeemed, the sacrifice had to be without sin.

Satan must have thought he did a pretty good job of messing up the plans of God, until Jesus. As the Son of God, Jesus was the only one that fulfilled all these requirements. When Jesus became Emmanuel, God with us in the flesh as the Son of Man, he then qualified to be our elder brother and nearest of kin. Since he was born of a virgin and lived a sinless life, he was not born into sin and was without spot or blemish.

The fact that Jesus was qualified in all respects under the law to be our kinsman redeemer provides the proof of his authority as our nearest of kin and proof that we are the natural children of God. As we discuss below, Jesus fulfilled all five obligations under the law. If we were not the natural children of God, Jesus would not have had the legal authority to redeem us, redeem the land, and provide for our salvation.

1. Kinsman Redeemer - obligation to redeem the land

The first obligation of the kinsman redeemer was to redeem the land. This requirement was established by God in Leviticus 25:25-28 (NASB):

> "If a fellow countryman of yours becomes so poor he has to sell part of his property, then his nearest kinsman is to come and buy back what his relative has sold. Or in case a man has no kinsman, but so recovers his means as to find sufficient for its redemption, then he shall calculate the years since its sale and refund the balance to the man to whom he sold it, and so return to his property. But if he has not found sufficient means to get it back for himself, then what he has sold shall remain in the hands of its purchaser until the year of jubilee; but at the jubilee it shall revert, that he may return to his property."

Land ownership was important to God. Each tribe of Israel was given a portion of land that was to stay in their family and never be sold. To keep this system, God instituted the year of Jubilee. Every fifty years, any land that had been sold was to revert to the original owner. Because of this, the selling of land was more of a lease since at the end of 50 years, it had to go back to the family. The problem is there is no record in Israel of this provision being implemented. Therefore, a family fallen upon hard times was put in an awkward position of regaining the land that had been sold.

The obligation of the kinsman redeemer was to buy back land that had been sold. This is a perfect picture of Jesus. When God created Adam and Eve, they were given dominion over the earth. Psalm 115:16 (KJV) says, "The heaven, even the heavens, are the Lord's: but the earth hath he given to the children of men." When Adam and Eve sinned, they sold their birthright and ownership of the land. Through the sacrifice of Christ, the earth and all that is in it was redeemed so it could be returned to the rightful owners. It is the reason Jesus could proclaim in Matthew 5:5 (NIV), "Blessed are the meek, for they will inherit the earth."

2. Kinsman Redeemer – obligation to provide an heir

The second obligation of the kinsman redeemer was to provide an heir. This requirement was established in Deuteronomy 25:5-6 (NASB):

> "When brothers live together and one of them dies and has no son, the wife of the deceased shall not be married outside the family to a strange man. Her husband's brother shall go in to her and take her to himself as wife and perform the duty of a husband's brother to her. It shall be that the firstborn whom she bears shall assume the name of his dead brother, so that his name will not be blotted out from Israel."

The only way for a man's family name to continue was to have a son. But what if a man died and did not have a son to receive his birthright and carry on his name? God made provision that the wife of the brother should not be married outside the family. Instead, the brother of the deceased husband would take his sister-in-law as his wife. Their firstborn son would then assume the name of his dead brother so his name and lineage would be carried on.

Jesus fulfilled this obligation as our elder brother. Hebrews 2:11 (NKJV) says:

> "For both He who sanctifies and those who are being sanctified are all of one, for which reason He is not ashamed to call them brethren, saying: I will declare Your name to My brethren; In the midst of the assembly I will sing praise to You. And again: I will put My trust in Him. And again: Here am I and the children whom God has given Me. Inasmuch then as the children have partaken of flesh and blood, He Himself likewise shared in the same, that through death He might destroy him who had the power of death, that is, the devil, and release those who through fear of death were all their lifetime subject to bondage."

Notice that Hebrews says the one who is being sanctified and the one who is sanctifying are all of one and for this reason Jesus could call us brothers. When Adam and Eve sinned, they died spiritually and were separated from God. They were no longer in the family. In other words, they were without. Jesus became the elder brother, and the church became the bride of Christ. Because of Jesus, the bride of Christ (the church) has been reunited to the family of God and granted the right to take back our name. II Corinthians 1:21-22 (KJ21) says, "Now He who establisheth us with you in Christ, and hath anointed us, is God, who hath also put His seal upon us, and given us the pledge of the Spirit in our hearts." God has placed upon us his seal. A seal displays the full legal name of the person who it belongs to. In this case, we have been sealed with the name of God and placed back in our original family to carry on his name.

3. Kinsman Redeemer – obligation to redeem the enslaved

The third obligation of the kinsman redeemer was to redeem the enslaved. This requirement was established by God in Leviticus 25:47-49 (NASB):

> "Now if the means of a stranger or of a sojourner with you becomes sufficient, and a countryman of yours becomes so poor with regard to him as to sell himself to a stranger who is sojourning with you, or to the descendants of a stranger's family, then he shall have redemption right after he has been sold. One of his brothers may redeem him, or his uncle, or his uncle's son, may redeem him, or one of his blood relatives from his family may redeem him; or if he prospers, he may redeem himself."

Under the Old Covenant, if an individual became poor, they could sell themselves to a stranger to work off their debts or to care for their family. While this may have been a common practice, God did not intend for a person to stay enslaved as a servant to another. Instead, he provided through the law a provision that a person's debt could be bought by their kinsman redeemer and set free. The law went on to establish that if he could not be redeemed, on the year of Jubilee (every 50th year), the person's debt would be satisfied, and the enslavement ended. This is a perfect picture of the nature of sin and the enslavement it brings upon the sinner. The Bible makes this truth clear. John 8:31-36 (NASB) says:

> "So Jesus was saying to those Jews who had believed Him, "If you continue in My word, then you are truly disciples of Mine; and you will know the truth, and the truth will make you free." They answered Him, "We are Abraham's descendants and have never yet been enslaved to anyone; how is it that You say, 'You will become free'? Jesus answered them, "Truly, truly, I say to you, everyone who commits sin is the slave of sin. The slave does not remain in the house forever; the son does remain forever. So if the Son makes you free, you will be free indeed."

The horrible conditions caused by the enslavement of sin can be seen all around us. Jesus became our kinsman redeemer and paid the price to redeem you from sin so you may be free and experience true liberty.

4. Kinsman Redeemer – obligation to avenge death

The fourth obligation of the kinsman redeemer was to avenge death. It is described in Numbers 35:16-21 (NASB):

> "But if he struck him down with an iron object, so that he died, he is a murderer; the murderer shall surely be put to death. If he struck him down with a stone in the hand, by which he will die, and as a result he died, he is a murderer; the murderer shall surely be put to death. Or if he struck him with a wooden object in the hand, by which he might die, and as a result he died, he is a murderer; the murderer shall surely be put to death. The blood avenger himself shall put the murderer to death; he shall put him to death when he meets him.

> If he pushed him of hatred, or threw something at him lying in wait and as a result he died, or if he struck him down with his hand in enmity, and as a result he died, the one who struck him shall surely be put to death, he is a murderer; the blood avenger shall put the murderer to death when he meets him."

The law established the criteria that required the kinsman redeemer to avenge the death of a family member if their death was the result of murder. It was considered murder if the act was committed out of hatred, by lying in wait for the person, or out of enmity. The kinsman redeemer then qualified to become the Blood Avenger.

The similarities between the Blood Avenger and Jesus are astonishing. The fall of humanity was the direct result of the serpent lying in wait for his prey. With enmity in Satan's heart against God's creation, he purposefully lied and deceived to bring about sin. As a result of their sin, death entered the human race. While speaking to his critics, Jesus gave us a deep insight to the motives of Satan in the deception of humanity. Jesus said in John 8:44 (NASB), "You are of your father the devil, and you want to do the desires of your father. He was a murderer from the beginning, and does not stand in the truth because there is no truth in him. Whenever he speaks a lie, he speaks from his own nature, for he is a liar and the father of lies."

It was Satan's desire to murder humanity and destroy God's plans. He had hatred in his heart against God and humanity and lied in wait for Adam and Eve. He used lies and deception to bring about their fall. After the fall, every child was born under the penalty of death. However, the death, burial, and resurrection of Jesus proves beyond the shadow of a doubt we are the natural children of God.

After his crucifixion and before the resurrection, Jesus descended into the heart of the earth and fulfilled the work of our Blood Avenger. Matthew 12:40 (KJV) says, "For as Jonas was three days and three nights in the whale's belly; so shall the Son of man be three days and three nights in the heart of the earth." While there, he conquered Satan, took the keys of death and Hell, and made an open show of his victory over darkness. Colossians 2:15 (KJV) says, "And having spoiled principalities and powers, he made a shew of them openly, triumphing over them in it." Finally, those held captive in hell were brought out by Jesus when he ascended into heaven. Ephesians 4:8-10 (KJV) says, "Wherefore he saith, When he ascended up on high, he led captivity captive, and gave gifts unto men. Now that he ascended, what is it but that he also descended first into the lower parts of the earth? He that descended is the same also that ascended up far above all heavens, that he might fill all things."

Jesus dealt with the sin problem to secure our freedom and avenged our death sentence upon the perpetrator. The fate of Satan is forever settled and one day, he will be cast into the lake of fire forever and forever (Revelation 20:10).

While Satan's fate is settled, what about humanity's sin. Numbers 35 made an interesting provision for those who were responsible for the death of another if there was no enmity in their heart. In this case, the slayer could go to a city of refuge if the court ruled them innocent. They had to stay in the city of refuge until the death of the high priest after which they could return to their land (Numbers 35:25).

The Bible declares we have all sinned and come short of God's glory (Romans 3:23). However, Jesus is our high priest and God is our refuge. Psalm 46:1 (KJV) says, "God is our refuge and strength, a very present help in trouble." As men and women born into sin, God is our refuge. Because of the death of Jesus our High Priest, we have been redeemed and declared innocent and will be returned to our land. Revelations 21:7 (KJV) says, "He that overcometh shall inherit all things; and I will be his God, and he shall be my son."

5. Kinsman Redeemer – obligation to be a trustee

The fifth and final obligation of the kinsman redeemer was to be a trustee. This requirement was established in Numbers 5:5-8:

> "And the Lord spake unto Moses, saying, Speak unto the children of Israel, When a man or woman shall commit any sin that men commit, to do a trespass against the Lord, and that person be guilty; Then they shall confess their sin which they have done: and he

> shall recompense his trespass with the principal thereof, and add unto it the fifth part thereof, and give it unto him against whom he hath trespassed. But if the man have no kinsman to recompense the trespass unto, let the trespass be recompensed unto the Lord, even to the priest; beside the ram of the atonement, whereby an atonement shall be made for him."

A trustee is a legal designation of a person who either holds property, authority, or a position of trust or responsibility for the benefit of another. In other words, a trustee acts on behalf of someone else. As our High Priest, Jesus is qualified to act on our behalf. Our part is to surrender our lives to the Lord and accept the recompense he made on our behalf.

We are God's natural sons and daughters because the Bible declares that we are

The definitive proof of everything we have discussed is that we are the natural sons and daughters of God because the Bible says we are. Let's add to our proof by examining more scripture to support the fact we are God's sons and daughters.

The gospel of John records an amazing account of Jesus as he entered the temple and was greeted by the Jews who wanted to know if he was the Messiah or not. They questioned Jesus in John 10:24 (NKJV), "Then the Jews surrounded Him and said to Him, How long do You keep us in doubt? If You are the Christ, tell us plainly." To answer their question, Jesus began to share with them that he had already answered them, but they would not believe him. So, he said to them in John 10:30 (KJV), "I and my Father are one."

When the people heard these words, they picked up stones to stone him to death. But Jesus said to them he showed them many mighty works and asked them for which of the good works did they seek to stone him. They answered Jesus in John 10:33-36 (NIV):

> We are not stoning you for any good work," they replied, "but for blasphemy, because you, a mere man, claim to

> be God." Jesus answered them, "Is it not written in your Law, 'I have said you are "gods"? If he called them 'gods,' to whom the word of God came - and Scripture cannot be set aside - what about the one whom the Father set apart as his very own and sent into the world? Why then do you accuse me of blasphemy because I said, 'I am God's Son'?"

It was certainly a revelation to the Jews that Jesus was declaring himself to be the Son of God. But the other interesting thing about Jesus' response was he challenged them about their own identity. He was quoting Psalm 82:6 (KJV), "I have said, Ye are gods; and all of you are children of the Most High." By quoting the Psalm, Jesus gave the explanation of who he was and who they were as well. They were the children of the Most High.

As another example, scripture says John the Baptist was the forerunner of the Messiah. John 1:6-7 (KJV) says, "There was a man sent from God, whose name was John. The same came for a witness, to bear witness of the Light, that <u>all</u> men through him might believe." The message of John the Baptist was ALL men through Christ might believe. In other words, John's message was not just to the Jews but to all men, Jew, and Gentile. Why is this important? It is important because John goes on to say in John 1:10-13 (KJV):

> "He was in the world, and the world was made by him, and the world knew him not. He came unto his own, and his own received him not. But as many as received him, to them gave he power to become the sons of God, even to them that believe on his name: Which were born, not of blood, nor of the will of the flesh, nor of the will of man, but of God."

Notice that God came unto his own. The word in the Greek is *idios*[95] and it means "pertaining to oneself, one's own," and "what pertains to one's property, family, dwelling, country." It is an emphatic adjective meaning uniquely one's own. In other words, God came to his own family, to his own children, to his own dwelling. We uniquely belong to God because we were created in his image and likeness as his children.

In this chapter, we uncovered the amazing truth and mystery of our relationship with God. We are his natural sons and daughters. We have been created in his image and likeness and the DNA of our daddy is in us. What the enemy sought to destroy; Christ redeemed to restore us to our original design so that we might *Walk in the fullness of I AM.*

Reflections of Who I AM

1. What is the single greatest mystery and revelation in the Bible?
2. What does the Bible say about us being the offspring of God and his DNA within us?
3. What is the mystery of being born again?
4. What is the significance of Jesus fulfilling all five obligations of a kinsman redeemer?
5. What do you believe is the most definitive proof in scripture that we were created to be the natural children of God?
6. Jesus said, "I AM the good shepherd" (John 10:11 NKJV). How can the information discussed in this Chapter help you apply the fullness of that truth in your daily life?

Prayer of Activation

Our Father in heaven, thank you for revealing to me who you created me to be. I believe that Jesus Christ is your son and that he came to this earth to be my kinsman redeemer. I am sorry for my sin and guilt. I repent and ask that you come into my heart and be my Lord, Savior, and redeemer. I freely accept the gift of life. From this day forward, I am a child of God. Teach me more fully who you are and who I am. Help me to walk in the fullness of my design as your child. I pray this in the name of Jesus, Amen.

Author's note: For everyone that just prayed this prayer, I encourage you begin your journey as a child of God by doing two things. Set aside a part of each day to read God's word and go to him in prayer. Ask him to teach you and reveal to you his truths. Finally, find a home church and become part of a church community where you can find fellowship with like-minded believers and become a disciple and follower of God. May God richly bless you and congratulations on receiving Christ. This is the most important decision you have ever made in life.

SECTION V
I AM the True Vine

> "I am the true vine, and my Father is the vinedresser…. I am the vine, you are the branches. He who abides in Me, and I in him, bears much fruit; for without Me you can do nothing" (John 15:1,5 NKJV).

The Greek word for "true" is *alethinos*[96] and it means "real and true, genuine." This is the opposite of what is counterfeit, fictitious, or imperfect. It comes from a root word that means "not hidden, unconcealed." The true and genuine vine is Jesus. He is the revealer of the Father, our connection to him, and the restorer of our true identity as his children. Every other way is a counterfeit to the truth and leads to a fictitious and imperfect reality.

The Greek word for "vine" comes from two root words. The first word is *amphoteroi*[97]and it means "both the one and the other." The second word is *halon*[98] and it means "a ground plot or threshing floor." As the true vine, Jesus came from God to restore us to himself and the kingdom. Because of Jesus, we have been restored to our original family and made one with him, the Father, and the Holy Spirit. He accomplished this through his death, burial, and resurrection. This work was long before prophesied by the Prophet Gad who told David to go to the threshing floor. Located on the sides of the north of Mount Zion, David bought the threshing floor, the temple mount where God's glory would dwell. In the fullness of time, Jesus became the Son of Man, and upon the threshing floor of Mount Moriah, Jesus was offered as the true and perfect lamb of God to take away the sins of the world.

As branches of the vine, we have been commissioned by God to proclaim the gospel of the kingdom. Through the power of the Holy Spirit, who raised Jesus from the dead, we can take authority over all the works of darkness including sin, sickness, and disease. He is the vine, and we are the branches. By ourselves we can do nothing. Through him our birthright has been restored and we can live in his presence and glory, *Walk in the fullness of I AM*, and bring forth much fruit as we fulfill the Great Commission. The Father is glorified when we bear much fruit.

THE GOSPEL OF THE KINGDOM

CHAPTER 15

The Recommission

"Go into all the world and preach the gospel to every creature" (Mark 16:15 NKJV).

The Great Commission is a central and vital message of the gospel, yet many churchgoers are unfamiliar with the term or what it means. The commission is recorded for us in Matthew 28:18-20, Mark 16:15-19, Luke 24:46-51, John 20:19-23, and Acts 1:8. What then is the Great Commission and why is it important to us today?

After the resurrection, Jesus stayed with the disciples for 40 days before his ascension. During that time, he commissioned them to go into all the world and preach the gospel. Ten days later 120 believers went to the upper room, the church was born, and the world has never been the same.

As previously discussed, the birthright, blessing, and Great Commission was originally given to Adam and Eve in the Garden. They were commissioned to multiply and have dominion over the earth. While the first Adam failed, the second Adam (Jesus) fulfilled all things. The chart below shows the link between the original blessing and mandate under the Old Covenant and the recommissioning Jesus gave his disciples and all subsequent believers.

Restoration of the Birthright, Blessing, and Great Commission	
Old Testament	**New Testament Restoration**
Birthright: Genesis 1:28 (KJV), "And God blessed them, and God said unto them, Be fruitful, and multiply, and re-plenish the earth, and subdue it: and have dominion."	Matthew 28:18-20 (NKJV), "All authority has been given to Me in heaven and on earth. Go therefore and make disciples of all the nations, baptizing them in the name of the Father and the Son and of the Holy Spirit, teaching them to observe all things that I have commanded you; and lo, I am with you always, even to the end of the age."
Blessing: Numbers 6:24-26 (NKJV), "The Lord bless you and keep you; The Lord make His face shine upon you, And be gracious to you; The Lord lift up His countenance upon you, And give you peace."	Luke 24:46-51 (NIV), "The Messiah will suffer and rise from the dead on the third day, and repentance for the forgiveness of sins will be preached in his name to all nations, beginning at Jerusalem. You are witnesses of these things. I am going to send you what my Father has promised; but stay in the city until you have been clothed with power from on high. When he had led them out to the vicinity of Bethany, he lifted up his hands and blessed them."
Commission: • Be fruitful – to bear fruit. • Multiply – to increase, make numerous. • Replenish – to fill, be full. • Subdue – to conquer, bring in subjection. • Dominion – to rule, prevail, subjugate.	Mark 16:15-19 (NKJV), "Go into all the world and preach the gospel to every creature. He who believes and is baptized will be saved; but he who does not believe will be condemned. And these signs will follow those who believe: In My name they will cast out demons; they will speak with new tongues; they will take up serpents; and if they drink anything deadly, it will by no means hurt them; they will lay hands on the sick, and they will recover."

When we read Matthew's account of the commission, Jesus said that all authority has been given to him. Notice he said all authority in heaven and in earth. Many times we tend to attribute power or authority to Satan; however, Jesus has stripped him of any and all authority and has commissioned us to go forth in his authority using his name. The gates of hell tremble at the authority of the believer and tries constantly to lie or use fear as tools of discouragement so that we don't utilize the authority that has been given to us.

When we read Luke's account of the commission, Jesus lifted up his hands and blessed the disciples. This was not a random gesture. He was giving the birthright and blessing to the disciples just like God did to Adam and Eve and Abraham did to his children. By doing so, he placed his name upon them and empowered them to use his name as they proclaimed the gospel. He let them know he would be with them. In other words, his face would shine upon them, and the borders of the kingdom would increase as they took the gospel to the ends of the earth. Everywhere they went, God would be with them, and supernatural signs and wonders would follow.

The blessing pronounced by Jesus upon the disciples and the giving of the Great Commission was a sign God was introducing his sons and daughters to the world. With the power of the Holy Spirit working in and through us, we demonstrate our oneness with Jesus and the Father. What was lost by Adam and Eve was restored by Christ.

Notice how Mark's account of the commission includes more than just sharing the message of salvation. It also includes the process of making disciples, teaching followers, and bringing the kingdom to others through the demonstrated power of the Holy Spirit. While it includes the water baptism of believers, it also includes using the name of Jesus to cast out demons, speaking with new tongues, healing the sick, and the promise of God's protection. Jesus confirmed the fullness of this gospel of the kingdom message when he said in Matthew 12:28 (NKJV), "But if I cast out demons by the Spirit of God, surely the kingdom of God has come upon you."

The question we must ask ourselves is what is the gospel of the kingdom? The Greek word for "gospel" is *euangelion*[99] and it means "good tidings." After Jesus was baptized and tempted in the wilderness,

Matthew 4:17 (NKJV) says, "From that time Jesus began to preach and to say, Repent, for the kingdom of heaven is at hand." From this passage we learn that the gospel includes a message of repentance. The Greek word used is *metanoeo*[100] and it means "to change one's mind for the better, heartily to amend with abhorrence of one's past sins." The Apostle Paul confirms the component of repentance in II Corinthians 7:10 (NIV), "Godly sorrow brings repentance that leads to salvation and leaves no regret."

So far we have learned that the gospel is good news, it involves Christ setting up his kingdom, and it includes being sorry for our sins and changing our minds for something that is better. This leads us to accept Christ as our savior and living a life without regret. But is there more to the gospel? Jesus told his disciples in John 14:12-13 (NKJV), "Most assuredly, I say to you, he who believes in Me, the works that I do he will do also; and greater works than these he will do, because I go to My Father. And whatever you ask in My name, that I will do, that the Father may be glorified in the Son."

Why did Jesus underscore the importance of his followers doing the same works he did and even greater? It's because the person experiencing sickness needs a healer. The person who is addicted needs deliverance. The person facing a problem without an answer needs wisdom and discernment. The person who has a need beyond the laws of the natural needs a miracle. This is the good news of the kingdom and a part of having dominion over the kingdom of darkness. Jesus connected the Great Commission with doing the works he did. In fact, Jesus' idea of preaching the gospel was demonstrated to us when he went about the whole region healing the sick, raising the dead, casting out devils, and proclaiming good news to all. The goal of the gospel of the kingdom is the restoration of what should be normal and natural. I John 3:8 (NKJV) says, "For this purpose the Son of God was manifested, that He might destroy the works of the devil."

Therefore, the gospel of the kingdom certainly includes the gospel of repentance and salvation, but it also includes the restoration of every born-again believer as the natural children of God and the destruction of the works of darkness. With the Holy Spirit in us, we are to go into all the world and proclaim this good news; and as we go, we are to heal the sick, raise the dead, cast out devils, tear down the strongholds of darkness, and walk in the supernatural power of God just as Jesus did. Paul adds another nuance to the gospel in Romans 14:17 (NKJV), "the kingdom of God is not eating and drinking, but righteousness and peace and joy in the Holy Spirit." The gospel of the kingdom is so much more than many have understood it to be.

SOZO

To bring more clarification to the topic of the gospel of the kingdom, it would help for us to have a deeper understanding of what it means to be "saved." The concept of salvation was brought up by an angel as he spoke to Joseph concerning the pregnancy of Mary. In Matthew 1:20-21 (NKJV), the angel said, "Joseph, Son of David, do not be afraid to take to you Mary your wife, for that which is conceived in her is of the Holy Spirit. And she will bring forth a Son, and you shall call His name JESUS, for He will save His people from their sins." The Greek word for "save" is *sozo*[101] and it is used 110 times in 103 verses in the New Testament. It is a powerful word that reveals to us the fullness of the gospel message. It means "to save, to keep safe and sound, to rescue from danger or destruction." It also means "to make well, heal, restore to health," "to deliver from the penalties of the Messianic judgment, to save from the evils which obstruct the reception of Messianic deliverance," "to make one a partaker of the salvation of Christ," and finally "to save and transport into."

One of the greatest deceptions of the enemy has been to limit the work of salvation and the gospel to include only the forgiveness of sins. As great and wonderful as that is, there is much more. When the Holy Spirit came upon Mary and she conceived, Joseph had misgivings about her story. He thought she had been unfaithful, and being an honorable man he was going to put her away privately and quietly. He planned to break off the engagement and divorce her. Instead, the angel of the Lord appeared to him in a dream with a message from God and declared Jesus would save his people from their sins. In doing so, the angel revealed the fullness of the message and just how complete is the work of salvation.

Why then have so many people limited the work of salvation to only the forgiveness of sins? Is it possible some have changed their theology to match their experiences? Some try to explain away God's promises because their prayers have not been answered. Their rationalization is that these works must not be for today or perhaps they passed away with the Apostles. If you have had such thoughts, allow the Holy Spirit to open your understanding and recall the words of Isaiah 53:4-6 (NKJV):

> "Surely He has borne our griefs And carried our sorrows; Yet we esteemed Him stricken, Smitten by God, and afflicted. But He was wounded for our transgressions, He was bruised or our iniquities; The chastisement for our peace was upon Him, And by His stripes we are healed. All we like sheep have gone astray; We have turned, every one, to his own way; And the LORD has laid on Him the iniquity of us all."

If that's not enough, Jesus said this about his himself in Luke 4:18-19 (NKJV):

> "The Spirit of the LORD is upon Me, Because He has anointed Me To preach the gospel to the poor; He has sent Me to heal the brokenhearted, To proclaim liberty to the captives And recovery of sight to the blind, To set at liberty those who are oppressed; To proclaim the acceptable year of the LORD."

When a man or woman is born-again, they are saved from sin and transported into the kingdom of God. In addition, their salvation provides for everything they need personally and everything they will need as they proclaim and minister the gospel to the world. This includes salvation from sin, health and healing from all sickness and disease, protection from all danger and destruction, and power over every demonic spirit and force in the kingdom of darkness. In short, the believer is both a recipient and carrier of all the goodness of God.

Since Jesus is our example, let's list a few scriptures that give an account of the works of Jesus:

- Jesus healed ALL the multitude (Luke 6:19).
- Jesus turned water into wine (John 2:1-11).
- The great catch of fish in the nets (Luke 5:1-11).
- Jesus stilled the storms (Matthew 8:23-27).
- Jesus opened blinded eyes (Matthew 9:27-31).
- Jesus fed 5,000 (Matthew 14:15-21).
- Jesus raised Lazarus from the dead (John 11-1-46).
- "And there are also many other things that Jesus did, which if they were written one by one, I suppose that even the world itself could not contain the books that would be written" (John 21:25 NKJV).

It is not too difficult for a believer to accept the fact that Jesus did many miracles, healings, signs, and wonders, but it is more difficult for some to believe we should be doing these same works. However, this is exactly what Jesus said to his followers. Therefore, we need to ask ourselves a sobering question. Are churches and believers performing the same works and miracles that Jesus did; and if we aren't even on par with the works Jesus did, what would it take for us to perform greater works than him? I believe as the fullness of times continue, we are going to see the supernatural on display and Christians doing greater works than Jesus. This will continue to be fulfilled as believers learn to *Walk in the Fullness of I AM*. This is the SOZO message and gospel of the kingdom.

Preliminary Definition of the Gospel of the Kingdom

Considering our discussions thus far, we are ready to offer a preliminary definition of the gospel of the kingdom:

> *The gospel, or good news of the kingdom is that God the Father sent his only begotten Son to destroy all the works of the devil in order to complete his original plans and*

design for creation, his family, and the kingdom. Through the rebellion of the angelic host, sin and darkness was born. This led to the desolation of the earth, the seven days of creation, and humanity's subsequent fall after yielding to the voice of the enemy. Through the virgin birth, God the Son became the Son of Man, one of us, the first born of many brothers, so he could meet all legal qualifications to become our kinsman redeemer. Through his birth, death, and resurrection, we can be born-again and restored to our original family as the natural sons and daughters of God and citizens of the kingdom. By accepting Christ, we receive the Holy Spirit and the down payment of all that is to come. This power working in us conforms us to his image and likeness, and enables us to Walk in the fullness of I AM, and fulfill the Great Commission to go into all the world and preach this good news of the kingdom. As we go, we have been commissioned to have dominion and authority over all sin, sickness, disease, and darkness that stands in opposition to God. In the fullness of time, Christ will return, and the kingdoms of this world will become the kingdoms of Christ and all of heaven and earth will be made new. All creation eagerly awaits the final revealing of the Sons and Daughters of God. As heirs and coheirs with Christ, we are made one with him and will rule and reign with him throughout eternity.

The Gifts of the Spirit – Ministry Gifts for Believers

How are you and I able to walk in this level of the supernatural and do the works of Jesus and even greater? There is only one way. It is recorded in Acts 1:8 (NKJV), "But you shall receive power when the Holy Spirit has come upon you; and you shall be witnesses to Me in Jerusalem, and in all Judea and Samaria, and to the end of the earth."

There has been much debate among Christians about when we receive the Holy Spirit, at salvation, or as a later encounter with God after salvation. The purpose of this Book is not to debate this issue.

Therefore, I'll share with you my belief and leave it up to you to seek God and come to your own conclusion.

I believe the Bible makes it clear that every believer receives the Holy Spirit at the moment of salvation. Romans 8:9 (NKJV) says, "But you are not in the flesh but in the Spirit, if indeed the Spirit of God dwells in you. Now if anyone does not have the Spirit of Christ, he is not His." This is further confirmed by I Corinthians 12:13 (NKJV), "For by one Spirit we were all baptized into one body - whether Jews or Greeks, whether slaves or free - and have all been made to drink into one Spirit."

While we receive the Holy Spirit when we are born again, there are scriptural examples of believers receiving the gift of the Holy Spirit subsequent to salvation. Let's list a few:

1. On the day of Pentecost – "And they were all filled with the Holy Spirit and began to speak with other tongues, as the Spirit gave them utterance" (Acts 2:4 NKJV).
2. The Gentiles at the house of Cornelius – "While Peter was still speaking these words, the Holy Spirit fell upon all those who heard the word. And those of the circumcision who believed were astonished, as many as came with Peter, because the gift of the Holy Spirit had been poured out on the Gentiles also. For they heard them speak with tongues and magnify God" (Acts 10:44-46).
3. The Ephesian believers - Acts 19:1-2 (NKJV), "And finding some disciples he said to them, Did you receive the Holy Spirit when you believed? So they said to him, We have not so much as heard whether there is a Holy Spirit."

I believe we receive the Holy Spirit when we are born again; however, there is a deeper infilling or gifting called the baptism in the Holy Spirit that is available to all believers subsequent to their salvation experience. For most people, the initial evidence of this gifting appears to be the speaking in tongues as recorded in the Book of Acts and other scriptures; however, I would not limit the infilling to this single gift, as important as it is. I would encourage each of you to seek God for the baptism of the Holy Spirit and the accompanying prayer language that comes with this infilling.

Paul said in I Corinthians 14:5 (NIV), "I would like every one of you to speak in tongues." Why, for what purpose? I Corinthians 14:2 and 4 (NKJV) says, "For he who speaks in a tongue does not speak to men but to God, for no one understands him; however, in the spirit he speaks mysteries.... He who speaks in a tongue edifies himself." And finally, Romans 8:26 (NKJV) says, "Likewise the Spirit also helps in our weaknesses. For we do not know what we should pray for as we ought, but the Spirit Himself makes intercession for us with groanings which cannot be uttered."

In addition to the language of tongues, there are also gifts of the Holy Spirit. The gifts of the spirit are different from the fruits of the spirit. Fruits require cultivation, planting, watering, and growing. A gift is something that is given. To equip the saints for the ministry of fulfilling the Great Commission, God gave gifts or offices unto men and women to help equip and train believers in the fullness of their relationship with God. It is recorded in Ephesians 4:11-13 (KJV):

> "And he gave some, apostles; and some, prophets; and some, evangelists; and some, pastors and teachers; For the perfecting of the saints, for the work of the ministry, for the edifying of the body of Christ: Till we all come in the unity of the faith, and of the knowledge of the Son of God, unto a perfect man, unto the measure of the stature of the fulness of Christ."

Notice how the Apostle Paul describes this as a process. He said in Ephesians 4:13 (KJV), "till we all come." In other words, this is a process that would take time. The implication is that this would come to pass in the fullness of times, or at the appointed time. We are on the cusp of this time when believers will walk in the fullness of Christ. Walking in the fullness of I AM can only occur through the power of the Holy Spirit.

When we read John 15:26, we learn that Jesus sends us the Holy Spirit from the Father, and the Spirit will testify of Jesus. In other words, the Holy Spirit will show us how to live like Jesus lived. John 16:13 (NKJV) says, "However, when He, the Spirit of truth, has come, He will guide you into all truth; for He will not speak on His own authority, but whatever

He hears He will speak; and He will tell you things to come." Walking in ALL truth is the equivalent to walking in the fullness of God.

In addition to the gifts of callings, there are also ministry gifts available to all believers, whether or not you have been called to be a Pastor, Evangelist, etc. These gifts are recorded in I Corinthians 12:4-11 (NKJV):

> "There are diversities of gifts, but the same Spirit. There are differences of ministries, but the same Lord. And there are diversities of activities, but it is the same God who works all in all. But the manifestation of the Spirit is given to each one for the profit of all: for to one is given the word of wisdom through the Spirit, to another the word of knowledge through the same Spirit, to another faith by the same Spirit, to another gifts of healings by the same Spirit, to another the working of miracles, to another prophecy, to another discerning of spirits, to another different kinds of tongues, to another the interpretation of tongues. But one and the same Spirit works all these things, distributing to each one individually as He wills."

The nine gifts of the Holy Spirit

Revelation Gifts

1. Word of wisdom – Supernatural insight on how to act, behave, or apply truth/knowledge.
2. Word of knowledge – Supernatural truth that you did not previously know.
3. Discerning of spirits – Supernatural insight to the spirit realm, whether of God or Satan. It can include seeing into this realm.

Power Gifts

1. Faith – Supernatural power that enables an extraordinary amount of faith for a specific circumstance.

2. Gifts of healings – Supernatural power to minister healing and deliverance to those who are sick or oppressed by the devil.
3. Working of miracles – Supernatural power to minister a creative or extraordinary act.

Speaking Gifts

1. Prophecy – A supernatural speaking, proclamation, or forth-telling a word from God about a past, current, or future event.
2. Tongues – An utterance of the Holy Spirit through the believer in an unknown tongue. It includes tongues of the spirit realm (unknown), or tongues of men (another language) not previously known by the person.
3. Interpretation of tongues – The supernatural understanding of a message or proclamation given in the gift of tongues.

Every believer has been given the Great Commission. Some believers have been given a ministerial Office (Apostle, Prophet, Evangelist, Pastor, Teacher) to help equip the church for the work of the ministry. Every believer can receive the gifts of the Holy Spirit. Through the power of the Holy Spirit in us, we can effectively proclaim the gospel of the kingdom to all the world and *Walk in the fullness of I AM.*

Reflections of Who I AM

1. Jesus declared that all authority in heaven and earth had been given to him (Matthew 28:18). What did Jesus do with this authority?
2. What was the giving of the Great Commission a sign of?
3. What is the significance of "Sozo" as it relates to our salvation, and why is this good news?
4. What is the gospel of the kingdom?
5. What are the gifts of the Holy Spirit?
6. Jesus said, "I AM the true vine" (John 15:1 NKJV). How can the information discussed in this Chapter help you apply the fullness of that truth in your daily life?

Prayer of Activation

Our Father in heaven, thank you for giving us your son. Help me to fully grasp the significance of the gospel of the kingdom and go into all the world and proclaim this good news. Fill me with your Holy Spirit as on the Day of Pentecost and help me to walk in the power and authority of Jesus. I receive the gifts of the Holy Spirit. Fill me with the prayer language of the Holy Spirit and enable me to be led by your spirit so that the works that Jesus did, I may do as well. You are the true vine and apart from you, I can do nothing. Help me to stay connected to you and bear much fruit for the kingdom. All honor and glory I give to you. I pray this in the name of Jesus, Amen.

CHAPTER 16

The Presence and the Anointing

"Glory and honour are in his presence; strength and gladness are in his place" (I Chronicles 16:27 KJV).

"And it shall come to pass in that day, that his burden shall be taken away from off thy shoulder, and his yoke from off thy neck, and the yoke shall be destroyed because of the anointing" (Isaiah 10:27 KJV).

The Great Commission compels every believer to share the good news of the kingdom to all the world. This passion is born from an unction within our spirit to proclaim the reality of kingdom living. This good news is not merely a philosophical way to live. Instead, it is the power of God that transforms the life of the believer by touching their whole spirit, soul, and body. Nothing short of the authenticity of God in their lives could sustain the whole-hearted commitment of Christ followers.

The certainty of this truth is demonstrated by the account of those who experienced first-hand the power of the gospel. I Thessalonians 1:5 (NKJV) says, "For our gospel did not come to you in word only, but also in power, and in the Holy Spirit." I Corinthians 2:4 (NKJV) says,

"And my speech and my preaching were not with persuasive words of human wisdom, but in demonstration of the Spirit and of power." And finally, I Corinthians 4:20 (NKJV) says, "For the kingdom of God is not in word but in power."

For every skeptic, doubter, and church goer who has watered-down their theology based upon the rationalization of their experiences rather than the truth of God's word, I want you to know there is more. The abnormal lifestyle of settling for something less than what is available has become common place in our world and in many churches. Many have never seen the power of God, and many have become anemic to what should be the conviction of their hearts based upon real-life encounters. Jesus himself said in John 14:12 (NKJV), "Most assuredly, I say to you, he who believes in Me, the works that I do he will do also; and greater works than these he will do, because I go to My Father." As we come into the fullness of time, I invite you to awaken to the good news of the gospel of the kingdom. Choose to want more.

For those who have already made this decision, they have experienced the presence of God, have had intimate encounters with him, and experienced his power and anointing. Witnessing his glory is something they long for and desire more than riches. They have experienced the truth of Psalm 34:8 (KJV), "O taste and see that the Lord is good."

His presence is so satisfying, it can reach from heaven to the core of who you are and activate heaven's promises. Consider for just a moment a partial list from God's word of what may be found in his presence: his voice, rest, glory, honor, strength, gladness, peace, help, the path of life, fullness of joy, eternal pleasure, God's secret place, salvation, and times of refreshing. Keep in mind, these are not ordinary run of the mill experiences such as a moment of pleasure or a temporary peace of mind. These are extraordinary and supernatural promises proceeding from God. For example, Jesus said in John 14:27 (NKJV), "Peace I leave with you, My peace I give to you; not as the world gives do I give to you. Let not your heart be troubled, neither let it be afraid." Jesus clearly communicated to his disciples that his giftings to them were not of this world nor could they be compared to the natural. When experienced, it leaves you full and content unlike anything else. How then do we experience these supernatural promises?

I want to share with you a truth that will take a lifetime to fully understand – Every good and perfect gift proceeds from the presence of God. Your key to walking in the fullness of I AM begins with being in his presence. Let's recall Ephesians 4:13 (NKJV), "till we all come to the unity of the faith and of the knowledge of the Son of God, to a perfect man, to the measure of the stature of the fullness of Christ." The only way to come to the stature of the fullness of Christ is through knowing him. This can only happen by spending time with the creator and having encounters with him. These repeated experiential encounters with God will change your life and allow you to mature and grow into his fullness. In other words, as you spend time with God and encounter him, he will teach you what it means to have an intimate relationship with him and live in the realms of the supernatural. It's all about the relationship!

Many who have grown in their relationship with God by spending time in his presence have also experienced his anointing and glory. Job 37:22 (AMP), says, "Out of the north comes golden splendor [and people can hardly look on it]; Around God is awesome splendor and majesty [far too glorious for man's eyes]." Since we already know that Heaven is located in the North, this scripture confirms that his splendor and glory proceeds from his presence. This verse reminds us of the vision recorded in Zechariah 4:12 (NIV), "What are these two olive branches beside the two gold pipes that pour out golden oil?" In scripture, oil is always connected with the Holy Spirit, God's anointing, and his power. In his presence, you will find the oil of the Holy Spirit for all that you need; but more importantly, you will have encounters with his splendor and the glory of heaven.

When you first become a Christian, it is important to spend time with God through prayer, studying his word, going to church, offering him praise and worship, and other such acts of service. In other words, a Christian should be committed to the spiritual disciplines to grow in their faith. But can I share with you an observation? I have seen believers who have committed their lives to Christ and the spiritual disciplines but have never or rarely experienced a supernatural encounter with God. Why settle when there is more? And if there is more, what are the keys to experiencing these encounters and walking in his fullness?

Presence

It all begins with being in God's presence. In that space, everything is possible. When we read the stories of Jesus, we see that when he came into people's lives they were never the same. He altered their life and those around them. Is this the type of encounters you desire?

What is the presence of God? The Hebrew word for "presence" is *panim*[102] and it means "face." The root of the word means "to turn." It's clear from this meaning that God's presence is something to be personally experienced and involves a tangible encounter with the creator.

Presence is the natural next step after coming to Christ through repentance. After your mind is changed and you turn away from what is not good, it is natural to turn towards what is better. At that point you turn your face and heart towards God, towards his way of thinking, and towards his face and presence. This is where the encounters begin.

Think for a moment about individuals in scripture who experienced the presence of God. What were their reactions? Moses' encounter with God in the burning bush began when he decided to turn aside to see why the bush was on fire but was not consumed. When Moses turned toward the burning bush he encountered God. His presence was so glorious that Moses hid his face because he was afraid to look upon him. When Ezekiel saw God, he said it was as the appearance of a rainbow in the clouds, like a surrounding radiance, and all he could do was fall on his face. When Daniel had an encounter with Gabriel, an Archangel of God, he was frightened and fell on his face. When Isaiah saw the Lord high and lifted up he fell on his face as a dead man. In the Gospels, the crowds wanted to stone Jesus when they asked him if he was God. When Jesus said I AM, his power knocked them off their feet. In the Book of Revelation when John saw Jesus he fell at his feet as though he was dead. When each of these individuals had a personal encounter with the presence of God, it was life changing. These experiences were not like an impersonal encounter you may have with someone you pass on the street by brushing up against them. These encounters were very different. They were tangible and powerful. They could be felt, and they went to the core of their being.

For our discussion, we need to make a distinction between the general presence of God and entering in or experiencing the presence of God. In a general sense, God's presence is everywhere. He made the heavens and earth, and they are all held together by him. From that standpoint, there is no place you can go to escape God's presence. He is everywhere.

While God's presence is everywhere, some people do not know it, recognize it, or avail themselves of its benefits. That's an amazing thought. All around the world, there are millions of people who are oblivious to the power of the presence of God. Their thoughts and life experiences are filled with anything and everything except the one who created all things. At the same time, there are believers who have a relationship with God who also go through their everyday lives unaware of the activities of God around them or just how close he is to them. I believe this saddens the heart of God. He longs for us to have encounters with him and experience him in a very real and personal way.

We must conclude then, there is a difference between the general presence of God and entering his presence. When you enter his presence, you have a tangible encounter where the physical realm touches the spiritual realm. You are often left undone and altered by his power. It causes you to change the way you think and will make you a serious disciple. Encounters with God's presence leaves you realizing that you have a destiny and purpose in life. Every encounter and taste of the heavenly realm leaves you wanting more.

For many Christians there is a mystery surrounding God's presence. What was meant to be routine and everyday has become mystified and confusing. Entering the presence of God should be an ordinary and routine experience for every believer. I want to challenge you to become purposeful and intentional about entering his presence. The question becomes how do you as a believer enter his presence? Let's turn to scripture for some examples:

1. God inhabits your praises - "But You are holy, Enthroned in the praises of Israel" (Psalm 22:3 NKJV). This is the picture of God sitting down, inhabiting, and abiding in that place. If you want to have an encounter with the presence of God, there is

no better way to start than to offer him praise from the depths of your soul.

2. The Holy Spirit invites us into his presence - "No one can come to Me unless the Father who sent Me draws him" (John 6:44 NKJV). The Holy Spirit will draw you to himself. I remember driving to work one day and wanting to use that time for prayer. I had a long list of items to pray about, mostly involving family and life situations. But as I began to pray, I heard the whisper of the Holy Spirit say, "*not now.*" just spend time with me. He touched the essence of my soul and drew me to himself. God wants to spend time with us in a deep meaningful relationship. Did you know that God misses being in your presence just as much as you miss being in his? Why else would the Holy Spirit draw you to him? In those moments, our ears become open to hear him and know his heart.
3. Seek his presence - "O God, You are my God; Early will I seek You; My soul thirsts for You; My flesh longs for You" (Psalm 63:1 NKJV). This Psalm was written by David when he was in the wilderness of Judah running from his son Absalom who was seeking to overthrow him as king. As heart breaking as the occasion was, David did not forget to rise-up early and seek God. The pressures of life will drive us to our knees to seek God. The comforting thought is that when we seek him, he will be found. James 4:8 (NKJV) says, "Draw near to God and He will draw near to you." Jeremiah 29:11-14 (NKJV) says, "Then you will call upon Me and go and pray to Me, and I will listen to you. And you will seek Me and find Me, when you search for Me with all your heart. I will be found by you, says the Lord." I would encourage every believer to have regular times of seeking God.
4. Recognize his presence - "Enter into His gates with thanksgiving, And into His courts with praise. Be thankful to Him, and bless His name" (Psalm 100:4 KJV). This psalm instructs us to enter his presence with thanksgiving and praise. Why would a person go into an empty room and speak to someone who was not there? That would not make sense. When you enter your local church and offer praise to God, recognize he is there. When

you fall on your knees and cry out to him, recognize he is there. When you call upon him, he is there. Be mindful of his presence. Know that he is not only near you, but he also lives within you. There's no closer place for him to be than in your heart.

5. We are seated in his presence - "And God raised us up with Christ and seated us with him in the heavenly realms in Christ Jesus" (Ephesians 2:6 NIV). Once you give your life to Christ, you are automatically seated with him in heavenly places. This is your rightful place and position as a believer. Don't ever think God is far away. You are right beside him.

Anointing

As wonderful as God's presence is, there is more. Have you encountered his anointing? Do you recall the first individual in the Bible God said was anointed? It was Lucifer. Ezekiel 28:14-16 (NKJV), "You were the anointed cherub who covers; I established you; You were on the holy mountain of God; You walked back and forth in the midst of fiery stones. You were perfect in your ways from the day you were created, Till iniquity was found in you." Before his fall, Lucifer was an anointed angel that covered the presence of God around his throne.

Why do you think Satan hates and fights the anointing of the Holy Spirit so much? He does not want you to experience the power of God like he once did when he lived in his presence. If you are a believer, Satan's goal is for you to be as anemic as possible. The moment you become a serious follower of Christ and begin to have encounters with his presence and anointing, you become a target of the enemy. It reminds him of the position he once held and the power of God that was taken away from him.

The Hebrew word for "anointing" is *Masha*[103] and it means an "unction, by implication, a consecratory gift." It comes from a root word that means "to spread over," "to rub," also "to paint." In the Greek, the word is *Chrisma*,[104] and it means a "smearing." Most Christians have heard about the anointing, but some do not understand what it is. Simply put, it is the power of God (an unction) that comes on (smeared on) a believer to operate in the realms of the supernatural to fulfill a calling or to minister to others. For example, if God has called you to be a Pastor, he will equip you for that Office. As you yield yourself to him, grow in him, and have encounters with him, he will equip you and anoint you with the Holy Spirit so that you can be empowered to fulfill that calling.

Another example would be if you encounter someone who is sick and in need of healing or a miracle. As a believer, you can pray for the sick using the prayer of faith and your trust in God. Every believer has this ability. However, this is different than praying for a sick person while under the anointing of God. In this instance, an unction from the Holy Spirit comes upon the believer and works through them to administer the gift of healing. Our success in praying for the sick through the prayer of faith is intermittent; however, when we pray under the anointing as a gift of the Holy Spirit, those prayers are 100% of the time successful.

When the woman with an issue of blood touched the hem of Jesus' garments, Jesus asked who touched him because he felt virtue go forth from him. In other words, he felt the unction and power of the Holy Spirit leave him to touch that woman. Many times, the anointing will work with a combination of the gifts of the Spirit. For example, God may give you a word of knowledge and combine that with the gift of healing. He may then lead you to pray for that person, and you will sense the unction of the Holy Spirit or his anointing flow through you to touch that person and bring about their healing or miracle. It's God's supernatural gift to the person in need, and he is using you to administer that gift.

The anointing of God is powerful. Isaiah 10:27 (KJV) says, "And it shall come to pass in that day, that his burden shall be taken away from off thy shoulder, and his yoke from off thy neck, and the yoke shall be destroyed because of the anointing." This verse gives us more insight to the power of the anointing. The mystery is concealed in the meaning of the word. As we previously discussed, the Hebrew word for anointing is *masha* and it means an unction or smearing. But there is another Hebrew word for anointing. It is found here in Isaiah 10:27 (KJV). The Hebrew word used in this verse is *semen*[105] and it means "fatness." Although this same word is used in other places in scripture, it is only translated as "anointing" one time, and it's here in Isaiah. What does this Hebrew word mean and what does it have to do with the anointing?

The use of this word is a metaphor of a yoke around a bull. In that day, a yoke was used around the neck of bulls or oxen to keep them together. Sometimes, the fat of the animals would become so large it would break off the yoke around the animal's neck. In the same way, the anointing of God will break the yoke of bondage. The purpose of the anointing coming upon an individual in this manner is to break the yoke of hinderance, sin, sickness, or disease.

This final question we need to ask is what is the purpose of the anointing? Jesus said in Luke 4:18-19 (KJV), "The Spirit of the Lord is upon me, because he hath anointed me to preach the gospel to the poor; he hath sent me to heal the brokenhearted, to preach deliverance to the captives, and recovering of sight to the blind, to set at liberty them that are bruised, To preach the acceptable year of the Lord." Notice how Jesus connected the Holy Spirit and the anointing. The Holy Spirit brings the anointing and Jesus said it was for six purposes:

1. To preach the gospel to the poor,
2. To heal the brokenhearted,
3. To preach deliverance to the captives,
4. To recover the sight of the blind,
5. To set at liberty them that are bruised, and
6. To preach the acceptable year of the Lord.

The presence and anointing deepens your relationship with God and equips you to be an overcomer. It is also directly connected with empowering you as a believer to fulfill the Great Commission and share with others the gospel of the kingdom.

Reflections of Who I AM

1. What truth is revealed in this chapter that will take you a lifetime to fully comprehend?
2. What is the difference between the presence of God which is everywhere and entering his presence?
3. How do we enter the presence of God?
4. What is the anointing?

5. What were the six purposes of the anointing Jesus revealed in Luke 4:18-19?
6. Jesus said, "I AM the true vine" (John 15:1 NKJV). How can the information discussed in this Chapter help you apply the fullness of that truth in your daily life?

Prayer of Activation

Our Father in heaven, I long to be in your presence. Everything proceeds from your presence. In your presence is glory, honor, strength, and gladness. As I learn to live in your presence, I pray for your anointing to reside within me that I may fulfill the Great Commission and bring your kingdom to others. Smear me with the presence and anointing of the Holy Spirit. Break every yoke and hinderance in my life, and help me lead others to this life of freedom. My life is yours. Use me to share this good news to others, and help me to bring forth much fruit as I stay connected to the vine of heaven. I pray this in Jesus's name, Amen.

CHAPTER 17

The Glory of God

"So the LORD said to Moses, I will also do this thing that you have spoken; for you have found grace in My sight, and I know you by name. And he said, Please, show me Your glory. Then He said, I will make all My goodness pass before you, and I will proclaim the name of the LORD before you" (Exodus 33:17-19 KJV).

We began our discussions with a description of the Ancient of Days when God's paradise on Earth was untouched by the curse of sin. That paradise is a far cry from the state of affairs in our present day. We live in an age where the casualties of war between good and evil are seen all around us. Every person will experience death, has been touched with sickness and tragedy, have had financial and emotional needs, and have seen the needs of others. As we watch governments failing and unable to work together, we are reminded that we live in an age of fear and uncertainty, and many people don't know where or who to turn to for the help they need.

What if in the middle of this chaos there was a way to experience God's goodness in our lives as he intended? I was reminded of this the other day as I was walking on a fitness trail. Along the way, there were exercise stations where a person could stop and focus on a specific area to strengthen. It was a beautiful path through the woods where you could experience nature and improve your health. But what if there was a different kind of path you could walk on, a path in the spirit focused on supplying every need in life? Instead of a station focused on a specific muscle, what if there was a spiritual station for miracles and healings, a station for financial blessings, a station for joy and peace, a station for adventure and fun, a station for receiving creative ideas? If there was such a path, you would quickly discover it was made possible by a designer. But what kind of designer could make that happen? It would have to be someone who had all power and knowledge, and the path would need to be designed so the participant could step into the wake of the designer who had gone before them to make it possible.

Such is the case for the glory of God. As you read the Bible, you will discover God's glory is talked about in both the Old and New Testaments. Many in our modern age have witnessed it. Entire congregations have given testimony describing the glory descending as a cloud or fog filling the room where they were gathered and accompanying it were manifestations of miracles and wonders. But for many this is something heard about or doubted but never encountered. Should you as a believer be able to experience for yourself the glory of God? If so, what is it and why should it be desired? The good news is the glory of God is relevant for our day and will have greater significance in the days ahead.

Moses was the first person to know God as I AM. As he continued to walk with God, he reached a point where he asked God to show him his glory. His heart was thirsty and longed for more. But what was this "more" he wanted?

To help us gain an understanding of God's glory, I want us to take a systematic approach to this topic by exploring the following questions:

A. What did Israel and Moses see when they saw the glory of God?
B. What was the key to Moses' encounter with God's glory?
C. What is the glory of God?

What did Israel and Moses see when they saw the glory of God?

Exodus Chapter 16 chronicles the first time Israel saw God's glory. In this narrative, we see God deeply concerned with the heart of humanity and their relationship with him. In stark contrast, Israel was mostly concerned about what God could do for them.

The backdrop of this story is remarkable. Israel had been in bondage for four hundred years, and each generation prayed for deliverance. Through Moses, God worked many mighty acts and wonders, including the plagues upon Egypt that led to their deliverance. Many scholars estimate there were over two million people that came out of Egypt, and they were no doubt thankful for their new-found freedom. But that's a lot of mouths to feed, and it did not take long for the character of their hearts to be tested.

In Exodus Chapter 16, Israel is just two and one-half months into their journey. They had left the area of Elim and came to the Wilderness of Sin on their way to Sinai. Their hunger pains were setting in, and they began to complain to Moses. Their desire for food, although legitimate, overshadowed their thankfulness for freedom and the presence of God they were experiencing. They complained to Moses they wished they had died by the hand of God in Egypt, because there they ate until they were full. How do you respond when you enjoy living in the blessings of God but at the same time encounter a significant need?

An entitlement mentality can be experienced in any circumstance. Its root is narcissism, the original sin of Lucifer. In their time of need, instead of thanking God for his blessings and seeking him for an answer they began to look for someone to blame. They came to Moses and Aaron and complained about their lack of food. The problem was God heard their murmurings, and he did not like it. In fact, God took their complaints against Moses personal.

God's response to their grumblings is recorded in Exodus 16:4 (RSV), "Then the Lord said to Moses, "Behold, I will rain bread from heaven **for you**; and the people shall go out and gather a day's portion every day, that I may prove them, whether they will walk in my law or not." Notice how God said he would do this for Moses' sake, and in doing so, he would test the people's hearts.

After hearing God's words, Moses spoke to Aaron and had him give the news to the people. As he did, something curious happened. Exodus 16:9-12 (NKJV) records the event:

> "Then Moses spoke to Aaron, Say to all the congregation of the children of Israel, Come near before the Lord, for He has heard your complaints. Now it came to pass, as Aaron spoke to the whole congregation of the children of Israel, that they looked toward the wilderness, and behold, the glory of the Lord appeared in the cloud. And the Lord spoke to Moses, saying, I have heard the complaints of the children of Israel. Speak to them, saying, At twilight you shall eat meat, and in the morning you shall be filled with bread. And you shall know that I am the Lord your God."

Israel's first encounter with God's glory is fascinating to say the least. Notice that everyone in Israel could hear God's voice; however, he did not speak directly to them. Instead, God spoke to Moses while they looked on. It was as if God wanted the people to know that Moses was his man, and he was answering their complaints for Moses' sake. Moses experienced God's glory while Israel sat on the sidelines eavesdropping. It would be like you setting in a room with a group of people, and the speaker addressed one individual about you instead of addressing you personally. You would say something like, "I'm right here, you can speak to me." I wonder what would have happened had their hearts been in the right position towards God. I'm sure God would have spoken to them directly, and they would have all experienced his glory. Instead, Moses had a direct encounter with God's glory, and the children of Israel were mere bystanders.

It is also interesting to note that all the people of Israel could visibly see God's glory as it appeared in a cloud. This was not an ordinary cloud. It was a visible manifestation of God. It could be seen and felt. What does this tell us? Many desire to see God's glory but their hearts are far from him. While God may allow you to see his glory, his desire is for you to personally experience it. May God give us all a revelation of what he truly desires, a heart that seeks relationship instead of one focused on asking him for things.

Jesus emphasized this point in Matthew 6:33 (KJV) when he said, "But seek ye first the kingdom of God, and his righteousness; and all these things shall be added unto you." This scripture has been misunderstood for ages. Some interpret it as a formula to receive answers to prayer. Put God first, pray, then he will answer after you have checked all the boxes. This mentality misses the point. Jesus had just taught them the Lord's Prayer, and afterwards, he began to teach them about what was in their hearts. He told them to not give their alms just to be seen of men. Instead, he taught them to give in secret. Likewise, he said they should enter their closets to pray. In other words, their prayers shouldn't be spoken to impress others. He said the same principle is true if you are fasting, it should be unto God and not for others to see.

What was the point of Jesus' message? He was telling his disciples to not worry and become anxious over the things they needed. God knows the things you need, even before you ask him. Jesus was teaching the disciples a great lesson. He was telling them that God would provide for all their needs because they were his children. He did not want them to worry over those things. Instead, he wanted them to seek first his kingdom and righteousness. Become a lover of God with your whole heart! God wants you to have lingering moments with him, spending time with him because you love him, not because you want something from him. This is one of the major keys to walking in the fullness of I AM and experiencing the glory of God.

Israel's first encounter with God's glory should have changed them, but sadly it did not. Their hearts continued to stray. We see it again in Exodus Chapter 24 when they came to Mount Sinai. They saw God's glory descend on the mountain like a consuming fire. Instead of this experience causing them to want more of God, they became restless and fearful when Moses was still on the mountain after forty days. In their fear, they convinced Aaron to make a golden calf for them to worship. It was a slap in the face to God. Over and over, they would repeat their straying from God. The message is clear, your heart must be changed to desire a real and meaningful relationship with God.

What was the key to Moses' encounter with God's glory?

What does the Bible tell us about Moses' relationship with God? Exodus 33:11 (NKJV) says, "So the LORD spoke to Moses face to face, as a man speaks to his friend." Have you thought about speaking to God face to face? What would that be like? Is it possible?

Before we continue discussing Moses' encounter with God, we need to pause for a moment to point out one of the mysteries in the Bible. While the Bible says God spoke with Moses face to face, a few verses later in Exodus 33:20 (NKJV), it says, "But He said, 'You cannot see My face; for no man shall see Me, and live.'" A possible explanation for this mystery is that Moses was allowed to talk to God face to face as a man would speak to his friend; however, the cloud of glory hid the appearance of God's face from being visibly seen. Moses was allowed to be in the full presence of God, hear his audible voice, and communicate with him as a friend. One day every believer will be allowed to see the face of God. Revelation 22:4 (KJV) says, "And they shall see his face; and his name shall be in their foreheads." How amazing is that?

Moses experienced God like few others have. Adam had this kind of relationship before the fall. God would walk with him in the cool of the day and they talked with each other. Jesus, as the Son of Man, communicated directly with his Father while here on earth. Could it be from these examples, God wants us to enjoy this privilege as well?

What was it about Moses that allowed him such closeness to God? I believe the key is found in Exodus 33:13 (NKJV), "Now therefore, I pray, if I have found grace in Your sight, show me now Your way, that I may know You and that I may find grace in Your sight." Here we see the character of Moses' heart was the key to his encounter with God. This prayer caught the attention of God and he responded in Exodus 33:17 (NKJV), "So the Lord said to Moses, I will also do this thing that you have spoken; for you have found grace in My sight, and I know you by name."

God said two things to Moses, you have found grace in my sight, and I know you by name. The Hebrew word for "grace" is *hen*[106] and it means "favor, goodwill." The Hebrew word for "name" is *sem*[107] and it means "fame," "a good name, reputation," "glory," or "renoun." The root of the word means to "put something upon," "lay hands on," "ordain," or "appoint." In other words, Moses made for himself a reputation to be celebrated, and God placed his name upon him. God was letting Moses know that his life and actions were honorable and trustworthy, and to celebrate who he was, God placed his hands and name upon him. Let that sink in for a moment. God answered Moses' prayer, and his reputation is recorded for us in Psalm 103:7 (KJV), "He made known his ways unto Moses, his acts unto the children of Israel." While the children of Israel looked for a sign, mighty acts, and deeds, Moses sought the ways of God. Because of that, his relationship grew to the point that he knew by experience the heart of God.

I want to encourage you to make this your goal. Your relationship with God is much more than what he can do for you. While we all want God to answer our prayers when times get tough, what does your relationship with the King of the World look like when you are not faced with a critical need? Do you take time to know him? Do you get excited about spending time with him and soaking in his presence? Do you enjoy communicating with him, praying to him, and listening for his voice? Your relationship with God can be as close or distant as you choose. Like Moses, you can be a friend of God. Let this be your reputation and heart's desire. With this as your heart's desire, God's favor will come, and you will experientially learn the ways of God and abide in his glory.

What is God's Glory?

What is the Glory of God? The Hebrew word for "glory" is *kabod*[108] and it means "majesty, glory, splendor," "abundance, riches," and "honor." The root of the word means to "be heavy, weighty," and to "be made heavy with abundance." In the Greek, the word is *Doxa*[109] and it has a similar meaning. It means "praise, honor," "splendor, brightness," "magnificence, excellence, preeminence, dignity." In other words, it is the magnificent display of God himself and his majesty. It is the mind of God on display. However, to fully understand it's meaning, let's examine Moses' encounter with God.

Even though Moses talked with God face to face, he was not satisfied, he wanted more. You have to love a man like this! His request and God's response is recorded for us:

> "And he said, Please, show me Your glory. Then He said, I will make all My goodness pass before you, and I will proclaim the name of the LORD before you.... And the LORD said, Here is a place by Me, and you shall stand on the rock. So it shall be, while My glory passes by, that I will put you in the cleft of the rock, and will cover you with My hand while I pass by. Then I will take away My hand, and you shall see My back; but My face shall not be seen" (Exodus 33:18-19, 21-23 NKJV).

> "Now the LORD descended in the cloud and stood with him there, and proclaimed the name of the LORD. And the LORD passed before him and proclaimed, The LORD, the LORD God, merciful and gracious, longsuffering, and abounding in goodness and truth, keeping mercy for thousands, forgiving iniquity and transgression and sin, by no means clearing the guilty" (Exodus 34:5-7 NKJV).

These verses open a door that allows us to see behind the veil of the natural and behold the mysteries of the indescribable glory of God. To see into this realm, we need to take hold of the deeper meaning of what is being said. Hidden in the meaning of each word is the revelation of what God is saying. To help us with this, I offer the following paraphrase of these scriptures based on their Hebrew meaning:

> *And Moses said, I beseech and pray, let me see and perceive the reverent and weighty abundance of your glory and power, the splendor of your honor. Then God said, I will make all my goodness, my best, my wealth and goods, my beauty and welfare, happiness, gladness, and cheerfulness pass before you. And I will cry out and herald in a loud voice the reputation, fame, and glory*

of the name of Jehovah before you. And Jehovah said behold, there is a place of habitation next to me. A place you can inhabit and live. It is a place of no delay. It is a place where you can take your stand. This place is a rock to fix yourself upon and be planted, settled, and ready. This rock next to me is solid and a place of refuge. It is also a sharp rock, as sharp as the edge of a sword. It is a place where the flesh is cut away as in circumcision, a place of covenant. I desire and have ordained you to be upon this rock and will place you there. While you are standing on the firm foundation of my covenant next to me, I will put a hedge around you. It will be a hedge to guard you and protect you like armor. Because you are next to me, I will cover you as my throne is covered by the angelic host. In that secret place you will be in the hollow of my hand while I cross over you. Then, I will turn aside my hand and grant you access to see what cannot be perceived by the eyes only. I will cause you to look at and perceive my glory, my light, and life. There you will see before me and behind me, the past and the future, but the full discovery of my glory by looking upon my face you will not see.

Now Jehovah came down in the midst of the cloud of glory and took a firm stand next to Moses and cried out with a loud voice the full and proper name of the unpronounceable name of God. And Jehovah crossed over him and cried out with a loud voice, Jehovah, the self-existing, eternal, strong and mighty one true God. I AM merciful and full of compassion, showing grace and favor, slow to anger, abounding in love and kindness, faithfulness, and divine instruction of truth, watching over my mercy and kindness for tens of thousands, forgiving and taking away the guilt of iniquity and penalty of rebellion and sin. Yet, I will not leave the guilty unpunished.

No wonder people fell down as dead men when they came into the presence of almighty God. Based on the Hebrew and Greek definitions of glory and the scriptures above, we are ready to develop a working definition of "glory."

> **Glory** - *The Glory of God is the manifestation or display of the power and fullness of God in person or in the fulfillment of his plans and designs. It is the fullness of who he is, his holiness, his love and kindness, his nature, and the manifestation of what he has planned on display. His glory brings heaven to earth and brings the unseen into what can be seen and experienced including his goodness, his very best, his happiness, joy and gladness, wealth, goods, beauty, health and welfare, and supernatural knowledge and wisdom concerning the past, present, and future. It is the secret place of the Most High where God resides and invites us to inhabit. His glory is tangible, weighty and manifests the consuming fire and light of his presence that cuts away and melts the sins of the flesh, leaving a firm foundation and covenant where we can take a stand and live as he abides in us and leads us to a life of holiness and freedom as God takes away all the guilt of sin.*

I don't know about you, but this definition changes the conversation for me about God's glory. At first reading, this may seem unapproachable or even scary. You may be wondering who can approach this place or question whether or not you want to experience his glory. It can seem overwhelming. Because of that, I want to unpack this definition a little further. When Moses asked God to show him his glory, God wanted Moses to understand the following principles:

1. God has invited you to live in his glory: God has invited you to live next to him, in his realm of glory, and abide there all the days of your life. Most of us have never seen the glory of God, much less think of it as a place to live. Most think of it as

something we may encounter once in a lifetime if we are lucky. But God wants you to live there 24/7. Exodus 33:21 (NKJV) says, "And the LORD said, Here is a place by Me, and you shall stand on the rock." When you research the Hebrew meaning of these words, you come to understand this is a place of habitation in the same glory realm where God lives. This place is so near to God, it is next to him. In Exodus 33:22 (NKJV), God says, "I will put you in the cleft of the rock." This is an invitation to let God take his hands and personally put you in this place he has ordained and established for you.

2. God's glory is the safest place in the world: God's glory is not a place of fear. It is the safest place in the world. When God described this place next to him, he said to Moses in Exodus 33:22 (NKJV) I "will cover you with My hand while I pass by." This realm of glory is in the palms of God's hands. It is a place of protection that means a hedge has been placed around you to guard and hide you in his glory. It also means to interweave, cover, and protect like the cherubim covered the ark of God. But there's more. Notice the end of the verse says, "while I pass by." Hidden in these few words are gems of revelation. The Hebrew root of the word "while" is *ad*[110] and it means "perpetuity of time, eternity." It means as long as you are in that secret place, his covering of protection will never end. But there is still more! The Hebrew word for "pass by" is *abar*[111] and it means "to pass over, to pass through," and "to pass by." It's the picture of the wind (of God) passing over you just like the waters overflow the banks or as an overflowing army. It also carries the meaning of being overwhelmed like a person overwhelmed by wine. In this secret place, you will be in the palms of God's hands. You will be covered and protected from harm while the wind of God passes over you and overwhelms you as though you were drunk with his spirit.
3. God's glory provides the resources for all your needs: God wants you to encounter his glory because he wants to share the treasures of heaven with you. In Exodus 33:18 (NKJV) God said, "I will make all My goodness pass before you." Can

you imagine having all the goodness of God pass before you. That word "goodness" in the Hebrew is *tub*[112] and it means "the goodness, i.e. the kindness of God," "good understanding," "that which is good, or best," "wealth, prosperity," "beauty," "welfare, happiness," and "gladness, cheerfulness." The root of the word means "to be beautiful, pleasant," "to be cheerful, merry," "to confer benefits," "to make fair, to adorn," and "to make cheerful." Does this sound like a place you want to live? Please do not misunderstand, this does not mean you will never encounter trials or troubles. You will. But God will be with you through every circumstance, make a table for you in the presence of your enemy, and strengthen you with his joy and presence. Like Romans 8:31 (NIV) says, "What, then, shall we say in response to these things? If God is for us, who can be against us?" And again, in Philippians 4:19 (NKJV), "And my God shall supply all your need according to His riches **in glory** by Christ Jesus." All the abundance of heaven is in his glory.

4. God's glory is merciful, longsuffering, gracious, and forgiving: While God's glory brings with it a weighty tangible presence of his holiness and purity, it is also merciful, longsuffering, gracious, and forgiving. Exodus 34:6-7 (NKJV) says, "The Lord, the Lord God, merciful and gracious, longsuffering, and abounding in goodness and truth, keeping mercy for thousands, forgiving iniquity and transgression and sin." Longsuffering means to be slow to anger and patient. While God wants you to walk upright and holy before him, he is a forgiving God and looks at your heart. Moses had a heart after God and always wanted more of him, but he was not a perfect man. You do not have to be perfect to live in his glory. His glory is not unapproachable or unobtainable. Rather, in his glory there is forgiveness of sin, and the guilt of our rebellion is removed. The good news is you do not have to be weighed down by your imperfections or bound by addictions. In God's glory, there is deliverance, freedom, and forgiveness. You can live in the favor of God without guilt or shame, forgiven, set free, and in right standing with the creator.

As we close this chapter, I encourage you to read Psalm 91, which sounds very much like living in God's realm of Glory. This is an amazing place to live, and God has personally invited us into this realm. As wonderful as this is, in the next chapter we will discuss living in a realm beyond God's glory.

Reflections of Who I AM

1. Why did the children of Israel only hear and see the glory of God while Moses personally experienced it?
2. What was the key to Moses' encounter with God's glory?
3. How would you define the glory of God?
4. When Moses asked God to show him his glory, what were the 4 truths God wanted Moses to Know?
5. What chapter in Psalm describes a life lived in God's glory?
6. Jesus said, "I AM the true vine" (John 15:1 NKJV). How can the information discussed in this Chapter help you apply the fullness of that truth in your daily life?

Prayer of Activation

Our Father in heaven, my heart's desire is to know your ways. While I have needs in my life and have pressing concerns for myself and family, my true longing is to spend time with you, to linger in your presence, and to know your heart. I accept your invitation to live by your side. I choose to trust you over all that I see, feel, or encounter in life. I don't want to just visit this place once in a while, instead, I want to dwell in your secret place. In this place, I want to see and experience your glory, your favor, and the best of who you are. Help me to live a life that builds your reputation through me. Help my life to display who you are and all the goodness of heaven. Give me supernatural insight to how I should think, act, and live. You are the true vine and I want to stay connected to you. Through this relationship, I can *Walk in the fullness of I AM* and who you have created and designed me to be. And may this all be done for your glory. I pray this in the name of Jesus, Amen.

CHAPTER 18

Beyond the Glory (Part 1)

"For now he towers above all creation, for all things exist through him and for him. And that God made him, pioneer of our salvation, perfect through his sufferings, for this is how he brings many sons and daughters to share in his glory" (Hebrews 2:10 TPT).

"For this light momentary affliction is preparing for us an eternal weight of glory beyond all comparison" (II Corinthians 4:17 ESV).

Years ago, the Holy Spirit spoke three words to my heart, "Beyond the Glory." Those words burned in my spirit, and I could not escape them. Though I spent time in prayer and study, I was unable to gain insight to its meaning. Years later my wife and I traveled to the Holy Land, and God began to speak to me again about this topic. During that trip, some of the insights of this mystery began to be revealed.

Why?

In Paul's letter to the Corinthians, he hinted at an eternal glory that was beyond all comparison to the things we have experienced. The key to discovering what is beyond the glory lies with an understanding of why God wants us to encounter his glory in the first place. Hebrews 2:10 (TPT) gives us clues to God's eternal plans, "for this is how he brings many sons and daughters to share in his glory."

As a career Auditor, I learned that asking the right questions often led to uncovering the truth. So then, why did God want to create humanity? Every mom and dad reading this book should ask themselves why they wanted children. The heart of God is that he is a Father who wants a family to share himself with. Standing outside of time he saw the end from the beginning, and his desire for a family was greater than all the obstacles that would emerge. Since the fall was foreseen, God's plan has always been the restoration of his sons and daughters to their original design.

The Apostle Paul asks the same question in a different way in Ephesians 3:9 (NKJV), "what is the fellowship of the mystery, which from the beginning of the ages has been hidden in God who created all things through Jesus Christ." The Greek word for "fellowship" is *koinonia*[113] and it means "joint participation, intercourse," and "to share which one has." Why did God want to share his glory with us? What else did he want to share? The answers to these questions have hidden in them the treasures of heaven and the mystery of our fellowship with the creator. But before we discuss these mysteries, we need to provide a little context for our discussion. To assist us with this, I want to share some of our encounters with God during our trip to the Holy Land.

Our Trip to Israel

In the fall of 2017, my wife and I had the privilege of traveling to Israel. It was an amazing trip that changed our lives, and the encounters we had with God began on our first day. We left the airport in Newark, New Jersey and thirteen hours later arrived in Tel-Aviv. After connecting with our tour group, we arrived in Jerusalem and stayed our first night at the Olive Tree Hotel. Our wake-up call was scheduled for 6:00 a.m.; however, something unexpected happened that first morning. At 5:00 a.m. I was awakened by the sound of someone blowing a shofar.

The shofar is mentioned seventy-two times in the Old Testament. It is a ram's horn that is blown like a trumpet. It was blown on Mount

Sinai when God gave the law to Moses. On that occasion, the glory of God descended, and the mountain was covered in a cloud of smoke. While the mountain quaked in God's presence, the shofar blew louder and louder as Moses spoke to God, and he answered with his audible voice. The shofar was also blown when Joshua and Israel marched seven times around Jericho, and the walls tumbled down. The shofar was used at festivals and during worship, at the coronation of a king, and during military battles. The shofar represents the voice of God, and one day soon, every believer who is anticipating the last trump will hear the blast from heaven and the dead in Christ will rise first, and we who are alive and remain will be caught up to meet the Lord in the air. Most Christians refer to this as the rapture. However, since the destruction of the second temple in 70 A.D., the shofar has lost its public use except on Rosh Hashana (Jewish New Year) and Yom Kippur (the Day of Atonement).

With that in mind, you can understand my surprise when I was awakened by the shofar at 5:00 a.m. on November 10th, 2017. It was not Rosh Hashanah or Yom Kippur. After the blasts stopped, I heard a man singing in English praises to God. I thought that was unusual since we were in Israel. I surmised it was one of the people from our tour group who wanted to begin their day, and everyone else's, with declarations to God. Therefore, I laid in bed and listened to him singing with intermittent sounds of the shofar. As I listened, I began to sense the presence of God, and I heard the Holy Spirit whisper, "the earth shall be filled with the glory of the Lord." I was instantly reminded of the prophecy recorded in Habakkuk 2:14. But then I heard something that took me aback. The Holy Spirit said, "*It has begun.*" Little did we know, this was just a few weeks before December 6, 2017, when the United States formally recognized Jerusalem as the Capital of Israel. On that day, President Donald Trump publicly recognized Jerusalem as the eternal capital of the Jewish people. This was a historic and prophetic day, and just 3 and a half weeks earlier God spoke to me that his glory would fill the earth, and that it had already begun.

It was no coincidence we were in Jerusalem that day, or that the Holy Spirit was speaking to me about his glory. On one of the days, we toured the city of Jerusalem. We sat upon the Mount of Olives, walked through the Garden of Gethsemane, visited Golgotha, entered in the empty tomb, and prayed at the western wall of the Temple Mount. Seeing these sights first-hand brought the scriptures to life. It was during these moments I began to understand a little more about what was beyond the glory; however, the context of that understanding was rooted in an awareness of the significance of the Temple Mount and the Holy of Holies.

Historical Significance of the Temple Mount

In scripture, the Temple Mount goes by more than one name. It is called the Holy Mountain of God, Mount Moriah, and Mount Zion. The Bible makes it clear that God loves this piece of real estate. In fact, Psalm 87:1-2 (NIV) says, "He has founded his city on the holy mountain. The Lord loves the gates of Zion more than all the other dwellings of Jacob." Why would God declare his love for this part of the earth over all others? Notice that scripture calls this place the holy mountain. In Psalm 24:3 (NIV), King David asks an interesting question, "Who may ascend the mountain of the Lord? Who may stand in his holy place?" God himself called this location holy, and the implication is how can a person stand in this place.

According to scripture, the Temple Mount is the epicenter of history and the center of the earth. As we have previously discussed, the foundation stone is located on this site. It was the center of Eden, and it was upon this stone God created Adam and Eve. This foundation stone was the designated throne of the earth and the seat of power upon which Lucifer wanted to be hailed as King when he led the rebellion against heaven.

After the fall of Adam and Eve, the Temple Mount is referenced again in the story of Abraham. God asked Abraham to offer up his only son Isaac. It's recorded in Genesis 22:2 (NKJV), "Then He said, "Take now your son, your only son Isaac, whom you love, and go to the land of Moriah, and offer him there as a burnt offering on one of the mountains of which I shall tell you." When Abraham took his son, he set out for the land of Moriah and as he came to the land on the third day, God pointed out to him the place he was to offer his son. Genesis 22:4 (KJV) says, "Then on the third day Abraham lifted up his eyes, and saw the place afar off." The Hebrew word for "afar off" is *rahoq*[114] and it means "remote," "from afar," and also "of time."

This location was picked out by God himself and it was not haphazard. What did Abraham see afar off? When Abraham looked up and God pointed out this location, he prophetically saw through the portals of time the crucified Christ. Jesus confirmed this to us in John 8:56-58 (NKJV), "Your father Abraham rejoiced to see My day, and he saw it and was glad. Then the Jews said to Him, "You are not yet fifty years old, and have You seen Abraham? Jesus said to them, Most assuredly, I say to you, before Abraham was, I AM." Abraham came to Mount Moriah and God showed him through the spirit the Messiah being offered for the sins of the world.

Abraham gave us another insight to the significance of this place in Genesis 22:14 (KJV), "And Abraham called the name of that place Jehovahjireh: as it is said to this day, In the mount of the Lord it shall be seen." So, God said to Abraham, from this place, it shall be seen. What shall be seen? What was he talking about? Hold on to this question and we'll come back to it.

As time continued, Isaac had children, and from Jacob the twelve tribes of Israel were born. Eventually, Israel ended up in Egypt, and God raised up Moses to deliver them from Pharoah. After God delivered Israel out of Egypt, he said to Moses in Exodus 25:8 (KJV), "let them make me a sanctuary; that I may dwell among them." When God instructed Moses to construct the Tabernacle, he provided the design and gave skills to those he called to perform the work. The Tabernacle was mobile and could go with them as they traveled in the wilderness. Everything was constructed precisely by design and was patterned after the things in heaven. Part of those instructions included a place called the Holy of Holies. The tabernacle was divided into two places, the Holy Place, and the Holy of Holies, which was the inner sanctuary.

Inside the Holy of Holies was the Ark of the Covenant that contained the two tablets on which God's finger wrote the ten commandments, Aaron's rod that was used to perform signs and wonders in Egypt, and a jar of manna that was saved from the manna that was given to them during their wilderness journey. On top of the Ark was the Mercy seat. God instructed Moses in Exodus 25 to make a Mercy Seat of pure gold with Cherubim on both ends. And God said to him in Exodus 25:22 (NKJV), "And there I will meet with you, and I will speak with you from above the mercy seat, from between the two cherubim which are on the ark of the Testimony, about everything which I will give you in commandment to the children of Israel."

Fast forward a few hundred years and we come to King David. Another name for the Temple Mount is Mount Zion. It's the name of the southern slope of the mountain. It is where the City of David is located. Its history goes back to a time when David had sinned. His sin was that he numbered the people of Israel against God's command, and because of that, it brought judgment to the nation. Therefore, the Prophet Gad went to David and instructed him to go to the threshing floor of Araunah the Jebusite and build an alter to atone for his sins (II Samuel 24). Can you guess where this threshing floor was? It was Mount Moriah, the Temple Mount. Despite all the arguments of who owns the Temple Mount, the Bible records that it was legally purchased by King David and therefore belongs to the Israelites. This location is confirmed for us as being the same place in II Chronicles 3:1 (KJV), "Then Solomon began to build the house of the Lord at Jerusalem in mount Moriah, where the Lord appeared unto David his father, in the place that David had prepared in the threshingfloor of Ornan the Jebusite."

While David wanted to build God a permanent structure, he was not allowed by God to construct the temple because of the many wars he had fought. However, his son Solomon was allowed to build the temple. After Solomon finished constructing the temple in the 10th Century BC, II Chronicles 7:1-2 (NKJV) says, "When Solomon had finished praying, fire came down from heaven and consumed the burnt offering and the sacrifices; and the glory of the Lord filled the temple. And the priests could not enter the house of the Lord, because the glory of the Lord had filled the Lord's house."

Each year, God called for a standing meeting to speak with his people. It took place on a specified day at a specified place. On Yom Kippur or the Day of Atonement, the High Priest of Israel would go to the Temple, constructed on the Temple Mount of Mount Moriah, and enter the Holy of Holies. There he would enter God's presence, encounter the glory of God, and speak personally with God on behalf of all the people of Israel. Needless to say, this was a solemn occasion and not taken lightly.

For the High Priest to be able to enter God's presence and glory, he had to go through a process of cleansing and preparation. If he did not properly prepare himself, it meant his sudden death. In fact, the fringes of the robe of the High Priest had bells attached to them, and a rope was tied around his waist before he entered this most holy place. As long as the priests on the outside could hear the bells ring, they knew he was still alive; however, should the bells stop ringing, they knew he had not properly prepared himself and had met an untimely death. In that case, they would pull him out by the rope they had tied around his waist. No doubt, the High Priest took this weighty responsibility with serious forethought.

To gain an appreciation for this task, let's describe what took place on this day each year. It was a day that every household was to be represented at the temple. As a person approached the Temple Mount from the Mount of Olives, they would first need to cross the Kings Valley or the Kidron Valley, and most likely enter through the Eastern Gate. As a side note, this gate is now enclosed, but one day it will be reopened and entered by Jesus Christ upon his return to earth. To keep Jesus from returning after his resurrection, the opening of the gate was sealed up by the Muslims and a graveyard constructed in front of the gate, because no good Jewish person will touch a dead corpse due to its uncleanness. Won't they be surprised when Jesus who is the resurrection and the life makes his entrance.

After entering the Eastern gate and upon approaching the temple, a person would first encounter the Outer Court or the Court of the Gentiles. Gentiles could come this far but no farther. The Jews were so zealous in their pursuit of purity that signs made of stone were placed along the fence separating the Outer Court from the Inner Court and threatened death to any gentile that dared enter. From the Outer Court, one would next enter the Beautiful Gate to the Women's Court. Unlike the gentiles, Jewish women were allowed to worship in this area of the temple but no farther than the Women's Court. To the west and opposite end of the Beautiful Gate were fifteen circular steps leading up to the Brazen Gate or the Nicanor Gate. It is taught that the Jewish priests would sing the 15 Songs of Ascent (Psalms 120 – 134) as they walked up the steps leading to the Inner Court or the Court of Israel. This is where all Jewish men would come to offer a sacrifice on behalf of their families.

This Court led to the temple itself which was divided into the Holy Place and the Holy of Holies. To enter the Holy Place, priests would proceed to a set of stairs that had 12 steps. On the 10th step of the stairs were two columns or pillars. The pillar on the right was named Jachin and the pillar on the left was named Boaz. As an interesting side note, these two pillars have significance in their naming. The Hebrew word for "Jachin" is *yakin*[115] and it means "God strengthens." The root of the word means "to be established." The Hebrew word for "Boaz" is *boaz*[116] and it means "fleetness" or quickness. As you recall, Boaz was an ancestor of King David and the kinsman redeemer of Ruth. Their names add meaning to the purpose and intent of the temple.

To go from the Holy Place to the Holy of Holies, the High Priest had to go through the veil of the temple. He was the one and only man that could enter this section of the temple and only one time each year. The veil was as thick as a person's hand. The Jewish historian Josephus describes Solomon's temple and the veil in Of the War - Book V, Chapter 5 verse 4:

> "As to the holy house itself, which was placed in the midst [of the inmost court], that most sacred part of the temple, it was ascended to by twelve steps; and in front its height and its breadth were equal, and each a hundred cubits, though it was behind forty cubits narrower; for on its front it had what may be styled shoulders on each side, that passed twenty cubits further. Its first gate was seventy cubits high, and twenty-five cubits broad; but this gate had no doors; for it represented the universal visibility of heaven, and that it cannot be excluded from any place. Its front was covered with gold all over, and through it the first part of the house, which was more inward, did all of it appear; which, as it was very large, so did all the parts about the more inward gate appear to shine to those that saw them; but then, as the entire house

> was divided into two parts within, it was only the first part of it that was open to our view. Its height extended all along to ninety cubits in height, and its length was fifty cubits, and its breadth twenty. But that gate which was at this end of the first part of the house was, as we have already observed, all over covered with gold, as was its whole wall about it; it had also golden vines above it, from which clusters of grapes hung as tall as a man's height. But then this house, as it was divided into two parts, the inner part was lower than the appearance of the outer, and had golden doors of fifty-five cubits altitude, and sixteen in breadth; but before these doors there was a veil of equal largeness with the doors. It was a Babylonian curtain, embroidered with blue, and fine linen, and scarlet, and purple, and of a contexture that was truly wonderful. Nor was this mixture of colors without its mystical interpretation, but was a kind of image of the universe; for by the scarlet there seemed to be enigmatically signified fire, by the fine flax the earth, by the blue the air, and by the purple the sea; two of them having their colors the foundation of this resemblance; but the fine flax and the purple have their own origin for that foundation, the earth producing the one, and the sea the other. This curtain had also embroidered upon it all that was mystical in the heavens, excepting that of the [twelve] signs, representing living creatures."[117]

Before entering the veil, the High Priest had certain duties that had to be carried out. Ten days preceding the Day of Atonement is Rosh Hashanah, the Jewish New Year. This day is celebrated as the anniversary of the creation of Adam. It is believed that on this day all the inhabitants of the world pass before God, who determines their outcome for the year. On Rosh Hashanah the shofar is blown to recognize God as King and as a call to repentance. Over the next 10 days leading up to the Day of Atonement (Yom Kippur), people were called to humble themselves, repent, and return to God.

Before entering the Holy of Holies, the High Priest had to be ceremonially prepared and clean. Seven days before the feast, the High Priest was taken aside and instructed on the specifics of his duties. The day before Yom Kippur, the High Priest would fast all day and night. On the next day, the High Priest began his duties by changing his clothes, immersing himself five times in water, and putting on gold clothing designed for the service. He then washed his hands and feet. He performed these acts ten times that day after which he sacrificed and offered an offering. He then burned incense and trimmed the temple lamps. After washing his hands and feet again, he also changed his clothes again and put on white garments for the day. The High Priest then laid his hands on a bull that had been selected for the sin offering for himself and his family as he made confessions to God. As he ended his confessions, he spoke aloud the sacred and unpronounceable name of God, the name Jehovah.

As a side note, it was believed that God's name was so holy that it could not be pronounced unless a person was ceremonially clean. Since the name of God contained no vowels, the pronunciation of the name was lost to all but the High Priest. When the High Priest pronounced the sacred name of God, the people responded by falling on their faces in worship to God.

Afterwards, the High Priest went to the two goats that had been set aside for this specific purpose. He cast lots (dice) for the goats (Leviticus 16:8). On one of the lots was the words "for the Lord," and on the other lot was the words "for Azazel." Once the goat "for the Lord" was selected, the High Priest would pronounce the goat to be the sin offering and utter once again the unpronounceable name of Jehovah. For the other goat (Azazel), a crimson red thread was tied around its neck, signifying it as the scapegoat. After returning to the bull set aside for the offering, the High Priest would once again lay his hands upon the offering and for a third time pronounce the ineffable name of Jehovah. Afterwards, the High Priest sacrificed the bull and let its blood drain in a bowl. The bowl was then given to another priest to stir so the blood would not clot. Afterwards, the High Priest used another pan and took burning coals from the bronze alter. With the coals of the alter in one hand and incense in the other hand, he entered the Holy Place. He passed between the table of showbread on his right and golden lampstand on his left as he went behind the veil of the temple into the Holy of Holies. Upon entering the Holy of Holies, he placed the pan of coals down between the poles of the Ark of the Covenant and put the incense upon the coals, and smoke filled the room. He then exited the Holy of Holies, back to the Holy Place where he said prayers. Afterwards, he took the blood of the bull and once again entered the Holy of Holies where he sprinkled the mercy seat with the blood. He sprinkled it upward one time and downward seven times before exiting. Next the High Priest sacrificed the goat "for the Lord;" however for this sacrifice, he did not pronounce the ineffable name of God.

After the sacrifice, the High Priest took its blood and once again entered the Holy of Holies and sprinkled its blood upon the Mercy Seat. After leaving the Holy of Holies, he took some of the remaining blood of the bull and goat and sprinkled them on the veil of the temple. He then mixed the remaining blood of the bull and goat together and went to the alter of incense and sprinkled the four horns of the alter, beginning with the Northeast horn and working counterclockwise to the remaining horns. Afterwards, he sprinkled the alter seven times and poured the remaining blood on the base of the bronze alter. While in the Holy of Holies, in addition to making sacrifice for atonement, he enquired of the Lord on behalf of the people. It is said that God's glory would fill the temple and God would commune with the High Priest as he was in his presence.

But what of the scapegoat? The scapegoat symbolically carried the weight of all the sins of the people. While the High Priest was in the Holy of Holies, the scapegoat stood on the outside looking eastward facing all the people. After the High Priest made atonement and exited the Holy of Holies, he came out and placed both his hands upon the head of the scapegoat. He said prayers to God and with the people laying prostate before him, he declared the people clean. The priests then led the sin laden goat through Solomon's Porch and through the Eastern Gate. The goat was led over an arched bridge to the Mount of Olives to a person appointed for the task. It was a stranger, a non-Israelite who would lead the goat to the wilderness.

The distance from Jerusalem to the wilderness was ten half Sabbath day's journey. At the end of each station someone was waiting with refreshments for the person leading away the scapegoat, who would then go with him to the next station. This allowed a trusted individual to go with the stranger but not walk more than a Sabbath's day's journey, half going and half returning. After reaching the edge of the wilderness, the goat was pushed over a cliff to its death, ensuring the sins of the people would not return to them in case the goat wandered back to Jerusalem. Once the goat was pushed over the cliff, a series of flags were raised from the wilderness back to the temple, letting the people know within minutes of the scapegoat's death and confirming to all the people their sins had been cast away to remember no more (See Psalm 103:12). Legend has it that the High Priest would put on the temple a piece of the crimson scarlet wool thread tied around the goat. From the time the goat left until it was pushed over the cliff, legend states that the crimson scarlet would turn white and fulfill Isaiah 1:18 (KJV), "Come now, and let us reason together, saith the LORD: though your sins be as scarlet, they shall be as white as snow; though they be red like crimson, they shall be as wool." It is also interesting to note that the 10 half day journeys equaled a total of 2 ½ days to reach the wilderness. This no doubt was prophetic and looking to Jesus who bore all our sins, who was crucified and did not raise from the dead until the third day. During that time period, he paid the price for our sins and carried them all upon himself.

As a side note, there is additional significance to the name of the scapegoat, Azazel. This is the name of one of the leading Angels that fell from heaven on Mount Hermon. He not only fell from heaven to cohabitate with women, but he was also responsible for introducing humanity to forbidden knowledge. The Book of Enoch says the following about Azazel:

> "And Azazel taught men to make swords, and knives, and shields, and breastplates, and made known to them the metals of the earth and the art of working them, and bracelets, and ornaments, and the use of antimony, and the beautifying of the eyelids, and all kinds of costly stones, and all colouring tinctures. And there arose

> much godlessness, and they committed fornication, and they were led astray, and became corrupt in all their ways"[118] (I Enoch 8:1-3).
>
> "And the whole earth has been corrupted through the works that were taught by Azazel: to him ascribe all sin"[119] (I Enoch 10:8-9).

When the scapegoat was selected to bear the sins of the people, there was a clear reference back to the fallen angel who was responsible for corrupting the human race. In Chapter 10 of the Book of Enoch, the Archangel Raphael binds Azazel hand and foot and casts him into darkness covered with jagged rocks to await the day of great judgment when he will be cast into the lake of fire. While sin entered the human race through the fall of Adam, it was the fallen angels and kingdom of darkness that corrupted humanity and led them astray. Thank God Jesus became our sin offering and paid the price for our sins. His work on the cross dealt with the sins of humanity as well as the kingdom of darkness, Satan, the fallen angels, and the realms of the demonic.

You may be wondering why I went into so much detail describing the temple and work of the priests and high priest to enter the Holy of Holies. I do so to bring home the truth that entering the presence and glory of God was no haphazard task or even something afforded to most humans. It was reserved for one man one day a year and only after much preparation and upon risk of death.

More Insight From our Trip to Israel

As we continued our tour of Jerusalem, the thought came to me, what is geographically beyond the Temple Mount? I began to realize that Solomon's Temple was constructed on the Temple Mount and specifically the Holy of Holies became the designated place for God's glory to be encountered. Then I realized, Golgotha is beyond the Temple Mount.

Although Golgotha is on the same general mountain range, it is beyond the proper limits of the Temple Mount. Realizing God does everything by design, I wondered why wasn't Jesus crucified on the

Temple Mount where millions of animals were sacrificed for the atonement of sin? Why was he crucified beyond the designated place of God's glory?

If you were to look at a map of Jerusalem, you would discover there are two possible locations for the site of Jesus' crucifixion. One site is Golgotha Dusatko, which is northeast of the Temple Mount and looks like a skull cap of a cranium. The other site is Gordon's Golgotha, which is due North of the Temple Mount and looks like the face of a skull within the cliffs of the mount. Our tour guide was convinced Gordon's Golgotha is the true site of the place where Jesus was crucified; however, both are north of the Temple Mount. Geographically speaking, beyond the Glory of the Temple Mount is Golgotha, the place where Jesus was crucified.

Let's put together some more of the puzzle pieces. Remember we read earlier Genesis 22:14 (KJV), "And Abraham called the name of that place Jehovahjireh: as it is said to this day, In the mount of the Lord it shall be seen." What can be seen from the Temple Mount? North of the temple is Golgotha. While the sacrifices under the Old Covenant were being performed on the Temple Mount on the alter, Jesus was crucified beyond that location on Golgotha. In other words, from the mount of the Lord it shall be seen. All those sacrifices pointed toward the Christ that was to come. Crucifixion on Golgotha also fulfilled the requirements of the ceremonial law recorded in Leviticus 1:10-11 (NKJV), "And if his offering be of the flocks, namely, of the sheep, or of the goats, for a burnt sacrifice; he shall bring it a male without blemish. And he shall kill it on the side of the altar northward before the Lord: and the priests, Aaron's sons, shall sprinkle his blood round about upon the altar."

Beyond the Veil of the Temple

We've answered the question of what is geographically beyond the Temple Mount. Now, let's look at another question. What happened at the precise moment Christ was crucified on Golgotha? It is recorded for us in Matthew 27:50-51 (NIV), "And when Jesus had cried out again in a loud voice, he gave up his spirit. At that moment the curtain of the temple was torn in two from top to bottom. The earth shook, the rocks split."

Let's recall the importance of the veil of the temple. Behind the veil was the Holy of Holies. It could only be entered by one man, the High Priest, and only on one day of the year. Think about the events surrounding Jesus' crucifixion. It was Passover and the creator of heaven and earth was brought before the High Priest and was condemned to death. In a short five and one-half months, that same High Priest would be needed on the Day of Atonement. How would he enter the Holy of Holies if the veil of the temple was torn in two? How would he be able to enter God's glory and hear from God himself if he couldn't recognize God's Son standing before him, who he had just condemned to be crucified? No doubt they put the veil back up. The Jewish sages teach there was a spare veil available should something happen to the veil of the temple. Each year, a new veil was woven to replace the veil from the prior year that had become stained with the blood of the sacrifices.

The lies of Satan will try to keep the veil up so no one can enter God's glory. How many veils have we put up to separate ourselves from God? What happens when the church fails to recognize the glory of God or wants to keep it behind the veil away from the masses? The religious spirit will always want to maintain order, check all the boxes, and make it impossible for the common person to experience the glory of God. But this is not the plan of God.

What does all this tell us? Legally speaking, humanity could not access God and was beyond his glory. When Jesus was crucified at Golgotha, a place geographically beyond the Temple Mount where God's glory descended, the veil of the temple tore and signified to all that access to God was now possible. This is what a loving Father does. The world can criticize and mock those of us who seek God, speak to him, and have the Holy Spirit speak to us; however, that privilege cost God and heaven everything.

God is moving beyond the realms of tradition and restoring all things to its original design. In this chapter, we have set the foundation for our conversation dealing with beyond the glory. In the next chapter, we will continue this theme and talk more about the Glory of God, what is beyond, and answer more fully the question why did God want to create humanity, and what is this mystery of the fellowship between us and God?

Reflections of Who I AM

1. What are the different names for the Temple Mount and the historical significance of this location?
2. Under the Old Covenant, who was allowed to enter the Holy of Holies to encounter the glory of God?
3. What is geographically beyond the Temple Mount and the glory of God?
4. Why did Jesus have to be crucified beyond the proper limits of the Temple Mount?
5. What is the significance of the veil being torn when Jesus was crucified?
6. Jesus said, "I AM the true vine" (John 15:1 NKJV). How can the information discussed in this Chapter help you apply the fullness of that truth in your daily life?

Prayer of Activation

Our Father in heaven, I stand in awe of you as I consider the bridges you built to make it possible for me to have a relationship with you. Since the begging of time, you had me in mind. When humanity was beyond the reach of your presence and glory, you made a way to bring your presence and glory to us. I thank you that I now have direct access to you. As a child of God, I am the temple of the Holy Spirit and your presence dwells in me. I come now before your presence and present myself to you. I can now live my life with you at the center. Let me never put up a veil of unbelief that would separate my life from yours. I pray this in the name of Jesus, Amen.

CHAPTER 19

Beyond the Glory (Part 2)

"To make all see what is the fellowship of the mystery, which from the beginning of the ages has been hidden in God who created all things through Jesus Christ" (Ephesians 3:9 NKJV).

"For [even the whole] creation [all nature] waits eagerly for the children of God to be revealed" (Romans 8:19 NKJV).

The thought of being able to share God's glory seems too good to be true. Yet, Jesus said in John 17:22-23 (NKJV), "And the glory which You gave Me I have given them, that they may be one just as We are one: I in them, and You in Me; that they may be made perfect in one, and that the world may know that You have sent Me, and have loved them as You have loved Me." God's longing to share his glory with us speaks volumes. Jesus confirmed this truth and at the same time showed the world the Father's hidden agenda and heart's desire. As unfathomable as it may sound, the Father loves us as much as he loves Jesus. He sent his son to pioneer our salvation so he could share his glory with us and thereby make us one with him as his power works within us to perfect us into his image and likeness. While many Christians speak of their desire to see the glory of God like Moses and the children of Israel in the Old Testament, there are many more hidden treasures beyond seeing his glory.

What are these hidden treasures? As we conclude our conversations on what is beyond the glory, there are three more questions we must discuss:

1. What is the Fellowship of the Mystery and Why Was it Hidden?
2. How Does God's Glory Shared with His Children Impact Their Lives?
3. How Will the Revealing of the Mystery Impact the World?

What is the Fellowship of the Mystery and Why Was it Hidden?

The Apostle Paul introduces us to the topic of the fellowship of the mystery and God's desire to share his glory with us. What's more, we are told this was part of God's long-term plans concealed from the beginning. What is this fellowship of the mystery? It sounds like something from a Tolkien novel. We understand the word "fellowship" implies a joint participation, an intimacy, a desire by God to share what he has. What does that mean? What are the depths of this mystery? Paul discusses this subject in Ephesians 3:9-21 (NKJV):

> "To make all see what is the fellowship of the mystery, which from the beginning of the ages has been hidden in God who created all things through Jesus Christ; to the intent that now the manifold wisdom of God might be made known by the church to the principalities and powers in the heavenly places, according to the eternal purpose which He accomplished in Christ Jesus our Lord, in whom we have boldness and access with confidence through faith in Him. Therefore I ask that you do not lose heart at my tribulations for you, which is your glory. For this reason I bow my knees to the Father of our Lord Jesus Christ, from whom the whole family in heaven and earth is named, that He would

> grant you, according to the riches of His glory, to be strengthened with might through His Spirit in the inner man, that Christ may dwell in your hearts through faith; that you, being rooted and grounded in love, may be able to comprehend with all the saints what is the width and length and depth and height - to know the love of Christ which passes knowledge; that you may be filled with all the fullness of God. Now to Him who is able to do exceedingly abundantly above all that we ask or think, according to the power that works in us, to Him be glory in the church by Christ Jesus to all generations, forever and ever. Amen."

In this short passage, the Holy Spirit has told us much. Front and center is the revelation that the fellowship of the mystery was hidden by God, and these mysteries have been hidden since eternity past. Why did God conceal something that was so good? The reasons trace back to the period before creation when everything was still in the mind of God. In those moments, he looked through the ages and foresaw the rebellion by Lucifer and one-third of the angelic host once they learned of his plans to create humanity.

In God's wisdom, he allowed the events to unfold, and after the creation of heaven and earth, he established the Divine Council from amongst the heavenly host to assist him in the administration of the kingdom. Talk about keeping your enemies close. During that early Period, the angels had access to heaven and earth, and Eden was established as the center of the earth. The throne of authority was set in Jerusalem, and work began on the New Jerusalem, which would become the headquarters of the kingdom.

Just as God foresaw, once the Divine Council learned of his plans to create humanity, Lucifer and one-third of the angels rebelled and wanted to overthrow God from his throne. No doubt there were many arguments presented to God as to why his plans were not good. No doubt they felt marginalized once they realized God intended to appoint a man to sit upon the seat of power in Eden. When their pride and narcissism reached a tipping point, they rebelled and there was war. The battlefields in heaven extended to the earth and the result was earth's destruction, chaos, and darkness covering the planet.

When God responded with his light and the six days of creation recorded in Genesis, the kingdom of darkness doubled down on their rebellion. The Watchers fell on Mount Hermon in Genesis 6, and the DNA of humans was corrupted through the Nephilim. Once again, their abominable actions led to the destruction of the planet, this time through a flood; however, the human race started again through Noah and his family.

The enemy was not deterred. Approximately 700 years after the flood, a mighty hunter rose up and founded a city. In Genesis 10, the Hebrew word used for the name of that city is *babel*[120] and it means "Babylon," or "confusion." This sounds familiar to the goals of the Watchers and the Nephilim. Under the leadership of Nimrod, and backed by the principalities and powers, the people came together and decided to build a tower to reach heaven. This was not a shovel ready jobs program. Instead, they were shaking their fists at God, and the tower was a symbol of their open defiance. Seeing their unity and knowing they could accomplish all they put their hearts too, God confounded their languages.

Afterwards, the tower project ceased, and the multitudes dispersed. Then in Genesis Chapter 10 we are given a genealogy and table of seventy nations that formed after the dispersion. In Genesis 10:32 and Deuteronomy 32:7-9, we learn that God set the boundaries of those nations and divided the land for their inheritance. While dividing the land, God enacted a key part of his plan and chose Israel for himself. Deuteronomy 32:9 (NKJV) says, "the Lord's portion is His people; Jacob is the place of His inheritance."

From among the seventy nations, only Israel worshipped God while the remaining nations worshipped the false gods of the principalities and powers, the fallen angelic host, and the Nephilim demigods. This gives us more insight to the temptations of Jesus recorded in Matthew 4:8-9 (NKJV), "Again, the devil took Him up on an exceedingly high mountain, and showed Him all the kingdoms of the world and their glory. And he said to Him, All these things I will give You if You will fall down and worship me."

The fallen angels and Nephilim thought they were superior to God and humans and sought to make themselves the rulers over creation. However, Jesus defeated darkness, took back the keys to death and hell, ruled out any resurrection for the Nephilim, paid the price for redemption, fulfilled every letter of the law, and became the one through whom the whole world may be saved. Jesus fulfilled the prophecy of Genesis 3:15 and the seed of the woman bruised the seed of the serpent.

It's important to recognize that even though God chose Israel as his inheritance, he did not forget about the other nations. Instead, he used Israel as an entry point to humanity to save them all. Regarding the Jews of Israel and the gentiles of the remaining sixty-nine nations, Ephesians 2:14-16 (NKJV) says, "For He Himself is our peace, who has made both one, and has broken down the middle wall of separation, having abolished in His flesh the enmity, that is, the law of commandments contained in ordinances, so as to create in Himself one new man from the two, thus making peace, and that He might reconcile them both to God." Through Jesus, the walls of separation were removed, and all could be born again, Jew and Gentile. This is the restoration of God's original plans to establish the fellowship.

Suddenly, the reason God concealed his plans from the beginning become clear. Ephesians 3:10-11 (NKJV) says, "to the intent that now the manifold wisdom of God might be made known by the church to the principalities and powers in the heavenly places, according to the eternal purpose which He accomplished in Christ Jesus our Lord." The eternal purposes of God were accomplished through Christ, and he put on full display the manifold wisdom of his plan. It was like God saying to the Divine Council and the principalities and powers, "*I told you so, can you see it now.*" God concealed his plans so the fallen could not abort them. God, as the great I AM, saw the end from the beginning and nothing or no-one would be allowed to prevent his eternal purposes from coming to pass.

With God's manifold wisdom on display, the fellowship of the mystery begins to come into focus. However, aspects of this mystery have continued to be hidden until these last days, until the fullness of time, when God is ready to put on full parade this fellowship to all of creation. In Romans 8:19 (AMP), God shows the fullness of his plans,

"For [even the whole] creation [all nature] waits eagerly for the children of God to be revealed." As the saying goes, you ain't seen nothing yet. So, get ready! Be prepared! Make sure you are part of the revealing when God makes known his sons and daughters to creation.

How Will God's Glory Shared with His Children Impact their Lives?

Now that we know what the fellowship of the mystery is and why it was hidden, we need to explore how God's glory shared with his children impact theirs lives. Let's begin by understanding the language used by Paul. The Greek word for "revealed" (or "manifestation" as it says in the KJV) is *apokalypsis*[121] and it means "an uncovering," "a laying bare," "a disclosure of truth, instruction, concerning divine things before unknown." The word is "used of events by which things or states or persons hitherto withdrawn from view are made visible to all." In other words, God is restoring the lives of his children to what he designed to be natural and normal.

This word also means "appearance" For this reason, the church has interpreted this scripture as a future event that would be fulfilled at the return of Christ. While the ultimate fulfillment of this scripture will occur on that day, the prelude or down payment of this revealing has begun in these last days. God is sharing his glory with his sons and daughters so they may be enabled to *Walk in the fullness of I AM* as they were designed from the beginning. This is the direct fulfillment of scripture. Haggai 2:9 (KJV) says, "The glory of this latter house shall be greater than of the former." II Corinthians 3:7-8 (NKJV) says, "But if the ministry of death, written and engraved on stones, was glorious, so that the children of Israel could not look steadily at the face of Moses because of the glory of his countenance, which glory was passing away, how will the ministry of the Spirit not be more glorious?" And also, II Corinthians 3:18 (NKJV) says, "But we all, with unveiled face, beholding as in a mirror the glory of the Lord, are being transformed into the same image from glory to glory." As God's sons and daughters, he has poured all of himself into all of you, "that you may be filled with all the fullness of God" (Ephesians 3:19 NKJV).

As a reminder, God's glory includes his fullness, his holiness, his love, his kindness, his nature, the manifestation of his plans, his goodness, his very best, his happiness, his joy, his gladness, his wealth, his goods, his beauty, his health, his welfare, and his supernatural knowledge and wisdom. God's glory shared with you is intended to transform your life. Think about all the goodness of God dwelling inside of you. Paul calls it the riches of his glory (Ephesians 3:16). And if these riches are not enough, being his son or daughter entitles you to some awesome benefits. Let's name a few:

Ephesians 3:12 - You have been granted access to the Father. This is good news because you no longer have to struggle with guilt and shame when you go to God. You have been made the righteousness of God (2 Corinthians 5:21) and can now come boldly to your Father's throne. This truth was signaled to the world when the veil of the temple was torn.

Ephesians 3:15 - He gave you his name. The whole family in heaven and earth is named after the Father. When God blessed Adam and Eve in the Garden, he knelt down before them, placed his hands upon them, and gave them his name. That name was restored to you when you were born again.

Ephesians 3:16 – Your inner man/woman has been strengthened with might. This includes your soul, conscious, affections, desires, and wants. They have all been strengthened with his might. The same Greek word for "might" in this passage is the same word used in Acts 1:8 (KJV) which says, "But ye shall receive power, after that the Holy Ghost is come upon you."

Ephesians 3:17 – Christ will dwell in your heart so you can be rooted and grounded in love. This speaks of your roots, your foundation. God is love and this is your foundation. Any of your actions or thoughts that goes against this nature will be quickened by your inner man/woman and a flag will go up giving you warning and pause.

Ephesians 3:18 – You will be able to comprehend the width, length, depth, and height of God and his love. This is the supernatural knowledge and wisdom of God. It is his power at work within you to conform you to his image so you may know him.

Ephesians 3:19 – That you may be filled with all the fullness of God.

If you look at yourself in the mirror and wonder how all of this is going to happen, Paul shares with you the secret, or process, of walking in his fullness. It's one thing to understand the plan of God but another thing for that plan to be enacted in your life. As previously noted, God introduced himself to Moses as I AM that I AM, which literally means, I AM Jehovah, I do note change, and I AM bringing to pass my word into existence. From eternity past, God declared you to be his son or daughter and he is in the process of bringing that to pass.

As you spend time in his presence, experience his anointing, and witness his glory, you begin the process of abiding in him and taking up your residence in that secrete place. Through the Holy Spirit, he shares with you his glory, and you begin to be rooted and grounded in love. It is only through the process of being rooted and grounded in love that you are able to comprehend the width, length, depth, and height of God so that you may be transformed from glory to glory and gain the capacity to walk in his fullness.

It would be easy for many of us to view this as beyond our ability. It would be easy for you to compare this glory against your own humanity. Can I share with you God understands this dilemma? This is the reason you received Christ by faith and not of works. This is the reason Jesus is our righteousness. This is the reason the just shall live by faith.

God anticipated all our doubts. The gap between our lives and God seems so big, and God knew it. This is the reason he sent his son. To help us with our humanity and to reveal the significance of his love for us, Romans 8:35 (NKJV) says, "Who shall separate us from the love of Christ?" I want you to think about the significance of this verse. The root of the Greek word for "separate" is *Chora*[122] and it means "the space lying between." In other words, there is no space between us and God's love, and there is no space between us and God himself. Let the power of that truth sink into your spirit and soul.

Think about two giant super magnets drawn together. As hard as it would be to separate the two, there would exist a thin microscopic crack or space between them. However, when it comes to our relationship to Christ, there is no space between, no crack, no thin line, no sliver of air between. Jesus said we are one with him and the Father and nothing can separate us.

With that question hopefully settled, let's think about a couple of questions. Does God seek to walk in the glory? Does God seek the fruit of the spirit or the gifts of the spirit. The answer is obviously No. They naturally proceed from God because they are part of his nature and character, the essence of who he is, and they naturally follow after him. Since we are created in the image and likeness of God, they should naturally flow from us just like they did from Jesus. Jesus declared this to be true in Mark 16:17 (NKJV), "these signs will **follow** those who believe." The Greek word for "follow" is *parakoloutheo*[123] and it means "to follow close, accompany," "to be always present, to attend one wherever he goes," and "a standard or rule, to conform oneself to." As your relationship with God grows, he will fill you with all of who he is, and the signs of the believer will naturally follow you and be the standard and rule to be conformed to. Churches that do not encourage these signs following the believer will have a difficult time with this scripture.

As the sons and daughters of God begin to be revealed to all of creation, we are going to see believers walk like and act like Jesus. We are in a transformation process. Realize the truth of who God is and who you are, and take hold of all God says about you. Let the power of love work in you. God is love (I John 4:8). Faith works by love (Galatians 5:6). Love never fails (I Corinthians 13:8). Love is the most powerful force there is and the key to knowing the Father, being conformed into his image, and walking in his fullness. As the fullness of Christ dwells in you, John 15:5 (NKJV) will become a natural byproduct of your life, "I am the vine, you are the branches. He who abides in Me, and I in him, bears much fruit; for without Me you can do nothing."

How Will the Revealing of the Mystery Impact the World?

The last question we need to ask is how will the revealing of the mystery impact the world? This goes to the heart of the Father's plans. It is so simple, it is ingenious. Ephesians 3:9 (NKJV) says, "to make all see what is the fellowship of the mystery." God wants all of creation to see the relationship he has with his sons and daughters. God's power working in his children will put on full display what all may have. All will want the

Christ within you. The Jesus in you will become irresistible. Colossians 1:26-29 (TPT), puts it this way:

> "There is a divine mystery—a secret surprise that has been concealed from the world for generations, but now it's being revealed, unfolded and manifested for every holy believer to experience. Living within you is the Christ who floods you with the expectation of glory! This mystery of Christ, embedded within us, becomes a heavenly treasure chest of hope filled with the riches of glory for his people, and God wants everyone to know it! Christ is our message! We preach to awaken hearts and bring every person into the full understanding of truth. It has become my inspiration and passion in ministry to labor with a tireless intensity, with his power flowing through me, to present to every believer the revelation of being his perfect one in Jesus Christ."

Conclusion

As we conclude this section, we are ready to answer the question of what is beyond the glory and finalize our definition of the gospel of the kingdom:

Question - What is beyond the glory?

Beyond the eyewitness accounts of God's glory is he shares his glory with us so that the essence of who he is, his power and all his goodness, works within us to conform us to his image that we may Walk in the fullness of I AM as his sons and daughters.

Question - What is the finalized definition of the gospel of the kingdom?

The gospel, or good news of the kingdom is that God the Father sent his only begotten Son to destroy all the works of the devil in order to complete his original plans and design for creation, his family, and the kingdom. In eternity past, God planned a family and a kingdom. Seeing the end from the beginning, God foresaw the rebellion of the angelic host that would occur once they learned of his plans to create humanity. Therefore, he hid his plans from all of creation, including the principalities and powers, in the mystery of the fellowship he planned for his family. Through the rebellion of the angelic host, sin and darkness was born. This led to the desolation of the earth, the seven days of creation, and humanity's subsequent fall after yielding to the voice of the enemy. Through the virgin birth, God the Son became the Son of Man, one of us, the first born of many brothers, so he could meet all legal qualifications to become our kinsman redeemer. Through his birth, death, and resurrection, Jesus became the pioneer of our salvation so he may bring many sons and daughters to share in his glory. By accepting Jesus Christ as Lord and Savior, we can be born-again and restored to our original family as the natural sons and daughters of God and citizens of the kingdom. By accepting Christ, we receive the Holy Spirit, the restoration of our fellowship with God, and the down payment of all that is to come. This mystery of Christ, now embedded within us, has become a heavenly treasure chest of hope filled with the riches of glory for his people, and God wants everyone to know it! Christ is our message! This power working in us conforms us to his image and likeness, and enables us to Walk in the fullness of I AM, and fulfill the Great Commission to go into all the world and preach this good news of the kingdom. As we go, we have been commissioned to have dominion and authority over all sin, sickness, disease, and darkness that stands in opposition to God. In the fullness of time, Christ will return, and the kingdoms of this world will become the kingdoms of Christ and all of heaven and earth will be made new. All creation eagerly awaits the final revealing of the Sons and Daughters of God. As heirs and coheirs with Christ, we are made one with him and will rule and reign with him throughout eternity.

The Greatest Revelation

This is the greatest revelation to be fully revealed to the earth.
It is the greatest revelation God has given to the world.
It is the most important thing to God and his greatest command.
It is the secret to walking in the fullness of I AM.
It is a mystery hidden since the foundations of the world.
Because of this, God dances over me.
Because of this, God etched my name in his hands.
By this one thing, All the gifts of the spirit operate and work.
By this one thing, we are marked as sons and daughters.
It is so powerful, there is no law against it.
It is so powerful, nothing in heaven, earth, or hell can oppose it.
It is so powerful, nothing can keep it from me.
By this one thing, I can know the ways of God.
By this one thing, I can hear his voice.
By this one thing, I can see him.
It is who God is.
It is why he does what he does.
It is why he went to the cross
It has the ability to permeate my heart and change me.
It has the ability to cause me to do God's will.
It is irresistible
GOD's LOVE FOR ME

Reflections of Who I AM

1. Who does God the Father love the most, Jesus or you?
2. What is the fellowship of the mystery, and why was it hidden?
3. How will God's glory shared with his children change their lives?
4. How will the revealing of this mystery impact the world?
5. What is the key to walking in his fullness?
6. Jesus said, "I AM the true vine" (John 15:1 NKJV). How can the information discussed in this Chapter help you apply the fullness of that truth in your daily life?

Prayer of Activation

Our Father in heaven, I come to you with complete surrender, humility, and thankfulness because you love me as much as you do Jesus. I thank you that I am your son/daughter and there is no space between you and me. I am in you, and you are in me. I ask that you help me be rooted and grounded in your love so that I may comprehend the width, length, depth, and height of who you are and the love you have for me and the world. Let your love completely fill me and change me from the inside out. Jesus, you are the true vine and without you, I can do nothing. Let the power of your love and the glory that you have shared with me complete its perfect work in my life. Help me bear much fruit for you and the kingdom. Let the expectation of your glory flood my life so that it becomes a treasure chest filled with your riches that all will want. Let it awaken me and all I come in contact with. I pray this in the name of Jesus, Amen.

SECTION VI
I AM the Door

"Then Jesus said to them again, Most assuredly, I say to you, I AM the door of the sheep" (John 10:7 NKJV).

The Greek word for "door" is *thyra*[124] and it means "an entrance, way or passage," "the door of the kingdom of heaven." Jesus revealed that he is the door to eternal life and abundant life. When doors are opened, they reveal what had been hidden or closed off. We can see what could not be seen, and we gain entry to what had not been accessible. When portals are opened, we move from the physical to the spiritual, from the natural to the supernatural, and gain access to new dimensions. Suddenly, impossibilities become possible, difficult things become easy, and new futures begin.

In Revelation 3:20 (NKJV), Jesus said, "Behold, I stand at the door and knock. If anyone hears My voice and opens the door, I will come in to him and dine with him, and he with Me." In this section, we will discuss access to intimacy with God, walking in his fullness, and sharing the good news of the gospel with others. We will talk about the difficulties of life and true freedom that comes through Christ. Jesus is not only the door to salvation; he is also the door to a new way of living. When you enter these gates, life will dramatically change, strongholds and hinderances can be overcome, and you can gain a new closeness with the creator.

Will you answer his knock at the doors of your heart? Open this door and you will never be the same. A whole new realm of possibilities is awaiting your response.

DOORS AND GATEWAYS

CHAPTER 20

Open the Gates for the King of Glory to Come In

"Lift up your heads, O you gates! Lift up, you everlasting doors! And the King of glory shall come in" (Psalm 24:9 NKJV).

I opened this book with a question, "have you ever wanted more?" It excites me to know we are coming to a time of walking in the fullness of God where we can experience greater intimacy in our relationship with the creator and the supernatural life he offers. Closely associated with this is God wants us to learn how to live life. Do you truly know how to live? Have you ever wondered about this or asked yourself this question? For example, what has happened to your joy and peace? What has happened to your discernment to know how to face obstacles? Is there a greater realm of possibilities available for you? These are profound questions many struggle with.

Have you ever thought about asking God to teach you how to live life? After all, since he is the author of life he may have an opinion on the matter. In fact, Jesus addressed this question head on when he declared himself to be the door. Jesus said there was only one way into the sheepfold and that was through him. He said all those who try to enter some other way is a thief and a robber. Keep in mind, Jesus was not just pontificating on the subject. He is the eternal I AM and creator of all things. Jesus said there have been others that came before him; however, they were all thieves, and the sheep did not hear them because his sheep know his voice. He said all who enter the sheepfold through him would be saved and will go in and out and find pasture. Jesus went on to say in John 10:10 (NKJV), "The thief does not come except to steal, and to kill, and to destroy. I have come that they may have life, and that they may have it more abundantly." God wants you to walk in his fullness so you may know how to live an abundant life. Abundance means over and above what is needed, more than enough. This is the heart of the good news.

Why would Jesus refer to himself as the door? It must be because doors and gates were erected to keep us from this way of life, from the life God designed for us. The kingdom of darkness has done everything it can to bring about dysfunction, death, and destruction. God sent forth his son to be the door and he declared to all of creation, "Lift up your heads, O you gates! And be lifted up, you everlasting doors! And the King of glory shall come in" (Psalm 24:7 NKJV). In Psalm 24:8 (NKJV), God asks, "Who is this King of glory? The Lord strong and mighty, the Lord mighty in battle." And if this isn't clear enough, James 2:1 (KJV) reveals to us that "Jesus is the Lord of Glory." This is the halleluiah moment that brings hope to all!

Jesus is Walking with You

Since Jesus is the Door and the one to give abundant life, by necessity, he is walking with you. Jesus told his disciples he would be with them always and would never leave them or forsake them. When you become born again, the Lord of Glory takes up residence in you and he is with you through every circumstance of life.

Have you figured out that even though you are born again, life's troubles still come your way? While the enemy uses his weapons of fear and doubt, we have the promise that he is not only with us but that he has gone before us. Think about walking in the wake of God's glory. Long after a ship has passed, it's wake can still be seen and followed.

Sometimes the wake is turbulent if the ship displaced a large amount of water. But after a while, the waves calm down, the waters become smooth again, and all that can be seen is the wake left by the ship. In other words, the ship that went before you prepared a path that initially was turbulent but eventually became smooth. Consider for a moment the words of Isaiah 45:1-2 (KJV):

> "Thus saith the Lord to his anointed, to Cyrus, whose right hand I have holden, to subdue nations before him; and I will loose the loins of kings, to open before him the two leaved gates; and the gates shall not be shut; I will go before thee, and make the crooked places straight: I will break in pieces the gates of brass, and cut in sunder the bars of iron: [3] And I will give thee the treasures of darkness, and hidden riches of secret places, that thou mayest know that I, the Lord, which call thee by thy name, am the God of Israel."

Since God said, "I will go before thee," this means he has already been where you are. The implication of this promise is mindboggling. Think about the circumstances you face in life today. Let's look at the words of Isaiah to Cyrus and unpack the revelation God wants you to receive.

1. You are God's anointed. Since Jesus is the Christ, the anointed one, and you are one with him, that makes you God's anointed. Like liquid gold, his anointing is spread over you. You are his consecrated one, filled with his presence and power.
2. God will strengthen you for the circumstances you face. As a child of the kingdom, God has given you the land to subdue. God will use you to reclaim the dominion of his kingdom.
3. Just like God loosened the loins of Kings before Cyrus, the plans and purposes of the enemy have been weakened, and they will be unprepared to do battle against one of God's chosen ones. In other words, God will disarm the enemy on your behalf. He is no match for the Jesus inside of you.

4. The two leaved gates will be opened. When Cyrus entered the gates of Babylon, the gates of the city by providence had been left open. Otherwise, they would have been trapped and defeated. The two leaved gates represent the gates of kings. They are the strongholds of the enemy. Where God commissions you and sends you, he will ensure the gates before you are left open. He has gone before you to secure your victory.
5. When God goes before you, he will make the crooked paths straight. You won't have to wonder which way to go, and the confusion and difficult paths caused by the enemy will be straightened.
6. God will break in pieces the gates of brass and the bars of iron. Again, this speaks to the strongholds of the enemy. However, there is another treasure in this verse. As a person entered the temple in Jerusalem to go to the holy of holies, they needed to pass through the women's court, up the fifteen steps, and through the Nikanor Gate. These were two gates of brass named after a convert to Judaism. This convert named Nikanor obtained the gates from Alexandria, Egypt and transported them by ship to Israel. When the ship encountered a life-threatening storm, they tossed overboard one of the doors, but Nikanor held on to the other. When taking his stand to protect the door, the winds calmed, and miraculously, they found the other door floating ashore when they landed. It is said that many miracles happened at the entrance of these two doors of the Nikanor Gate. Whatever your need, miracles still happen today and there is nothing too hard for God. No shut doors, no iron bars, and no weapon or stronghold of the enemy can stand against you if God is on your side. His glory has gone before you and you are walking in the wake of all his goodness.
7. When Cyrus entered the gates of Babylon, he obtained the treasures and riches of the city. God will provide for all your physical and spiritual needs, will open to you the hidden treasures, and make known to you the secrets of his mysteries.

Two Spiritual Laws Working for You

There are two spiritual laws we need to consider as we think about navigating life as a child of God and walking in his fullness. The first of these laws is found in Romans 8:2 (NKJV), "For the law of the Spirit of life in Christ Jesus has made me free from the law of sin and death." Think for a moment about the law of sin and death. The moment Satan and one-third of the angelic host rebelled against God, darkness and evil were born. Once Adam and Eve partook of the forbidden fruit, the evil spirits of sin and death gained legal access to earth and humanity. Therefore, the law of sin and death encompasses everything that is evil, bad, and destructive, including death and separation from God. All sickness, poverty, lack and want is part of the law of sin and death. All addictions, depression, mental illnesses, wars, and poverty are part of the law of sin and death. In other words, all evil comes under this law. The good news is that when Jesus came, he instituted a higher law to supersede the law of sin and death. As the door to abundant life, Jesus brought about a new law called the law of the Spirit of life in Christ Jesus, and this law sets us free from the law of sin and death.

This cannot be accomplished in the flesh or on your own. You need a gateway, a door, a supernatural entrance to escape the law of sin and death. Jesus is that door to abundant life. As you continue your journey of walking in the fullness of I AM, learn to call upon the law of the spirit of life. Lift up your head, open up the gates and let the king of glory come in to transport you to a new way of living life.

The second spiritual law is found in Acts 17:28 (KJV), "For in him we live, and move, and have our being." All of your life is in Christ. Do you suppose for one moment that God is baffled by the circumstances you find yourself in? Could it be he does not have an answer or a solution for your problems? Of course not. He has already gone before you to make the crooked paths straight and has an answer for every circumstance. He has counsel and direction for the choices and decisions you should be making that will produce the results of the destiny he has planned for you. Your task is to go to him, go to the door, go to the gateway. Through those doors is your breakthrough, victory, and treasures of heaven.

Greater than these

As the sons and daughters of God walk through the doors Jesus has for them, their true identity will be revealed to all of creation. As this happens, we are going to see believers walk like and act like their elder brother. We are quickly approaching the "greater works than these" days. Jesus said to his disciples in John 14:12 (NKJV), "Most assuredly, I say to you, he who believes in Me, the works that I do he will do also; and greater works than these he will do, because I go to My Father."

We could write volumes of books on the things Jesus did, but for brevity's sake, let's list a few. What did Jesus do?

1. Healed the sick, even of uncurable diseases.
2. Performed miracles.
3. Cast out devils.
4. Fed 5,000 with five loafs of bread and two fishes.
5. Walked on water and calmed the storms.
6. Preached and taught about the kingdom of God.
7. Loved everyone.
8. Spent time with the Father.
9. Knew the hearts and minds of people as the Spirit revealed them to him.
10. Raised the dead.

Let's be honest with ourselves, do we see churches doing the works of Jesus? At best, we catch glimpses of some of these things. As we survey the church world, we see many types of churches. Some claim to be "the church," and unless you are a part of their denomination you're not part of the true church. Some churches focus on ritual, form, and tradition, and many people find comfort and security in time honored methods. However, II Timothy 3:5 (NKJV) warns that in the last days, many will be characterized as "having a form of godliness but denying its power." Some churches struggle with the Holy Spirit, and they debate whether or not the gifts of the Spirit are for our day or if they were done away with when the Apostles died. They focus on leading people to Christ and that is the entirety of their DNA. Their motto is I Corinthians 14:40

(KJV), "Let all things be done decently and in order." They fear the supernatural will provoke a negative reaction from people and so they quench the workings of the Holy Spirit. Paul didn't say "Let nothing be done." Instead, he said let them be done "decently and in order." In some churches, we see Christianity is approached in a seeker friendly manner. They want everyone to feel comfortable, and they rarely, if ever, challenge congregants with topics related to repentance, salvation, or holiness. I'm afraid for many, the second greatest commandment has replaced the first (See Matthew 22:36-40). On the other hand, there are many churches and ministries who are pressing into the things of God and seek after him with their whole hearts. They desire all that God has for them, including the supernatural. They want more of him in their lives.

We can debate whether or not churches are doing the works of Jesus, but we are hard pressed to find the church world doing greater works than Jesus. I want to challenge every church and every believer to embrace the words and promises of Christ in John 14:12. When Jesus said "greater works" his meaning was clear. He meant more, larger, stronger, greater in number, power, and authority. We are approaching these days and as we enter those doors, we will see the fulfillment of Habakkuk 2:4 (NKJV), "For the earth will be filled with the knowledge of the glory of the Lord, as the waters cover the sea."

On the day of Pentecost in Acts Chapter 2, Peter stood up and began to share with the onlookers what had just happened. He shared how Jesus fulfilled the prophecies of scripture and had been raised up and seated at the right hand of the Father. He told them they were witnessing the outpouring of the Holy Spirit spoken of by the Prophet Joel. The words of Peter combined with the witnessing of the supernatural convinced them the message was true.

Their response to Peter's words are recorded in Acts 2:37 (KJV), "What shall we do?" This is the question everyone reading this book needs to ask themselves. What is God asking of you? My encouragement is to make sure Jesus is both savior and Lord of your life. Ask God to fill you with the gift of the Holy Spirit. Like Moses, seek to know the ways of God. Like Jesus, spend time with the Father and do the things you see him do and say the things you hear him say.

As you seek and spend time with the Father, Son, and Holy Spirit, he will lead you into his fullness. He will fill you with his glory and you will begin to do the works of Jesus and even greater. As God's children begin to walk in his fullness, the church will fulfill the words of Jesus in Matthew 24:14 (NKJV), "This gospel of the kingdom will be preached in all the world as a witness to all nations, and then the end will come."

Reflections of Who I AM

1. Do you know how to truly live life the way God intended? If not, what is God saying to you?
2. Why did Jesus refer to himself as the door?
3. What are the situations in your life that you need God to go before you and make straight?
4. What are the two spiritual laws working for you?
5. After hearing Peter's message on the day of Pentecost, the people asked in Acts 2:37 (KJV), "what shall we do." What is God asking of you today?
6. Jesus said, "I AM the door" (John 10:7 NKJV). How can the information discussed in this Chapter help you apply the fullness of that truth in your daily life?

Prayer of Activation

Our Father in heaven, I am so thankful that you sent your son Jesus to be the door in my life and the door for the whole world. As I look to you, I ask that you show me the doors you have set before me. Help me to walk through them. Fill me with your fullness so that I might be conformed to your image and likeness. I choose you and I choose life. Go before me in each circumstance I listed above, and make those crooked paths straight. I receive your promises for me. I receive healing, miracles, your intervention, direction, and guidance. I trust you with the cares of my life because I know all of my life is in you. Show me all that you want me to do. I pray this in the name of Jesus, Amen.

CHAPTER 21

Come Away with Me – The Secret Stairs

"The voice of my beloved! Behold, he comes Leaping upon the mountains, skipping upon the hills. My beloved is like a gazelle or a young stag. Behold, he stands behind our wall; He is looking through the windows, gazing through the lattice. My beloved spoke, and said to me: "Rise up, my love, my fair one, and come away" (Song of Solomon 2:8-10 NKJV).

Over the years, I've talked to many Christians who have felt weary or restless in their walk with God. Sometimes they feel that their relationship has grown stale. Have you ever found yourself in this position? Is there something tugging at your heart for more? Perhaps that restlessness is the voice of the Father drawing you deeper. There were times in Jesus' life that he needed to get away to spend time with the Father.

In this chapter we are going to discuss a key to open the doors of greater experiences with God and Walking in the Fullness of I AM. It's a discussion that explores his voice calling you to come away with him. It is his invitation for you to abide in the secret place. In this place, your relationship with him matures. In this place, you will be taken on an adventure, and the dull and routine will be replaced with excitement and purpose. You will begin to experience the "suddenly" moments of life. Suddenly, old things will pass away, and all things will be made new. Your former life of the "natural" will become a life of the supernatural.

The key to this door begins with an understanding of the depth of God's love. It knows no boundaries and is unrestrained in its pursuit for you.

God's Unrestrained Love

For many people, the Song of Solomon is a book that causes pause and raises questions. The Book is also called the Song of Songs. The chapters are songs about a man and the woman he loves. The man was Solomon, the King of Israel, and the woman's name is unknown. She is simply called "the Shulamite" (Song of Solomon 6:13).

Before this Book became part of the cannon of scripture, it was heavily debated among rabbi scholars who questioned the contents of the book and whether or not it was scripture. The matter was finally settled that it should be included in scripture, and the reason was best summed up by Rabbi Akiba. He said in Mishnah Yadayim 3:5, "The whole world is not worth the day on which the Song of Songs was given to Israel, for all the Scriptures are holy, but the Song of Songs is the Holy of Holies."[125]

As we have discussed, the Holy of Holies was where the presence and glory of God dwelled. It was the inner sanctuary, the secret place, where God talked directly with the High Priest. Metaphorically, it was the cleft of the rock where Moses saw the glory of God. The rabbi scholars concluded that the Song of Songs represented the most intimate message of God and was comparable to the Holy of Holies.

The Song of Songs describes the unrestrained love between a man and a woman. What else can better describe God's love for us? Throughout scripture we see God's unbridled love for us. John 3:16 (KJV) says, "For God so loved the world, that he gave his only begotten Son, that whosoever believeth in him should not perish, but have everlasting life."

Ephesians 5:25 (KJV) says, "Husbands, love your wives, even as Christ also loved the church, and gave himself for it."

God's love for us is unrelenting, and he desires to be with us. In Matthew 25, Jesus spoke of the kingdom of heaven as ten virgins who went out to meet the bridegroom. The Apostle John saw the vision of this day and said in Revelation 19:7 (KJV), "Let us be glad and rejoice, and give honour to him: for the marriage of the Lamb is come, and his wife hath made herself ready." And if this is not clear enough, Isaiah 54:5 (NKJV) says, "For your Maker is your husband - the LORD Almighty is his name - the Holy One of Israel is your Redeemer; he is called the God of all the earth."

There is nothing like the love of God. It is the most perfect of loves. It is wild and untamed. It will not relent and will never give up. In fact, I Corinthians Chapter 13 not only describes what true love is, but it also describes God's love for us. I Corinthians 13:4-8 (NIV) says:

> "Love is patient, love is kind. It does not envy, it does not boast, it is not proud. It does not dishonor others, it is not self-seeking, it is not easily angered, it keeps no record of wrongs. Love does not delight in evil but rejoices with the truth. It always protects, always trusts, always hopes, always perseveres. Love never fails."

First and foremost, God's love for you is patient. He will wait for you. He will pursue you your entire life if that is what it takes for you to come to know him. How many times have you felt like you exhausted the patience of God? Those feelings are usually our self-disappointment. The truth is God's love toward you is unending. This does not mean the consequences of sin will not be experienced. The Bible makes clear there are wages to sin, and we reap what we sow. This is the natural course of life. However, God's love is slow to anger, slow to wrath, and he has great patience towards us. There are times our sin causes God's hand to be removed from our life, and he allows us to experience the results of our actions. In turn, many have mistakenly blamed God for the fallout of their own bad behavior. They ask why God allowed those things to happen to them instead of realizing that

Satan, the enemy of their soul, was all along seeking to rob, kill, and destroy them. In fact, God has gone to extraordinary lengths to secure our salvation and forgive sin, so that we may enjoy his presence and experience his love.

It deeply saddens the heart of God when we experience the consequences of sin. You recall the occasion when Jesus was looking over Jerusalem. He said in Matthew 23:37 (NKJV), "Jerusalem, Jerusalem, you who kill the prophets and stone those sent to you, how often I have longed to gather your children together, as a hen gathers her chicks under her wings, and you were not willing."

God's love is not only patient, but it is also kind. This means his love is pleasant, virtuous, and benevolent. It means he does not treat you harshly, or with bitterness. There is no one kinder than God, and he wants the very best for you.

Once we experience God's love, we understand he does not envy or boast. He is not angry at you, nor does he treat you with indignation. Instead, he seeks to promote you and advance you. Nothing can tear you away from his love. He is zealous in his pursuit of the plans and purposes he has for your life. His favor overshadows you and goes before you.

He keeps no record of your wrongs. When we confess our sins to him, he cast them as far away as the east is from the west to remember no more (Psalm 103:12). God rejoices to watch you walk in his truth and uncover his secrets and mysteries. He loves it when you search out his ways and know his heart. He longs for you to know him and dwell in the secret place he has for you. He is the protector you can trust. He will bestow his trust upon you as he tries your ways, and you draw close to him. You can always hope in him, for he will never let you down. His love for you will preserver and endure all things. Know for certain that his love for you will never fail. It will never cease. It will never be exhausted. He is good, and just like the Song of Solomon shows, his love for you is unrestrained.

A Call to Come Away

The Song of Solomon not only describes God's unrestrained love for you, but it also reveals another secret. It is the mystery of God's voice calling you to come away with him. Song of Solomon 2:10 (KJV) says, "My beloved spake, and said unto me, Rise up, my love, my fair one, and come away." This is the voice of the bridegroom calling out to his love. It reminds us of what Jesus said in John 10:27 (KJV), "My sheep hear my voice, and I know them, and they follow me."

In this text, we see that the groom comes leaping and skipping upon the mountains and hills. In other words, he comes to his bride readily and swiftly, with excitement and pleasure. Did you know that God can't wait to be with you? He doesn't want to wait until after this life is over or after the end of days. He desires and longs to be with you now. He wants you to be in his presence. You are his, and he is yours. Regardless of any hills or mountains in the way, God's love for you will not be stopped by obstacles. Instead, he will come for you swiftly, leaping, and skipping over mountains to find his true love.

Some scholars have said Chapter 2 of the Song of Solomon is a reference to the Feast of Passover when God called Israel out of Egypt, which foreshadowed the cross and the resurrection of Easter. It represents the communion of the believer's awakened soul with Christ, who calls us into a fuller communion with him.

In verse nine, the groom is standing behind a wall outside the house peeking through the lattice. After leaping and skipping upon the mountains and hills to reach the one he loves, he peeks through the holes of the lattice to catch a glimpse of his bride. He can't wait to get to her. Looking through the lattice, the bride only catches glimpses of the groom, because the lattice blocks her view of him. She sees that he longs to be with her, but there is a wall in the way.

Under the Old Covenant, people could only catch glimpses of God through ceremony on special occasions. At times, the spirit of God would come upon an individual but would not stay. This Old Covenant was between God and the Jewish people. It left out the gentiles. When God established his covenant with Abraham and his descendants, it wasn't because he did not love the world. Instead, it was because Abraham was the only man that dared to believe God. God saw in him a man through whom he could pierce the darkness and enter the world, a man whose decedents would follow him until the day he could redeem all. The covenant with Abraham was God's entrance to our lives.

The lattice represented the divide between Jew and Gentile and the partition between humanity and God. We have discussed the veil that separated the Holy of Holies from those outside. Only the High Priest could come into God's presence. The other Jews could only come so far but not beyond the veil. The gentiles could only come as close as the courts of the gentiles. Women were only allowed so far. There were barriers that kept humanity away from God. There were walls and partitions that kept Jews and Gentiles separated. That all changed with the coming of Christ. The groom would not remain outside the wall to just catch glimpses of his bride.

Ephesians 2:13-14 (NASB) says, "But now in Christ Jesus you who formerly were far off have been brought near by the blood of Christ. For He Himself is our peace, who made both groups into one and broke down the barrier of the dividing wall." Jesus removed the barrier between Jew and Gentile so that we may be one new man/woman. He also tore down the barriers between himself and humanity. Do you realize how amazing this is? Can you see that throughout history God's love for humanity was persistent, and he would not let anything stand in his way of coming to you. The Father, Son, and Holy Spirit longs to be with you. God enjoys being with you as much as you enjoy being with him.

But there is more. In verse ten, the groom speaks to the bride and invites her to come away with him. He says in Song of Solomon 2:10 (KJV), "Rise up, my love, my fair one, and come away." His request is for her to leave everything behind, and be with him. He is saying to us today, lay aside your problems and cares of life. Lay aside all questions, doubt, and fear. Lay aside the hurts and pains of life that isolates and causes wounds and hurts. Rise up from your sleep. Wake up from your slumber. You are my love, my fair one. Come away with me. I stand at the door and knock. Don't shut me out. Open the door and come away. I want to take you to a secret place.

God is saying, the time of waiting is over. I am here, now. Notice the significance of his call. The good news of the gospel is that you do not have to wait until you meet God after this life is over to be with him. In this present life, before the return of Christ, you are called to an incredible journey with God. You are called to be with him, learn of him, journey with him, and know him closely and intimately. You are called to steal away from the cares of life and come into the secret place.

The Secret Stairs

What is this secret place? In this text, the groom calls for his bride to come away with him, and the text speaks of the mystery of the secret place, or may we say the secrets of the secret place. In Song of Solomon 2:13-14 (KJV), it says "The fig tree putteth forth her green figs, and the vines with the tender grape give a good smell. Arise, my love, my fair one, and come away. O my dove, that art in the clefts of the rock, in the secret places of the stairs."

We saw the secret place in the Book of Exodus when Moses asked God to show him his glory, and God placed him in the cleft of the rock and covered him with his hand. While there, God caused all his goodness to pass before him as he revealed himself to him. We also saw this secret place in Psalm 91:1. The Hebrew word for "secret" in both the Song of Solomon and in Psalm 91 is *seter*[126] and it means "a hiding place; hence something secret, clandestine, hidden." It also means "a veil, covering," and "protection, defense." However, in Song of Solomon, God tells us the cleft of the rock is in the secret places of the stairs. This is something new.

What is the secret place of the stairs? The Hebrew word for "stairs" is *madrega*[127] and it means "a steep mountain, which one has to ascend by steps, as though it were a ladder." It reminds us of Jacobs dream when he saw a ladder descend from heaven and angels ascending and descending. The angels came directly from heaven to earth and back up to heaven. What were these stairs and what is the mystery God is trying to reveal to us?

The Song of Solomon gives us more clues to the secret of the stairs. Song of Solomon 2:13 (KJV) says, "The fig tree putteth forth her green figs, and the vines with the tender grape give a good smell. Arise, my love, my fair one, and come away." What does this mean? The Hebrew word for "putteth forth" is *hanat*[128] and in this case it means "fills its fruit with aromatic juice, to mature." In other words, it means to mature or ripen. While in the cleft of the rock, you will experience a time of maturity. As you behold all the goodness of God and experience his glory, it will cause you to ripen, to come of age, to ascend the stairs to a higher level. It will give you history with God. It will give you experiential knowledge that just reading about him can never give you. These experiences will be your testament. They will be your testimony, your life experiences with God that cause you to ripen and mature and know from experience the goodness and faithfulness of God first-hand.

The Hebrew word for "green fig" is *pag*[129] and it means "unripe figs." It refers to the figs that hang on the tree through the winter. This is significant and gives us clues to the mystery. Fig trees produce an early fig and a late fig. The early figs are called paggim, and they grow on old vines. They take about four months to ripen towards the end of June. Although these figs ripen early, they have an inferior taste. In Hosea 9:10, God speaks about his first calling of Israel. He said they were like the early figs; they turned from God and went after idols. The fruit was inferior and not the best the vine could put forth.

It is the early fruit that grows from old vines. As a child of God, you will go through seasons in your life. Remember, it is the Father's desire that you produce much fruit. When you are first introduced to God, you lack experience. As a new believer, you are grafted into the older vines, and you begin to bear fruit from the substance you get from those vines. However, God wants you to produce much fruit. As you abide in the secret place, he will begin to prune you. Everything in your life that does not bear fruit, he cuts back and prunes. Your old way of thinking, old habits, and character traits will be pruned. Some of them produced fruit, but they were early fruit and not your best. Because of his love for you, he cuts back the old so the new may grow. And with maturity, you begin to grow new vines.

While the early figs ripen towards the end of June, the late figs grow on the new vines and ripen after August. They are a better harvest with a better taste. As you mature in Christ and grow new vines, the fruit of those vines will be much better and more plentiful. They will produce a greater harvest. God has uniquely designed you with gifts and talents tailor made for you. He wants you to come into your own self, the person he has designed you to be. That mature person will bear much fruit.

As the fig season progresses, some figs stay unripen through the winter and only become ripe in the spring. As springtime approaches, the once green figs begin to ripen and become darker with a partly red and violet color. They are called the winter figs due to them going through the harsh winter months before they matured. Their color is now mature, and they are filled with the juice and spice of its fruit and ready to be eaten. These are the very best of the best of the fruit. These are the *pag* spoken of in our text. As you continue your walk with God, some fruit will take longer to mature. It will not happen quickly, instead it will mature over time and through much travail and hardship. This fruit will stand the test of time and the hardships of the winter seasons of life. Psalm 30:5 (NKJV) says, "weeping may endure for a night, but joy comes in the morning." Galatians 6:9 (NKJV) says, "And let us not grow weary while doing good, for in due season we shall reap if we do not loose heart."

You may be wondering why your fruit has not ripened or if you will ever see the results of your efforts. You have gone through the trials and troubles of life and have endured much for the kingdom of God. It may seem like all that you have done has not amounted to much. But God wants you to know that the fruit of your labor has been called to endure the winter months. Perhaps you are waiting on a spiritual breakthrough that seems to be delayed. Rest assured that the greater the battle, the greater the victory. The fruit after these delays will be the early spring harvest filled with the juice and spice of life. Your fruit will be the best of the best. Do not grow weary, you are about to reap a harvest, and the fruit will be beyond anything you can imagine.

But that is not all, Song of Solomon 2:13 (KJV) goes on to say, "the tender grape give a good smell". Once again, it speaks of the coming of spring. The vines are in bloom and the tender grapes give off its aroma and fragrance that is a soothing sacrifice to God. The first time this word is used in Scripture is in Genesis 8:21. It was after the flood of Noah. God caused a wind to blow over the whole earth to dry up the flood waters. Finally, after the waters had abated Noah removed the covering of the ark, and God told him and his family to leave the ark and go forth on dry ground. After leaving the ark, Noah built an alter and offered up a sacrifice to God. Genesis 8:21 (KJV) says, "And the Lord smelled a sweet savour; and the Lord said in his heart, I will not again curse the ground any more for man's sake." It spoke of a new beginning, a fresh start. The air was clear, and the sacrifices made were a sweet aroma to God.

As his bride, you are the fair one in God's eyes. He is calling you to come away with him to the secret place. He desires to be with you, to see you, to enjoy you. Come away with him to the secret place of the Most High. Come away with him to the cleft of the rock where you will be overshadowed and protected, and all his goodness will pass before you. Come away with him where you will experience the riches of heaven, and there you will mature and produce much fruit. There in the cleft of the rock you will find the secret place of the stairs. Just like Jacob saw a ladder descending from heaven, our bridegroom is the portal. He is the door to all new things and the fruit to be enjoyed. The lingering times will be worth the wait.

Jesus is your passage of ascension to produce winter figs. While the steps are steep, and the journey requires endurance and the hardships of the winter months, the fruit is the best of the best, and the aroma of the fruit is soothing to God.

Jesus is also your door and stairway to the heavenly realms. In Revelation 3:20-21 (NKJV), Jesus said, "Behold, I stand at the door and knock. If anyone hears My voice and opens the door, I will come in to him and dine with him, and he with Me. To him who overcomes I will grant to sit with Me on My throne, as I also overcame and sat down with My Father on His throne." May I share with you that you do not have to wait until eternity to enter the throne room of God. Ephesians 2:6 (NIV) says, "And God raised us up with Christ and seated us with him in the heavenly realms in Christ Jesus."

God's message is clear. He wants you to be like the winter fig. He does not want you to mature before your time. There are higher heights and deeper depths in your relationship with God. A new season is coming. Springtime is on the way. The tender grapes are emitting a sweet-smelling aroma and the aroma is irresistible. Psalm 34:8 (KJV) says, "O taste and see that the Lord is good: blessed is the man that trusteth in him."

Reflections of Who I AM

1. Who are the two main characters in the Song of Solomon, and who do they depict?
2. What does the lattice in the Song of Solomon represent?
3. What are the secret stairs in the cleft of the rock?
4. What did the early figs or *paggim* represent?
5. What do the winter figs or *pag* represent?
6. Jesus said, "I AM the door" (John 10:7 NKJV). How can the information discussed in this Chapter help you apply the fullness of that truth in your daily life?

Prayer of Activation

Our Father in heaven, I come to you with a hungry heart for more. I want more of you. I hear you calling me away to be with you. I know that you long to be with me and my heart longs to be with you. I have purposed in my heart that I will dwell in the secret place of the stairs. Jesus is my door and portal to the heavenly realms. Seated with Christ in the heavenly realms, I will grow and mature into his image. I will endure the seasons of life. I will be patient as you cause my fruit to mature in its appointed season. I ask that you let my life be a sweet-smelling aroma to you. I will not grow weary in well doing. Instead, I sense a new season and I will wait for the full maturity of the fruit you are growing in my life. I can do all things through you, and the fruit you cause to grow in my life will be an abundant harvest and the best of the best. Together, we will leap for joy over every obstacle and all glory and honor I give to you in the name of Jesus. Amen!

CHAPTER 22

Freedom is a Big Idea

"Therefore if the Son makes you free, you shall be free indeed" (John 8:36 NKJV).

If you are truly going to live life as a revealed son or daughter of God in his fullness, then you must understand what it means to live in freedom. God's idea of freedom is really big and goes beyond what most of us can imagine. To grasp this idea, I want to challenge your mindset to think outside the box of traditional reasoning. When God developed his plan of salvation, it was not only to redeem you from something, but more importantly, it was to redeem you FOR something? The moment you realize God has redeemed you FOR his kingdom, your concept of salvation will begin to change, and you will come to understand freedom is a BIG IDEA!

To set the stage for this conversation, let's reflect back on our discussions about creation. In Genesis 1:2-3 (KJV) the Bible says, "And the earth was without form, and void; and darkness was upon the face of the deep. And the Spirit of God moved upon the face of the waters. And God said, Let there be light." As previously discussed, this passage describes the aftermath of the fall of Lucifer and the angels that conspired with him when they decided to rebel against God. The results of this fall were chaos and destruction, darkness and evil. In response, God said, let there be light. From that moment, God has been bringing light into dark places and restoring freedom to humanity and creation. Full restoration cannot take place devoid of freedom.

In Luke 4:18 (KJV) Jesus said, "The Spirit of the Lord is upon me, because he hath anointed me to preach the gospel to the poor; he hath sent me to heal the brokenhearted, to preach deliverance to the captives, and recovering of sight to the blind, to **set at liberty** them that are bruised." The heart cry of those enslaved is freedom. God wants you to walk in complete freedom because without liberty and freedom, it is extremely difficult to view yourself as an image bearer of God. Based on this truth and the good news of the gospel, we can conclude freedom is a possibility within our reach.

Hindrances of Freedom

To gain a proper understanding of freedom, we must first think about the hinderances to the liberty we seek. Let's discuss a few of the major hinderances:

Cares of Life - Each of us come face to face with the cares of life, and they can greatly impact our level of freedom. They include the stress, worry, and fear we encounter when we face daily challenges. For example, parents may worry about their children, their health, their friends, and grades in school. Sometimes we worry about our parents as they begin to age, or a loved one that is sick. Sometimes we worry about our finances or the loss of a job. You may become stressed when you hear instances of abuse, terrorism, or observe a generation focused only on themselves. The cares of life can consume our thinking and the way we live.

Addictions - Do you or someone you know struggle with addictions? The sin that began small can envelop a person's life and captivate their every thought. Many try hard over and over again only to find themselves failing once again. Willpower alone will never be enough. With each failing comes the guilt and shame from letting yourself and others down. It is crippling. It will hinder your walk with God and the fulfillment of his plans for your life. Addictions can become so strong;

many have succumbed to the belief that the best they can hope for is to keep their failings to a manageable level. Many do not believe they can ever be free. Addictions are the devil's playground and barriers to liberty.

Generational Sins - The ravages of addictions and sin in some instances are passed down from one generation to the next. They show up as behavioral patterns that repeat themselves in successive generations. As a result, discussions often center around who is to blame. Is it our fault, our parents, or are we a victim? Generational sins or curses need to be broken before freedom can come. They do not have to become a way of life, and we do not have to repeat the sins of our parents or forefathers.

Financial Debt - Financial struggles can be devastating. Couples who argue over finances have a greater probability of divorce. Finances can be some of the hardest areas for couples to talk about, even harder than religion, politics, or death. It is a problem that has engulfed our society and governments. Many have turned to bankruptcy, which then passes the loss to the creditor, which in turn passes those losses to consumers. It's a spiraling disease that cripples the person and our society. The seeds of poor behavior, walking in no restraint, and failed economic policies have led to a bondage of debt. Our nation is past swimming in debt and is now drowning in it. It is a national catastrophe.

Unrealistic Obligations - Unrealistic or unobtainable obligations can lead you to excessive stress and difficulties. Have you made promises you can't keep? Is your schedule so busy you do not have enough time for your spouse, your children, yourself, not to mention time for God? More and more our society has become bound to calendars and schedules as a lifestyle. Is it wrong to be busy or make commitments? No, unless it has become a source of bondage that robs you of your freedom and your inability to function.

Moral Decay of Society - As behaviors of communities have continued to decline, we find our society in moral decay. Nations and people have turned from God and no longer have the proper guidance to lead them through the maze of life. Without a compass, many people sail through life not knowing which way to turn. Without the foundational principles of God's word, many rely upon their intellect or luck. Some people live from their soul rather than from their spirit. After some time, lifestyles of empty hearts and empty lives catches up with society, and it becomes difficult to distinguish disfunction from what should be normal.

As we consider these hinderances, it becomes confusing when we consider what the Bible says on one hand and the reality of life on the other. For too many, the reality of freedom becomes fuzzy when faced with everyday life. Therefore, I want to ask you a difficult question. Has your theology about freedom been developed by your life experiences, or do you question your experiences against what God says? I'm afraid that many go through the struggles of life not giving much thought to freedom, or viewing it as a life goal that can never actually be achieved.

God wants to challenge your theology on freedom. The good news is these hinderances can be overcome, and you can live a life totally and literally free. I believe God is calling us to a life of freedom like we have never experienced before. This kind of freedom is so radical, it has the potential to revolutionize the world and give birth to a great awakening.

With that in mind, I want to challenge you to begin a quest for freedom. Since God's concept of freedom is really big, I suspect most of us will not grasp it all at once. But as you begin this journey, you will catch glimpses of the truth. Little by little, you will see what it looks like and will begin to grasp the greatness of what freedom offers. With that in mind, I want us to discuss 5 concepts of Freedom:

Concept No 1 - If Jesus sets you free, you will be free indeed

John 8:36 (KJV) says, "If the Son therefore shall make you free, ye shall be free indeed." The word "free" in the Greek is *eleutheros*[130] and it means "set at liberty," "to liberate from bondage." The root of the word means "free, exempt, unrestrained, not bound by an obligation," "so that one may now do what was formerly forbidden." Do you know anyone who lives in this degree of freedom? I told you freedom was a big idea.

Are you free from restraint? In its strictest form, it means to be in chains or held down. It can also mean that you have a desire to go somewhere or do something, but you are being kept from that activity by someone or something. While it can be the picture of chains or handcuffs, it can also be the picture of boundaries or methods. When someone is free of restraint, they are boundless. They can walk and move around freely and employ multiple methods and means to accomplish their intended will. Did you know that God is not restrained by anything other than this own word? God can and does move in many ways to accomplish his will, and with him there is always liberty and freedom from constraint.

Are you free from sin? True freedom does not mean you are free to live and act in a sinful manner. God hates sin because of the devastating impact it has on your life. Behaviors that are sinful will always lead to a loss of liberty. God's idea of freedom is for you to pursue life with the liberty and freedom of how to live without the restraints of sin.

Are you free from the law? This does not mean the law no longer applies to you. It does and always will. It is God's perfect will. In fact, true freedom only comes when you are not guilty of breaking the law. When you are walking in compliance with the law, you are free from the consequences of disobeying it. It is liberating, refreshing, and clean. It is light and not heavy. It is living with a clean and clear conscious. Freedom allows you to walk upright in God's law without the fear of failure. If you should fail, you can receive forgiveness through Christ. He paid the price for our sins and declared us free with our debt paid in full.

Other than Jesus, has the world ever seen a man or a woman walk in total freedom? I suspect most of us live in partial freedom. Your first major challenge is to accept the possibility that you can live a life of freedom since the Bible says Jesus can and will set you free. Before we go further, I think it important to clarify that living a life in freedom does not mean you will not encounter hinderances or obstacles. You definitely will. The good news is that God will give you victory through them all.

God is always careful about the words he uses. When God says something in his word, he means it. Hidden in his words are the keys and secrets of the kingdom. When he said free, he meant free. It was not an allegory, an illusion, or a goal to strive to achieve. It was a promise given that can be received and walked in. John 8:36 (KJV) said, "If the Son therefore shall make you free, ye shall be free indeed. What does it mean to be free indeed? The word "indeed" is the Greek word *ontos*[131] and it means "truly, in reality, in point of fact." In other words, God makes it clear that freedom is not a metaphor. He is not talking about approaching freedom or having freedom as a goal. He means truly, in reality, in point of fact free. FREE INDEED!

This is mind boggling. If we accept the possibility of living life in true freedom; where we are truly, in reality, in point of fact free indeed, then the concept of FREEDOM is a really big idea. And, if this is true, how could something this big have escaped us for so long? My life experience tells me that life doesn't even come close to resembling this kind of freedom, yet we know that God does not lie.

Why do we fall short of our potential? I believe the answer to this question comes down to two words: Lies and Fear. Let's ask ourselves, what is a lie? A lie is a false statement made with the intent to deceive, an intentional untruth, a falsehood. A lie desires to create a false or misleading impression. A key to understanding this concept begins with identifying the source of all lies. John 8:44 (NIV) says, "You belong to your father, the devil, and you want to carry out your father's desires. He was a murderer from the beginning, not holding to the truth, for there is no truth in him. When he lies, he speaks his native language, for he is a liar and the father of lies."

The father and author of all lies is the devil. Whether it is the kingdom of darkness speaking to your soul or the enemy using another human being or circumstances to speak to you, Satan never tells the truth. We can always judge the truth by what God says in his word and what the Holy Spirit is speaking to us. Another indicator is the presence of fear. II Timothy 1:7 (NIV) says, "God has not given us a spirit of fear, but of power and of love and of a sound mind." The presence of fear is always a good indicator the enemy is lying to us about our circumstance.

Concept No 2 - Truth Breaks the Power of the Lie

John 8:32 (NKJV) says, "You shall know the truth, and the truth shall make you free." The first step toward walking in the fullness of freedom begins with truth. Why does knowing the truth make you free? The answer is simple, it breaks the power and grip of the deception. Once exposed, it has no more power over you. Think about this, a lie believed produces fruit, and that fruit is fear and doubt. It brings you to a place of being afraid. When you entertain the thoughts of "what if," the fruit is fear. When you entertain the thoughts of "maybe this isn't true," the fruit is doubt.

Once you know the truth about a lie, the guessing games are over, and fear and doubt have no more power. Let me give you an example. A person goes to the doctor and their preliminary exam points to cancer. When they entertain the thoughts of "what if," fear and doubt set in, and their world is turned upside down. Once the same person goes back for more extensive tests that come back negative, the fear and doubt leaves. The follow-up tests reveal the truth and there is no more reason to fear or doubt. They are free of the lie.

Hebrews 11:1 (KJV) says, "Now faith is the substance of things hoped for, the evidence of things not seen." Why is this scripture true? It is true because Romans 10:17 (NKJV) says, "So then faith comes by hearing, and hearing by the word of God." Faith comes from the word of God, and the word is truth. Truth heard, received, and accepted as truth will not receive a lie that would contradict it. Why? Because if anything is spoken to the contrary, you know it is not true. The truth of good news wipes out all fear. It tears down the walls of hopelessness and restores hope, faith, and liberty. It sets you free. It's that simple.

Concept No 3 - You are Right Now Free

Let's dig a little deeper and talk about the unpleasant things in life. Let's discuss the person that is dealing with a confirmed sickness, disease, or addiction. Let's discuss the person that just lost their job, and their bank account is empty. How can that person live in freedom in those circumstances? It's easy to be free of a lie once you know the truth, but what if the reality of something bad confronts you head on?

This brings us to concept No. 3. What if God's word is not lying? What if you can be free indeed? If you think Freedom is a big idea, wait until you hear this. What if the truth is that right now YOU ARE FREE? I don't mean a metaphorical freedom but a real point in fact freedom. You are probably thinking how is this possible since I don't feel or act free, and the reality of my circumstance has been confirmed?

Earlier, we defined a lie as a false statement made with the intent to deceive; an intentional untruth; a falsehood. What if your bank account really is empty, you really do struggle with an addiction, and the doctor has confirmed a sickness, how can you be free under those circumstances? Consider this, what if there is a different kind of lie, one that is different than we traditionally think about? What if it is possible to live a lie? This can be manifested in two different ways. The first is a circumstance where you are deceived, and you live your life based on an untruth. The circumstances you face are in fact true; however, they are caused by living a life based on a lie. You are not intentionally lying. Instead, the deception has altered your life and you are living out the lie. The second way this can be manifested is when the circumstance itself is contradictory to what God says. For example, the test results came back positive, and you have been confirmed to have a disease or sickness. If God's word is the truth and your circumstance is contrary to that truth, then the circumstance you are experiencing is challenging the validity of God's word. In these instances, our circumstances and conditions are not aligned with what God says, which makes them a lie. Think about it this way. There is a difference between what is true and what is THE TRUTH. Remember, freedom is a BIG IDEA and God wants you to know it. The truth is that through Jesus Christ, you are Free RIGHT NOW. Not in the future free. Not free one day. Not free if all the circumstances change. But right now you are free. You may not know it, your body may not know it, your bank account may not know it, but it doesn't mean it isn't true. A lie can seem very real but not based on truth. What you live, accept, act out, and experience are all real. It's just that they may not be based on what is true. What if the lie is your circumstances, and the truth is what God's word says? For example:

- What if the lie being lived is the sickness that has trespassed and attached itself to your body, but the truth is Isiah 53:5 (KJV), "with his stripes we are healed?"
- What if the lie being lived is the bondage to sin and addictions, but the truth is Romans 6:14 (KJV), "For sin shall not have dominion over you?"

- What if the lie being lived is my child may never accept Christ, but the truth is Acts 16:31 (NKJV), "Believe in the Lord Jesus, and you will be saved, you and your household?"
- What if the lie being lived is I can never get out of financial debt, but the truth is Deuteronomy 8:18 (NIV), "But remember the Lord your God, for it is he who gives you the ability to produce wealth, and so confirms his covenant?"
- What if the lie is, how can God love me, but the truth is Zephaniah 3:17 (NIV), "The LORD your God is with you, the Mighty Warrior who saves? He will take great delight in you; in his love he will no longer rebuke you, but will rejoice over you with singing?" Rejoice means he dances over you.

In each of these circumstances, there is a greater truth than the reality of what we are facing. You may not have your answer today, but God is not slack concerning his promises, and faith is the substance of the things we hope for.

Concept No 4 - Truth is Not Bound by Time or Circumstances

The fourth concept is truth is not bound by time or circumstances. God told Abraham that he and Sara would have a child, but it wasn't until he was one hundred years old that Isaac was born. The promise was true the first day it was spoken. There are 100s of Bible prophecies that have come to pass that were spoken many years before they happened. Why, because God's word is truth.

God stands outside the dimensions of time and space. He sees the ending from the beginning, and what he says is truth. Jesus said heaven and earth will pass away, but my words will never pass away. God's word is eternally true regardless of the circumstances. This is why you can proclaim the truth of what God said, even if your circumstances are different. You aren't lying to yourself or others, you are proclaiming a truth that God is going to bring into realization. Knowing this truth exposes the lie, breaks its power, and sets you free to live at rest and peace until your answer comes.

Concept No 5 - Freedom is Given, Received, and Maintained through the Holy Spirit

This brings us to the final concept, freedom is given, received, and maintained through the Holy Spirit. Jesus is your door to freedom, and you cannot receive and walk in this truth on your own, it takes the power of God. II Corinthians Chapter 3:17-18 (KJV) says, "Now the Lord is that Spirit: and where the Spirit of the Lord is, there is liberty. But we all, with open face beholding as in a glass the glory of the Lord, are changed into the same image from glory to glory, even as by the Spirit of the Lord."

When God's spirit is present, there is FREEDOM. You are free because God's word says you are. Period, end of story. Walking in the Spirit allows you to live in the conduit of God's presence, all his promises, and to hear and receive truth. When you live and pray in the spirit, your ears are open to hear heaven. The Holy Spirit is your source of power to overcome every obstacle and live a life of freedom.

When you KNOW the TRUTH, and LIVE in the SPIRIT, you WILL walk in ABSOLUTE LIBERTY and FREEDOM, and it will absolutely revolutionize your life and the world.

Reflections of Who I AM

1. Why is Freedom such a BIG IDEA?
2. What does it mean to be free indeed?
3. How does the truth set us free?
4. What are some of the ways we can live a lie?
5. If your circumstances are true but they contradict what God says, how can you gain freedom in those conditions?
6. Jesus said, "I AM the door" (John 10:7 NKJV). How can the information discussed in this Chapter help you apply the fullness of that truth in your daily life?

Prayer of Activation

Our Father in heaven, I thank you that through Jesus, I am free indeed. I thank you that your word is true no matter what my circumstances indicate. I thank you that your truth is not bound by time or the details of what I am encountering. Right now, I submit my entire life to you, and I step through the door that Jesus opened for me. Father, I speak to the circumstance(s) of (fill in the blank) in my life and declare that God's word is the truth, and it breaks the power of the lie. Your word says (select the scripture that speaks to your need), and this breaks the power of the lies of the enemy. I declare that my circumstances must align with God's word, and I receive freedom through the power of the Holy Spirit and the door opened up for me by Jesus. All honor and glory I give to you in the name of Jesus. Amen!

SECTION VII

I AM the Resurrection and the Life

"Jesus said to her, "I am the resurrection and the life. He who believes in Me, though he may die, he shall live" (John 11:25 NKJV).

In the first I AM statement of Jesus; he is the bread of life and creator of all things. Out of nothing he created everything. Lucifer and the kingdom of darkness thought they had destroyed the plan of God. In the last I AM statement of Jesus; he reveals that he is the resurrection and the life. Jesus brought to life what the enemy thought he destroyed. The Greek word for "resurrection" is *anastasis*[132] and it means "raised to life again," to "rise from the dead."

In this last section, we will complete the story of us and God's plan for the restoration of all things. Let there be no doubt in the minds of those who are looking at the battles they face in life or the chaos and evil they see in the world. The end of our story has already been decided, and our future is exciting. The kingdom of God is at hand, and the final days of our story will prove to be victorious and filled with adventure. Only God knows what is beyond, but we are given an amazing promise in I Corinthians 2:9 (NKJV), "Eye has not seen, nor ear heard, Nor have entered into the heart of man The things which God has prepared for those who love Him."

Take courage and be of good cheer, the best is yet to come.

THE NEW BEGINNING

CHAPTER 23

The Restoration of All things, Joint Heirs with Christ

> "whom heaven must receive until the period of restoration of all things about which God spoke by the mouth of His holy prophets from ancient time" (Acts 3:21 NKJV).

Every story has an ending except ours. The good news of the gospel is that we are promised a new beginning. For those who have accepted Jesus Christ as Lord and savior, congratulations, your future is secure and filled with anticipation. If you have not, I encourage you to become a follower of the one who offers you eternal and abundant life.

Jesus said in Matthew 24:14 (NKJV), "And this gospel of the kingdom will be preached in all the world as a witness to all the nations, and then the end will come." For a lot of people, this is scary; however, I want to encourage you to not be afraid that everything will cease to exist. This is not the case. The Bible declares plainly that the world and the kingdom of God will never come to an end. As Ephesians 3:21 (NKJV) says, "Unto him be glory in the church by Christ Jesus throughout all ages, world without end. Amen."

As we close out this book, I want us to look at four final topics: the end of this present age, the final judgment, the restoration of all things, and God's children becoming heirs and joint heirs with Christ.

The End of this Present Age

I truly believe God has saved the best for last. As we continue in the last days, we will see a glorious church without spot or blemish coming into its own. The followers of Christ are awakening to the truth of who they are and God's plans for his kingdom. We are entering a time where the routine and common are about to change. The new normal will be defined by God as he presents to the world his sons and daughters walking in the fullness of their design. I believe we will see the darkness continue to grow darker while the light will get brighter. Perhaps it is this contrast that will cause more people to seek Jesus as the church begins to do the works of Christ and greater.

What do you imagine walking in the fullness of I AM will look like in these last days? At times it will be filled with supernatural encounters and the power of God. At other times, it may look different than you expect. Jesus was walking in the fullness of I AM when he bore our punishment and went to the cross. As the enemy throws everything he has at you, it may feel like you are on the battlefield for your life. The good news is God will prepare a table for you in the middle of your battlefield. While there may be casualties all around and others are giving up in exhaustion, there is a tent of refreshing set for you in in the middle of the battle. You can step into this tent and find nourishment, rest, and peace as the Captain of the Host (Jesus) comes to your aid and rescue. As Psalm 23:4-5 (NKJV) says, "Yea, though I walk through the valley of the shadow of death, I will fear no evil; For You are with me; Your rod and Your staff, they comfort me. You prepare a table before me in the presence of my enemies; You anoint my head with oil; My cup runs over."

These last days are sure to be exciting, adventurous, and maybe a little scary; but they will be filled with victory, joy, and peace like you have never experienced. Allow the fullness of I AM to prepare you for what is ahead. Be strengthened with the power of his might, and walk in his presence, anointing, and the wake of his glory. You can do all things through Christ who will strengthen you (Philippians 4:13 NKJV).

We are not sure how long this period of time will last, but it will be characterized by a great harvest of souls and a time of the greater glory outpouring on believers. These times will continue until the restrainer is removed. Paul writes about the coming of the Lord in II Thessalonians 2:7-8 (NKJV), "For the mystery of lawlessness is already at work; only He who now restrains will do so until He is taken out of the way. And then the lawless one will be revealed, whom the Lord will consume with the breath of His mouth and destroy with the brightness of His coming." The church is the restrainer, and her influence will continue until the rapture. While some believe in a mid or post tribulation rapture, I am convinced it will take place prior to the tribulation period.

Paul describes the event in I Thessalonians 4:16-17 (NKJV), "For the Lord Himself will descend from heaven with a shout, with the voice of an archangel, and with the trumpet of God. And the dead in Christ will rise first. Then we who are alive and remain shall be caught up together with them in the clouds to meet the Lord in the air. And thus we shall always be with the Lord." This is the last shofar to be blown, and this is the event the Bible refers to as the resurrection of the just (Luke 14:14). At this time, the followers of God who have already passed away will be resurrected first, then those who are alive at his appearing will be transformed, and together we will be caught away with Christ into heaven in our new glorified bodies. Paul described our new bodies in I Corinthians 15:53-55 (KJV):

> "For this corruptible must put on incorruption, and this mortal must put on immortality. So, when this corruptible shall have put on incorruption, and this mortal shall have put on immortality, then shall be brought to pass the saying that is written, Death is swallowed up in victory. O death, where is thy sting? O grave, where is thy victory?"

Can you imagine the resurrection? One day, we are going to be like Jesus (I John 3:2). All over the world dead bodies will be transformed, glorified, and brought back to life as they are reunited with their soul and spirit. Your new body will be free from all flaws. People who have had near death experiences say in heaven everyone appears to be in their early thirty's. They are young, alive, and look really good. This will happen because the same spirit that raised Jesus from the dead dwells in you and will also resurrect your body (Romans 8:11).

Can you imagine the impact this will have upon the earth when millions of believers are suddenly gone? The world will be thrown into chaos as the antichrist and his kingdom take advantage of the absence of the church's influence on world affairs. The world will be hurled into a 7-year period of tribulation, and God will judge the kingdoms of this world.

While the world is experiencing a great tribulation, the raptured Saints of God will be enjoying the marriage supper of the lamb described in Revelation 19:6-9. During this time, we will receive our rewards and crowns for our service to God. This will be our judgment. At the conclusion of this 7-year period, Christ and the church will return to execute judgment.

Revelation 20:1-2 (KJV) says, "And I saw an angel come down from heaven, having the key of the bottomless pit and a great chain in his hand. And he laid hold on the dragon, that old serpent, which is the Devil, and Satan, and bound him a thousand years." With the binding of Satan, Jesus will set up his government and will reign over the earth with the saints of God for 1,000 years. Those that came through the tribulation and did not submit to the mark of the beast will continue to live their lives, have children, and enjoy life.

At the conclusion of the millennial reign, Satan will be loosed for a season to deceive the nations once again. He will gather together the armies of the earth for one final battle against the Saints of God. The battle will take place at the temple mount area of Jerusalem and the armies will gather against God's people and the beloved city. God will send down fire from heaven to devour them and afterwards, Revelation 20:10 (KJV) says, "And the devil that deceived them was cast into the lake of fire and brimstone, where the beast and the false prophet are, and shall be tormented day and night for ever and ever."

The Final Judgment

After Satan's judgment, the Bible describes the Great White Throne Judgment (Revelation 20:11-15). Everyone appearing before this final judgment will be judged for not following Christ. The followers of God will have already received their rewards/judgment during the marriage supper of the lamb. The Bible says the books will be opened along with the Book of life. The books in heaven containing the design and plans for each person will be opened and they will be judged based on their books and the fact that they did not become followers of God. Then the Book of Life will be opened to confirm their names have been erased.

Death and hell along with all those not found written in the Book of Life will be cast into the lake of fire for eternity. Revelation 20:14 calls this the second death, eternal separation from God. This is a place that was originally prepared for Satan and his angels, but all those not following God will spend eternity in this horrible place. If you have not already done so, I urge you to accept Christ as your savior and Lord.

The Restoration of All Things

As our story concludes, this present age will end, and a new age will begin. This will be the time spoken of in Acts 3:21. God will restore all things to his original design and plan.

One of the things that will be restored is the singularity of heaven. After the rebellion of Satan and the birth of darkness, God created the firmament to divide the heavens and separate the darkness from the light. In the final restoration, Isaiah 34:4 (KJV) says, "And all the host of heaven shall be dissolved, and the heavens shall be rolled together as a scroll." The firmament of the second heaven will be rolled back like a scroll and the singularity of heaven will be restored. Revelation 6:16 tells us those witnessing God's final judgment will be in fear because they can look into heaven and see God setting upon his throne.

In addition to the restoration of heaven, the earth will be made new. Revelation 21 tells us there will be a new heaven and a new earth. The earth will be refashioned and made new much like it was during the six days of creation recorded in the beginning of our story. The New Jerusalem will come down from heaven and become the center of the kingdom. From the beginning of creation, God planned a kingdom, a family, and a throne. Jesus as the Son of God and Son of Man will set upon this throne in the New Jerusalem. Revelation 21:5-6 (NKJV) says,

"Then He who sat on the throne said, Behold, I make all things new. And He said to me, Write, for these words are true and faithful. And He said to me, It is done! I am the Alpha and the Omega, the Beginning and the End."

In this new earth, Eden will be restored. At the center of the New Jerusalem will be the throne of God, the river of life, and the tree of life. The tree of the knowledge of good and evil will not be in the restored Eden, every curse will be gone, and the kingdom will be restored. It is recorded for us in Revelation 22:1-5 (NKJV):

> "And he showed me a pure river of water of life, clear as crystal, proceeding from the throne of God and of the Lamb. In the middle of its street, and on either side of the river, was the tree of life, which bore twelve fruits, each tree yielding its fruit every month. The leaves of the tree were for the healing of the nations. And there shall be no more curse, but the throne of God and of the Lamb shall be in it, and His servants shall serve Him. They shall see His face, and His name shall be on their foreheads. There shall be no night there: They need no lamp nor light of the sun, for the Lord God gives them light. And they shall reign forever and ever."

Heirs and Joint Heirs with Christ

Forever and ever is hard for us to comprehend. While we may not know exactly what will be included in eternity, we are given some clues. Jesus said in Matthew 25:34 (NKJV), "Then the King will say to those on His right hand, 'Come, you blessed of My Father, inherit the kingdom prepared for you from the foundation of the world." I want you to notice the word inherit. As the natural children of God, we have an inheritance. It was prepared for us from the ancient of days before the creation of earth. But it is more than you have ever imagined. If you want more, just wait, you haven't seen nothing yet. Let's catch a glimpse of what is in store for our inheritance.

Joint heirs with Jesus – Romans 8:17 (KJV) says we are, "joint-heirs with Christ." Do you know what that means? It means everything Jesus inherits, you do too. For those of you that want it all, God has a future for you. Hebrews 1:2 (NKJV) says God has spoken to us in these last days through his son Jesus, "whom He has appointed heir of all things, through whom also He made the worlds." There won't be any desire to argue over the last will and testament, we inherit everything with Jesus. By the way, this inheritance is incorruptible, eternal, and will never fade away (I Peter 1:3-4 - NKJV).

Celebrated with Jesus Forever – Romans 8:17 (NKJV) says, "and if children, then heirs—heirs of God and joint heirs with Christ, if indeed we suffer with Him, that we may also be glorified together." The phrase "glorified together" is the Greek word *syndoxazo*[133] and it means "to approve together." The root of the word means "to praise, extol, magnify, celebrate," "clothe with splendor," to "hold in honor," and "to make renowned." Of course, we can all imagine honoring Jesus, but did you know that you will be honored and clothed in splendor with him. Your renown will be celebrated throughout eternity.

A New Name – Revelation 2:17 (NKJV) says, "To him who overcomes I will give some of the hidden manna to eat. And I will give him a white stone, and on the stone a new name written which no one knows except him who receives it." Your new name will be uniquely yours. It will describe the essence of who you are, your identity, and everything the Father feels about you.

The Earth – Matthew 5:5 (KJV), "Blessed are the meek: for they shall inherit the earth." This is the real estate deal of a lifetime. Just imagine inheriting the earth and living in a mansion or multiple mansions. Each of your mansions will be uniquely designed just for you. You will host others as you fellowship with the saints throughout eternity.

Listing of Inheritance – In addition to the inheritance noted above, here is a listing of other things we will inherit and encounter in eternity:

- Eternal Life (Matthew 19:29).
- Access to the tree of life (Revelation 2:7).
- Crown of life (Revelation 2:10).
- Clothed in white garments, your name confessed to the Father (Revelation 3:5).

- Jesus will write upon you the name of God, the name of the New Jerusalem, and Jesus' own new name (Revelation 3:12).
- You will set with Jesus upon his throne (Revelation 3:21).
- The nations (Psalm 2:8).

Conclusion

The Book of Enoch 62:15-16 says, "And the righteous and elect shall have risen from the earth, And ceased to be of downcast countenance. And they shall have been clothed with garments of glory, And these shall be the garments of life from the Lord of Spirits: And your garments shall not grow old, Nor your glory pass away before the Lord of Spirits."[134] In eternity, you will be clothed in light and the glory of God just as Adam was in the garden. Because of Jesus, we have a blessed hope of a new beginning unlike anything we can imagine.

As we conclude our discussions, I want to remind you of the words of God to Moses during his encounter with God at the burning bush. Exodus 3:14 (KJV) says, "And God said unto Moses, I Am That I Am: and he said, Thus shalt thou say unto the children of Israel, I Am hath sent me unto you." I leave you with one final invitation. I invite you to begin to *Walk in the Fullness of I AM* and join me and the Apostle Paul as he declared in I Corinthians 15:10 (KJV), "But by the grace of God I am what I am."

Reflections of Who I AM

1. What must happen before the end will come?
2. What is the rapture?
3. Describe the resurrection?
4. How is the judgment of the believer different from the Great White Throne Judgment?
5. What does it mean to be an heir and joint heir with Christ?
6. Jesus said, "I AM the resurrection and the life" (John 11:25 NKJV). How can the information discussed in this Chapter help you apply the fullness of that truth in your daily life?

Prayer of Activation

Our Father in heaven, I thank you for sending your son, Jesus. Because he is the resurrection and the life, and because I have accepted Christ as my Lord and Savior, I have eternal life. I choose from this day forward to *Walk in the Fullness of I AM*. Lead me and guide me in all I do. Give me boldness and favor to declare this good news of the kingdom to those around me. I am excited about my future in this life and the one to come. All honor and glory I give to you in the name of Jesus. Amen!

END NOTES

1 "G3339 - metamorphoō - Strong's Greek Lexicon. https://www.blueletterbible.org/lexicon/g3339/kjv/tr/0-1/.

2 "G4138 - plērōma - Strong's Greek Lexicon (kjv)." Blue Letter Bible. https://www.blueletterbible.org/lexicon/g4138/kjv/tr/0-1/.

3 "G740 - artos - Strong's Greek Lexicon (kjv)." Blue Letter Bible. https://www.blueletterbible.org/lexicon/g740/kjv/tr/0-1/.

4 "G2222 - zōē - Strong's Greek Lexicon (kjv)." Blue Letter Bible. https://www.blueletterbible.org/lexicon/g2222/kjv/tr/0-1/.

5 "H430 - 'ĕlōhîm - Strong's Hebrew Lexicon (kjv)." Blue Letter Bible. https://www.blueletterbible.org/lexicon/h430/kjv/wlc/0-1/.

6 "H3068 - Yᵊhōvâ - Strong's Hebrew Lexicon (kjv)." Blue Letter Bible. https://www.blueletterbible.org/lexicon/h3068/kjv/wlc/0-1/.

7 "H1254 - bārā' - Strong's Hebrew Lexicon (kjv)." Blue Letter Bible. https://www.blueletterbible.org/lexicon/h1254/kjv/wlc/0-1/.

8 "Ex nihilo." *Merriam-Webster.com Dictionary*, Merriam-Webster. https://www.merriam-webster.com/dictionary/ex%20nihilo.

9 "H7225 - rē'šîṯ - Strong's Hebrew Lexicon (kjv)." Blue Letter Bible. https://www.blueletterbible.org/lexicon/h7225/kjv/wlc/0-1/.

10 "H7218 - rō'š - Strong's Hebrew Lexicon (kjv)." Blue Letter Bible. https://www.blueletterbible.org/lexicon/h7218/kjv/wlc/0-1/.

11 "G165 - aiōn - Strong's Greek Lexicon (kjv)." Blue Letter Bible. https://www.blueletterbible.org/lexicon/g165/kjv/tr/0-1/.

12 Caryle Murphy, "Most Americans believe in heaven and hell." Pew Research Center, 10 November, 2015, https://www.pewresearch.org/fact-tank/2015/mm/10/most-americans-believe-in-heaven-and-hell/.

13 "H8064 - šāmayim - Strong's Hebrew Lexicon (kjv)." Blue Letter Bible. https://www.blueletterbible.org/lexicon/h8064/kjv/wlc/0-1/.

14 "H4325 - mayim - Strong's Hebrew Lexicon (kjv)." Blue Letter Bible. https://www.blueletterbible.org/lexicon/h4325/kjv/wlc/0-1/.

15 "H7549 - rāqîaʿ - Strong's Hebrew Lexicon (kjv)." Blue Letter Bible. https://www.blueletterbible.org/lexicon/h7549/kjv/wlc/0-1/

16 "G2537 - kainos - Strong's Greek Lexicon (kjv)." Blue Letter Bible. https://www.blueletterbible.org/lexicon/g2537/kjv/tr/0-1/.

17 "H4397 - mal'āḵ - Strong's Hebrew Lexicon (kjv)." Blue Letter Bible. https://www.blueletterbible.org/lexicon/h4397/kjv/wlc/0-1/.

18 R. H. Charles, The Apocrypha and Pseudepigrapha of the Old Testament, ed. Joshua Williams Northwest Nazarene College, 1995, https://www.ccel.org/c/charles/otpseudepig/enoch/ENOCH_1.HTM.

19 "H5712 - ʿēḏâ - Strong's Hebrew Lexicon (kjv)." Blue Letter Bible. https://www.blueletterbible.org/lexicon/h5712/kjv/wlc/0-1/.

20 "H1966 - hêlēl - Strong's Hebrew Lexicon (kjv)." Blue Letter Bible. https://www.blueletterbible.org/lexicon/h1966/kjv/wlc/0-1/.

21 "H4473 - mimšaḥ - Strong's Hebrew Lexicon (kjv)." Blue Letter Bible. https://www.blueletterbible.org/lexicon/h4473/kjv/wlc/0-1/.

22 "H5345 - neqeḇ - Strong's Hebrew Lexicon (kjv)." Blue Letter Bible. https://www.blueletterbible.org/lexicon/h5345/kjv/wlc/0-1/.

23 "H4540 - mᵊsukâ - Strong's Hebrew Lexicon (kjv)." Blue Letter Bible. https://www.blueletterbible.org/lexicon/h4540/kjv/wlc/0-1/.

24 "H7617 - šāḇâ - Strong's Hebrew Lexicon (kjv)." Blue Letter Bible. https://www.blueletterbible.org/lexicon/h7617/kjv/wlc/0-1/.

25 "H7632 - šāḇîḇ - Strong's Hebrew Lexicon (kjv)." Blue Letter Bible. https://www.blueletterbible.org/lexicon/h7632/kjv/wlc/0-1/.

26 "H3958 - lešem - Strong's Hebrew Lexicon (kjv)." Blue Letter Bible. https://www.blueletterbible.org/lexicon/h3958/kjv/wlc/0-1/.

27 "H2492 - ḥālam - Strong's Hebrew Lexicon (kjv)." Blue Letter Bible. https://www.blueletterbible.org/lexicon/h2492/kjv/wlc/0-1/.

28 "G1 - alpha - Strong's Greek Lexicon (kjv)." Blue Letter Bible. https://www.blueletterbible.org/lexicon/g1/kjv/tr/0-1/.

29 "G3184 - methyō - Strong's Greek Lexicon (kjv)." Blue Letter Bible. https://www.blueletterbible.org/lexicon/g3184/kjv/tr/0-1/.

30 "Where no man has gone before," Wikipedia, last modified April 24, 2022, https://en.wikipedia.org/wiki/Where_no_man_has_gone_before.

31 "G2602 - katabolē - Strong's Greek Lexicon (kjv)." Blue Letter Bible. https://www.blueletterbible.org/lexicon/g2602/kjv/tr/0-1/.

32 R. H. Charles, The Apocrypha and Pseudepigrapha of the Old Testament, http://www.pseudepigrapha.com/jubilees/8.htm.

33 "H1961 - hāyâ - Strong's Hebrew Lexicon (kjv)." Blue Letter Bible. https://www.blueletterbible.org/lexicon/h1961/kjv/wlc/0-1/.

34 "H8414 - tôû - Strong's Hebrew Lexicon (kjv)." Blue Letter Bible. https://www.blueletterbible.org/lexicon/h8414/kjv/wlc/0-1/.

35 "H922 - bôû - Strong's Hebrew Lexicon (kjv)." Blue Letter Bible. https://www.blueletterbible.org/lexicon/h922/kjv/wlc/0-1/.

36 "H2822 - ḥōšeḵ - Strong's Hebrew Lexicon (kjv)." Blue Letter Bible. https://www.blueletterbible.org/lexicon/h2822/kjv/wlc/0-1/.
37 "H6440 - pānîm - Strong's Hebrew Lexicon (kjv)." Blue Letter Bible. https://www.blueletterbible.org/lexicon/h6440/kjv/wlc/0-1/.
38 "H8415 - t^{ə}hôm - Strong's Hebrew Lexicon (kjv)." Blue Letter Bible. https://www.blueletterbible.org/lexicon/h8415/kjv/wlc/0-1/.
39 "G12 - abyssos - Strong's Greek Lexicon (kjv)." Blue Letter Bible. https://www.blueletterbible.org/lexicon/g12/kjv/tr/0-1/.
40 "G443 - anthrōpoktonos - Strong's Greek Lexicon (kjv)." Blue Letter Bible. https://www.blueletterbible.org/lexicon/g443/kjv/tr/0-1/.
41 "H3556 - kôḵāḇ - Strong's Hebrew Lexicon (kjv)." Blue Letter Bible. https://www.blueletterbible.org/lexicon/h3556/kjv/wlc/0-1/.
42 "H7363 - rāḥap¯ - Strong's Hebrew Lexicon (kjv)." Blue Letter Bible. https://www.blueletterbible.org/lexicon/h7363/kjv/wlc/0-1/.
43 "H914 - bāḏal - Strong's Hebrew Lexicon (kjv)." Blue Letter Bible. https://www.blueletterbible.org/lexicon/h914/kjv/wlc/0-1/.
44 "H996 - bayin - Strong's Hebrew Lexicon (kjv)." Blue Letter Bible. https://www.blueletterbible.org/lexicon/h996/kjv/wlc/0-1/.
45 "H3117 - yôm - Strong's Hebrew Lexicon (kjv)." Blue Letter Bible. https://www.blueletterbible.org/lexicon/h3117/kjv/wlc/0-1/.
46 "H3915 - layil - Strong's Hebrew Lexicon (kjv)." Blue Letter Bible. https://www.blueletterbible.org/lexicon/h3915/kjv/wlc/0-1/.
47 Rashi, M. Rosenbaum and A.M. Silberman, London, 1929-1934, https://www.sefaria.org/Rashi_on_Genesis.1.8?vhe=Rashi&lang=bi.
48 "H784 - 'ēš - Strong's Hebrew Lexicon (kjv)." Blue Letter Bible. https://www.blueletterbible.org/lexicon/h784/kjv/wlc/0-1/.
49 "G4442 - pyr - Strong's Greek Lexicon (kjv)." Blue Letter Bible. https://www.blueletterbible.org/lexicon/g4442/kjv/tr/0-1/.
50 "H6754 - ṣelem - Strong's Hebrew Lexicon (kjv)." Blue Letter Bible. https://www.blueletterbible.org/lexicon/h6754/kjv/wlc/0-1/.
51 "H6459 - pesel - Strong's Hebrew Lexicon (kjv)." Blue Letter Bible. https://www.blueletterbible.org/lexicon/h6459/kjv/wlc/0-1/.
52 "H1823 - d^{ə}mûṯ - Strong's Hebrew Lexicon (kjv)." Blue Letter Bible. https://www.blueletterbible.org/lexicon/h1823/kjv/wlc/0-1/.
53 "H3335 - yāṣar - Strong's Hebrew Lexicon (kjv)." Blue Letter Bible. https://www.blueletterbible.org/lexicon/h3335/kjv/wlc/0-1/.
54 "H6083 - 'āp̄ār - Strong's Hebrew Lexicon (kjv)." Blue Letter Bible. https://www.blueletterbible.org/lexicon/h6083/kjv/wlc/0-1/.
55 "H5301 - nāp̄aḥ - Strong's Hebrew Lexicon (kjv)." Blue Letter Bible. https://www.blueletterbible.org/lexicon/h5301/kjv/wlc/0-1/.

56 "H5397 - nᵊšāmâ - Strong's Hebrew Lexicon (kjv)." Blue Letter Bible. https://www.blueletterbible.org/lexicon/h5397/kjv/wlc/0-1/.

57 "H2416 - ḥay - Strong's Hebrew Lexicon (kjv)." Blue Letter Bible. https://www.blueletterbible.org/lexicon/h2416/kjv/wlc/0-1/.

58 "H120 - 'āḏām - Strong's Hebrew Lexicon (kjv)." Blue Letter Bible. https://www.blueletterbible.org/lexicon/h120/kjv/wlc/0-1/.

59 "H5315 - nep̄eš - Strong's Hebrew Lexicon (kjv)." Blue Letter Bible. https://www.blueletterbible.org/lexicon/h5315/kjv/wlc/0-1/.

60 Scripture taken from THE MIRROR, Copyright 2012, Used by permission of The Author Francois du Toit.

61 William Whiston M.A.. The Genuine Works of Flavius Josephus The Jewish Historian, University of Cambridge, London 1737, https://penelope.uchicago.edu/josephus/index.html.

62 "H5828 - 'ēzer - Strong's Hebrew Lexicon (kjv)." Blue Letter Bible. https://www.blueletterbible.org/lexicon/h5828/kjv/wlc/0-1/.

63 "H5826 - 'āzar - Strong's Hebrew Lexicon (kjv)." Blue Letter Bible. https://www.blueletterbible.org/lexicon/h5826/kjv/wlc/0-1/.

64 "H1288 - bāraḵ - Strong's Hebrew Lexicon (kjv)." Blue Letter Bible. https://www.blueletterbible.org/lexicon/h1288/kjv/wlc/0-1/.

65 "G3598 - hodos - Strong's Greek Lexicon (kjv)." Blue Letter Bible. https://www.blueletterbible.org/lexicon/g3598/kjv/tr/0-1/.

66 "G225 - alētheia - Strong's Greek Lexicon (kjv)." Blue Letter Bible. https://www.blueletterbible.org/lexicon/g225/kjv/tr/0-1/.

67 "H1847 - da'aṯ - Strong's Hebrew Lexicon (kjv)." Blue Letter Bible. https://www.blueletterbible.org/lexicon/h1847/kjv/wlc/0-1/.

68 "H3045 - yāḏa' - Strong's Hebrew Lexicon (kjv)." Blue Letter Bible. https://www.blueletterbible.org/lexicon/h3045/kjv/wlc/0-1/.

69 "H5175 - nāḥāš - Strong's Hebrew Lexicon (kjv)." Blue Letter Bible. https://www.blueletterbible.org/lexicon/h5175/kjv/wlc/0-1/.

70 "G1228 - diabolos - Strong's Greek Lexicon (kjv)." Blue Letter Bible. https://www.blueletterbible.org/lexicon/g1228/kjv/tr/0-1/.

71 Charles, The Apocrypha and Pseudepigrapha of the Old Testament, https://www.ccel.org/c/charles/otpseudepig/enoch/ENOCH_1.HTM.

72 "H5303 - nāp̄îl - Strong's Hebrew Lexicon (kjv)." Blue Letter Bible.

73 "H7497 - rᵊp̄ā'îm - Strong's Hebrew Lexicon (kjv)." Blue Letter Bible.

74 Charles, The Apocrypha and Pseudepigrapha of the Old Testament, https://www.ccel.org/c/charles/otpseudepig/enoch/ENOCH_1.HTM.

75 The Book of Jasher. J.H. Parry & Company. 1887. https://www.holybooks.com/wp-content/uploads/Book-of-Jasher.pdf.

76 Charles, The Apocrypha and Pseudepigrapha of the Old Testament, https://www.ccel.org/c/charles/otpseudepig/enoch/ENOCH_1.HTM.

77 "G1504 - eikōn - Strong's Greek Lexicon (kjv)." Blue Letter Bible. https://www.blueletterbible.org/lexicon/g1504/kjv/tr/0-1/.
78 "G2342 - thērion - Strong's Greek Lexicon (kjv)." Blue Letter Bible. https://www.blueletterbible.org/lexicon/g2342/kjv/tr/0-1/.
79 "G5480 - charagma - Strong's Greek Lexicon (kjv)." Blue Letter Bible. https://www.blueletterbible.org/lexicon/g5480/kjv/tr/0-1/.
80 "G5482 - charax - Strong's Greek Lexicon (kjv)." Blue Letter Bible. https://www.blueletterbible.org/lexicon/g5482/kjv/tr/0-1/.
81 "G706 - arithmos - Strong's Greek Lexicon (kjv)." Blue Letter Bible. https://www.blueletterbible.org/lexicon/g706/kjv/tr/0-1/.
82 "G444 - anthrōpos - Strong's Greek Lexicon (kjv)." Blue Letter Bible. https://www.blueletterbible.org/lexicon/g444/kjv/tr/0-1/.
83 "G5516 - chxϚ - Strong's Greek Lexicon (kjv)." Blue Letter Bible. https://www.blueletterbible.org/lexicon/g5516/kjv/tr/0-1/.
84 "G4742 - stigma - Strong's Greek Lexicon (kjv)." Blue Letter Bible. https://www.blueletterbible.org/lexicon/g4742/kjv/tr/0-1/.
85 "H4135 - mûl - Strong's Hebrew Lexicon (kjv)." Blue Letter Bible. https://www.blueletterbible.org/lexicon/h4135/kjv/wlc/0-1/.
86 "G4166 - poimēn - Strong's Greek Lexicon (kjv)." Blue Letter Bible. https://www.blueletterbible.org/lexicon/g4166/kjv/tr/0-1/.
87 "G1577 - ekklēsia - Strong's Greek Lexicon (kjv)." Blue Letter Bible. https://www.blueletterbible.org/lexicon/g1577/kjv/tr/0-1/.
88 "H1538 - gulgōleṯ - Strong's Hebrew Lexicon (kjv)." Blue Letter Bible. https://www.blueletterbible.org/lexicon/h1538/kjv/wlc/0-1/.
89 "G1085 - genos - Strong's Greek Lexicon (kjv)." Blue Letter Bible. https://www.blueletterbible.org/lexicon/g1085/kjv/tr/0-1/.
90 "G3439 - monogenēs - Strong's Greek Lexicon (kjv)." Blue Letter Bible. https://www.blueletterbible.org/lexicon/g3439/kjv/tr/0-1/.
91 "G1096 - ginomai - Strong's Greek Lexicon (kjv)." Blue Letter Bible. https://www.blueletterbible.org/lexicon/g1096/kjv/tr/0-1/.
92 "G5207 - yhios - Strong's Greek Lexicon (kjv)." Blue Letter Bible. https://www.blueletterbible.org/lexicon/g5207/kjv/tr/0-1/.
93 "G5087 – tithēm.i - Strong's Greek Lexicon (kjv)." Blue Letter Bible. https://www.blueletterbible.org/lexicon/g5087/kjv/tr/0-1/.
94 "H1350 - gā'al - Strong's Hebrew Lexicon (kjv)." Blue Letter Bible. https://www.blueletterbible.org/lexicon/h1350/kjv/wlc/0-1/.
95 "G2398 - idios - Strong's Greek Lexicon (kjv)." Blue Letter Bible. https://www.blueletterbible.org/lexicon/g2398/kjv/tr/0-1/.
96 "G228 - alēthinos - Strong's Greek Lexicon (kjv)." Blue Letter Bible. https://www.blueletterbible.org/lexicon/g228/kjv/tr/0-1/.

97 "G297 - amphoteroi - Strong's Greek Lexicon (kjv)." Blue Letter Bible. https://www.blueletterbible.org/lexicon/g297/kjv/tr/0-1/.
98 "G257 - halōn - Strong's Greek Lexicon (kjv)." Blue Letter Bible. https://www.blueletterbible.org/lexicon/g257/kjv/tr/0-1/.
99 "G2098 - euangelion - Strong's Greek Lexicon (kjv)." Blue Letter Bible. https://www.blueletterbible.org/lexicon/g2098/kjv/tr/0-1/.
100 "G3340 - metanoeō - Strong's Greek Lexicon (kjv)." Blue Letter Bible. https://www.blueletterbible.org/lexicon/g3340/kjv/tr/0-1/
101 "G4982 - sōzō - Strong's Greek Lexicon (kjv)." Blue Letter Bible. https://www.blueletterbible.org/lexicon/g4982/kjv/tr/0-1/.
102 "H6440 - pānîm - Strong's Hebrew Lexicon (kjv)." Blue Letter Bible. https://www.blueletterbible.org/lexicon/h6440/kjv/wlc/0-1/.
103 "H4888 - māšḥâ - Strong's Hebrew Lexicon (kjv)." Blue Letter Bible. https://www.blueletterbible.org/lexicon/h4888/kjv/wlc/0-1/.
104 "G5545 - chrisma - Strong's Greek Lexicon (kjv)." Blue Letter Bible. https://www.blueletterbible.org/lexicon/g5545/kjv/tr/0-1/.
105 "H8081 - šemen - Strong's Hebrew Lexicon (kjv)." Blue Letter Bible. https://www.blueletterbible.org/lexicon/h8081/kjv/wlc/0-1/.
106 "H2580 - ḥēn - Strong's Hebrew Lexicon (kjv)." Blue Letter Bible. https://www.blueletterbible.org/lexicon/h2580/kjv/wlc/0-1/.
107 "H8034 - šēm - Strong's Hebrew Lexicon (kjv)." Blue Letter Bible. https://www.blueletterbible.org/lexicon/h8034/kjv/wlc/0-1/.
108 "H3519 - kāḇôḏ - Strong's Hebrew Lexicon (kjv)." Blue Letter Bible. https://www.blueletterbible.org/lexicon/h3519/kjv/wlc/0-1/.
109 "G1391 - doxa - Strong's Greek Lexicon (kjv)." Blue Letter Bible. https://www.blueletterbible.org/lexicon/g1391/kjv/tr/0-1/.
110 "H5703 - ʿaḏ - Strong's Hebrew Lexicon (kjv)." Blue Letter Bible. https://www.blueletterbible.org/lexicon/h5703/kjv/wlc/0-1/.
111 "H5674 - ʿāḇar - Strong's Hebrew Lexicon (kjv)." Blue Letter Bible. https://www.blueletterbible.org/lexicon/h5674/kjv/wlc/0-1/.
112 "H2898 - ṭûḇ - Strong's Hebrew Lexicon (kjv)." Blue Letter Bible. https://www.blueletterbible.org/lexicon/h2898/kjv/wlc/0-1/.
113 "G2842 - koinōnia - Strong's Greek Lexicon (kjv)." Blue Letter Bible. https://www.blueletterbible.org/lexicon/g2842/kjv/tr/0-1/.
114 "H7350 - rāḥôq - Strong's Hebrew Lexicon (kjv)." Blue Letter Bible. https://www.blueletterbible.org/lexicon/h7350/kjv/wlc/0-1/.
115 "H3199 - yāḵîn - Strong's Hebrew Lexicon (kjv)." Blue Letter Bible. https://www.blueletterbible.org/lexicon/h3199/kjv/wlc/0-1/.
116 "H1162 - bōʿaz - Strong's Hebrew Lexicon (kjv)." Blue Letter Bible. https://www.blueletterbible.org/lexicon/h1162/kjv/wlc/0-1/.

117 Whiston, The Genuine Works of Flavius Josephus The Jewish Historian, https://penelope.uchicago.edu/josephus/index.html.
118 Charles, The Apocrypha and Pseudepigrapha of the Old Testament, https://www.ccel.org/c/charles/otpseudepig/enoch/ENOCH_1.HTM.
119 Charles, The Apocrypha and Pseudepigrapha of the Old Testament, https://www.ccel.org/c/charles/otpseudepig/enoch/ENOCH_1.HTM.
120 "H894 - bāḇel - Strong's Hebrew Lexicon (kjv)." Blue Letter Bible. https://www.blueletterbible.org/lexicon/h894/kjv/wlc/0-1/.
121 "G602 - apokalypsis - Strong's Greek Lexicon (kjv)." Blue Letter Bible. https://www.blueletterbible.org/lexicon/g602/kjv/tr/0-1/.
122 "G5561 - chōra - Strong's Greek Lexicon (kjv)." Blue Letter Bible. https://www.blueletterbible.org/lexicon/g5561/kjv/tr/0-1/.
123 "G3877 - parakoloutheō - Strong's Greek Lexicon (kjv)." Blue Letter Bible. https://www.blueletterbible.org/lexicon/g3877/kjv/tr/0-1/.
124 "G2374 - thyra - Strong's Greek Lexicon (kjv)." Blue Letter Bible. https://www.blueletterbible.org/lexicon/g2374/kjv/tr/0-1/.
125 Kathryn M. Schifferdecker, What in the world is this doing in the Bible?, https://www.workingpreacher.org/commentaries/revised-common-lectionary/ordinary-22-2/commentary-on-song-of-solomon-28-13-2.
126 "H5643 - sēṯer - Strong's Hebrew Lexicon (kjv)." Blue Letter Bible. https://www.blueletterbible.org/lexicon/h5643/kjv/wlc/0-1/.
127 "H4095 - maḏrēḡâ - Strong's Hebrew Lexicon (kjv)." Blue Letter Bible. https://www.blueletterbible.org/lexicon/h4095/kjv/wlc/0-1/.
128 "H2590 - ḥānaṭ - Strong's Hebrew Lexicon (kjv)." Blue Letter Bible. https://www.blueletterbible.org/lexicon/h2590/kjv/wlc/0-1/.
129 "H6291 - paḡ - Strong's Hebrew Lexicon (kjv)." Blue Letter Bible. https://www.blueletterbible.org/lexicon/h6291/kjv/wlc/0-1/.
130 "G1658 - eleutheros - Strong's Greek Lexicon (kjv)." Blue Letter Bible. https://www.blueletterbible.org/lexicon/g1658/kjv/tr/0-1/.
131 "G3689 - ontōs - Strong's Greek Lexicon (kjv)." Blue Letter Bible. https://www.blueletterbible.org/lexicon/g3689/kjv/tr/0-1/.
132 "G386 - anastasis - Strong's Greek Lexicon (kjv)." Blue Letter Bible. https://www.blueletterbible.org/lexicon/g386/kjv/tr/0-1/.
133 "G4888 - syndoxazō - Strong's Greek Lexicon (kjv)." Blue Letter Bible. https://www.blueletterbible.org/lexicon/g4888/kjv/tr/0-1/.
134 Charles, The Apocrypha and Pseudepigrapha of the Old Testament, https://www.ccel.org/ccel/charles/otpseudepig/enoch/ENOCH_2.HTM.